MW01713931

Softdesk® ARCHITECTURE 2 Certified Courseware

Softdesk Technical Resource Team

ONWORD® PRESS

SOFTDESK®

Softdesk® Architecture 2 Certified Courseware

By the Softdesk Technical Resource Team for Softdesk 7.2 and 7.5

Published by OnWord Press
2530 Camino Entrada
Santa Fe, NM 87505-4835 USA

SAN 694-0269
First Edition, 1996

10 9 8 7 6 5 4 3 2 1

Printed in the United States of America

Library of Congress CIP data is available

ISBN 1-56690-100-6

This document created by the *Technical Resources Group* at Softdesk, Inc., Henniker, NH.

Softdesk Technical Resources

This book represents one of the many ways that the Softdesk Technical Resource Team is helping you develop your full potential with Softdesk engineering and design software products. This book and the Softdesk *Level II Certification Exam** give you the skills and professional recognition as a knowledgeable Softdesk user.

Softdesk gratefully acknowledges the work of everyone who contributed to this book, including the *Softdesk Resellers, Softdesk Registered Consultants,* and *Softdesk Employees* who took the extra time to test and comment on these materials. The contributors to this book represent an international team of design and educational leaders, including the Softdesk Technical Resource Group staff and *Softdesk Registered Consultants.*

- ✔ Walter Kappelmann
- ✔ Jonathan Solomon
- ✔ Ken Krupa
- ✔ Reid M. Addis
- ✔ Tony Tedder
- ✔ Softdesk employees in the STR group

... and all *Softdesk Registered Consultants* who helped conduct the QA/QC on this project.

* The Softdesk certification exams are available at Sylvan Prometrics testing centers across North America. For more information on the Softdesk certification exam, call 1-800-716-EXAM.

Warning and Disclaimer

This book is designed to provide information about Softdesk Auto-Architect applications. Every effort has been made to make this book complete and as accurate as possible; however, no warranty or fitness is implied.

The information is provided on an "as-is" basis. The authors and OnWord Press shall have neither liability nor responsibility to any person or entity with respect to any loss or damages in connection with or rising from the information contained in this book.

OnWord Press

OnWord Press is dedicated to the fine art of professional documentation. In addition to the author who developed the material for this book, other members of the OnWord Press team make the book end up in your hands. In addition to those listed below, thanks to Suzanne Henry, Randall Mix, Dwight Chase, Debora Willford, and Zeke Olguin.

Dan Raker, Publisher and President
Janet Leigh Dick, Associate Publisher
David Talbott, Director of Acquisitions
Daniel Clavio, Director of Market Development
Rena Rully, Senior Manager
Ed Lorusso, Senior Editor
Carol Leyba, Production Manager
Patrice Werner, Production Editor
Lynne Egensteiner, Cover Designer
Kristie Reilly, Indexer

Table of Contents

Introduction

Softdesk Architecture Level 2 Certified Courseware

The skills that you develop in the *Softdesk Architecture 2 Certified Courseware* give you the ability to solve complex design problems with powerful design tools. To say you are Level II Certified means you have excelled in your building design abilities with Softdesk products.

This book gives you the skills you need so you can truly say "I can solve design problems with Softdesk *Auto-Architect* and *Details* modules. To get the maximum benefit from this book, you should use it during training from an Authorized Softdesk Reseller or Training Center. You can also use it as a follow-up self-study guide. Either way, it helps you prepare for the Softdesk *Building Design & Engineering Level II Certification Exam*. You cannot, however, simply read this book and expect to pass the examination.

This book includes goals and objectives that show what skills you should have as a result of this training. Read these goals. Make sure you understand the software features presented. Consider how they enhance the design process. Practice the steps, try your own variations of the exercises, and focus on developing proficiency with the commands and procedures. If you can *perform* the skills presented in this book, you should be able to pass the examination and proudly claim to be Level II Certified for Softdesk *Building Design & Engineering*.

Course Goals

To use the Softdesk *Building Design & Engineering* modules, you must be well versed in the design principles that apply to the various tasks that the software performs. This book assumes you are familiar with these design principles. You must also be able to use the Softdesk *Building Design & Engineering* software modules described in the Softdesk *Architecture 1 Certified Courseware.* You should have successfully passed the Softdesk *Building Design & Engineering Level I Certification Exam* before you begin this training.

After completing the *Softdesk Architecture 2 Certified Courseware*, you should be able to:

- ✔ Manage space area information with linked labels.
- ✔ Place columns on an existing building grid and draw walls that automatically clean up column enclosures.
- ✔ Solve complex design problems with wall styles.
- ✔ Use advanced window and door style features.
- ✔ Solve commercial stair design and annotation problems.
- ✔ Design toilet stalls that meet the requirements of the ADA.
- ✔ Create a ceiling grid for three-dimensional model-ing.
- ✔ Design complex roofs with roof generator.
- ✔ Create detail libraries and sheets.
- ✔ Manage material and detail libraries.

Note:

You should refer to the Softdesk documentation for the respective modules referred to in this training guide to help you accomplish these goals.

How to Use This Book

Each chapter in this book includes concepts, steps, and examples that show you how to achieve the course goals.

- ✔ Read the objectives at the beginning of the chapter.
  - ✗ These objectives tell you what skills you should be able to perform as a result of the training.
- ✔ Read the bulleted concept lists at the beginning of each topic to find key facts pertaining to that topic.
- ✔ Complete all of the *Hands-on* examples in the book on your computer.
  - ✗ Use the hands-on sections to see the procedures for using each feature.
  - ✗ Use the illustrations within the hands-on sections to check your progress on your computer.
- ✔ Read the *Notes* sections.
  - ✗ Each note gives you facts to help you understand the procedures or use other options within the procedures.
- ✔ Review each step when you finish each hands-on section.
  - ✗ Make sure you understand what you did in each step and why you did it.
- ✔ Review the concepts before the hands-on section to make sure you understand how the facts pertain to the procedure.
- ✔ Reread the objectives when you finish each chapter and ask yourself the following questions:

- ✗ Can I do the task stated in each objective?
- ✗ Do I understand the facts related to each objective?
- ✗ Can I complete the procedure related to each objective?

Typographical Conventions

This book presents information in the following format:

- ✔ Pull-down menu items appear in square brackets; an arrow separates each menu item:

  Select [File New...] from the pull-down menu.

- ✔ Keyboard key names appear between pointed brackets.

  Press <Enter> to continue.

- ✔ Values that you should type on the keyboard or select from a dialog box appear as bold characters.

  Type **LEVEL II CERTIFIED** for the description.

- ✔ Labels, buttons, or prompts on a dialog box or a command prompt line appear in quotation marks.

  Choose the "Edit" button under "Styles" in the dialog box.

- ✔ Computer file names and directory paths appear in italics.

  <drive>:\sdsk\macros.lsp

Softdesk Data Set CD-ROM Installation

The data sets for the exercises in the hands-on portions of the book are stored on the CD-ROM in the directory *\sdsk* and *\sdskproj*. Copy these files to your hard drive using the [Xcopy] command in MS-DOS, in the Windows File Manager, or in Windows 95 Explorer.

Make sure that the files do not maintain the read-only attribute that is assigned to them on the CD-ROM.

Steps to copy the files using Xcopy:

Step 1: Exit Windows or use the MS-DOS icon to access the MS-DOS command prompt.

Step 2: Change to the root directory of the hard drive where you want to install the files.

```
C:\>
```

Step 3: Put the CD-ROM in your CD-ROM drive and change to the root directory on that drive.

```
C:\> d:
D:\>
```

Step 4: Copy the \sdsk directory to your hard drive.

```
D:\> xcopy sdsk c:\sdsk\ /s /v
```

Step 5: Copy the \sdskproj directory to your hard drive.

```
D:\> xcopy sdskproj c:\sdskproj\ /s /v
```

Step 6: Change into each data set directory on your hard drive and issue the following command:

```
C:\sdskproj> attrib *.* -r /s
```

You are now ready to start the Softdesk modules and complete the hands-on portions of the self-study guide.

Chapter 1

Advanced Space Planning Tools

Objectives

To manage space area information with linked labels, you should be able to:

- ✔ Link space boundaries and labels.
- ✔ Maintain and edit space boundary and label links.
- ✔ Update space areas and label links.

Introduction

This chapter shows you how to use the intelligent relationship between a space boundary and room label on a space plan created with *Auto-Architect*. The skills you develop in this chapter will not only help you create space plans from scratch, they will help you

- ✔ Use information from existing projects to create new space plans.
- ✔ Use space planning tools to make design changes at later stages of your projects.

As you complete the exercises, notice how *Auto-Architect* creates and maintains a relationship between a space boundary and a room label on a drawing. If you begin your designs with a space plan, you establish a database of information that will help you quickly calculate areas later in your project. You should also focus on how to establish the link between a space boundary and a label on an existing drawing. This can help you make design changes and create space plans with drawings from earlier versions of *Auto-Architect* or another CAD system.

Another concept that you should focus on is the difference between defining space boundaries with gross or net area. By understanding the difference between gross and net area, you will have more flexibility to lay out complex floor plans and generate walls. You should always verify the area values that *Auto-Architect* places with a room label to make sure it is showing net or gross area.

Linking Space Boundaries and Labels

Auto-Architect allows you to

- ✔ Link space boundaries to room labels using the "Find Boundary" or "Draw" options.
- ✔ Calculate areas using a "Net" area calculation method or a "Gross" area calculation.

In *Auto-Architect,* net area is the useable area in a room or space that stops at the wall surface.

- ✔ Gross area is the net area plus the area occupied by one half the width of the walls around the space.

✔ Do not confuse the *Auto-Architect* definition with the architectural design definition where net area is the rentable area in a building.

Draw Boundary

Use the "Draw Boundary" option to create new space plans.

✔ You can convert the results of the space to walls, and thus the space boundaries become the centerlines of the eventual walls.

✔ The "Draw Boundary" option creates gross areas by default.

Hands-on:

Step 1: Open the file *\sdskproj\workshop\dwg\int1b.dwg*.

Step 2: Zoom in on the top left corner; leave plenty of clear drawing space.

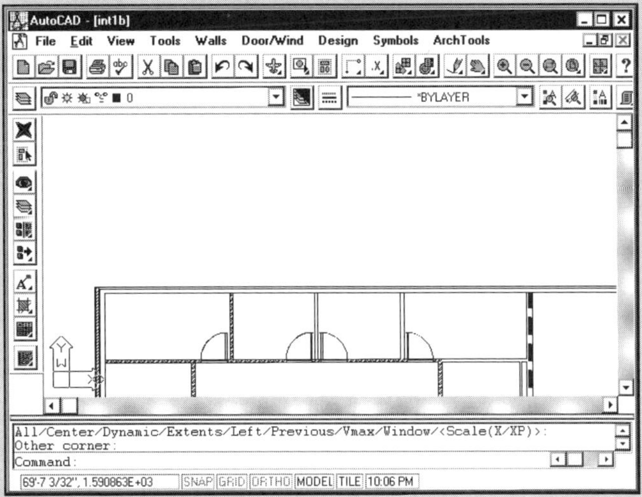

Step 3: Choose [Design ⇨ Spaces and Rooms ⇨ Create Space or Labels...] from the pull-down menu.

Step 4: Choose the description "OFFICE - STANDARD COM." to set the area label automatically.

Step 5: Select the "Gross Area" option and enter an area of **150**.

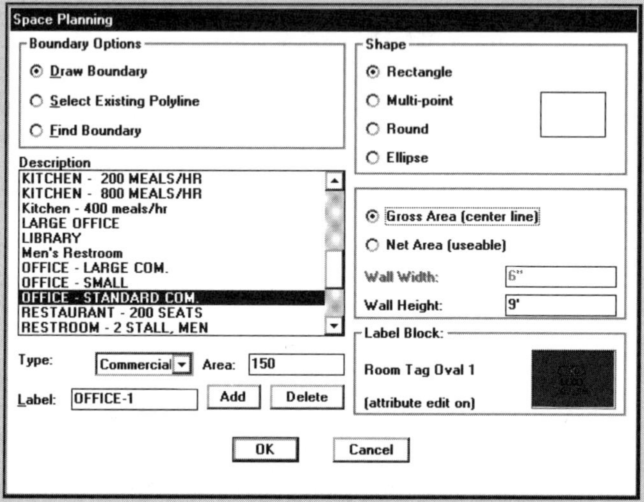

Step 6: Create a space by picking a point and then specifying an edge point by entering **@16′,0**.

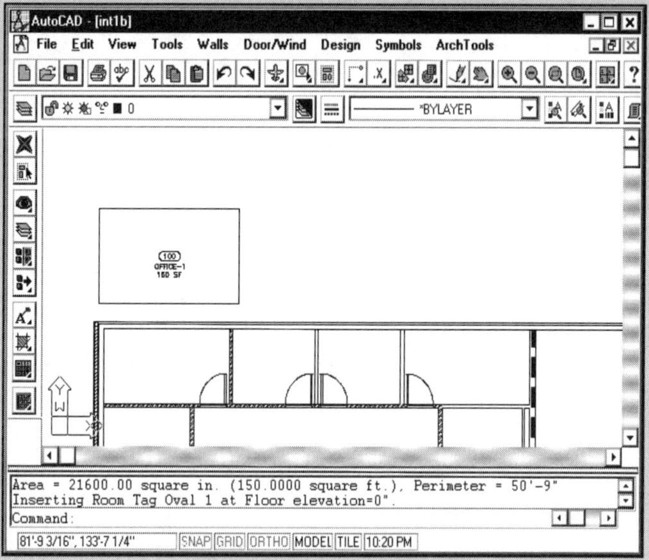

Step 7: Choose the "Next" button to view the "Net Offset" value.

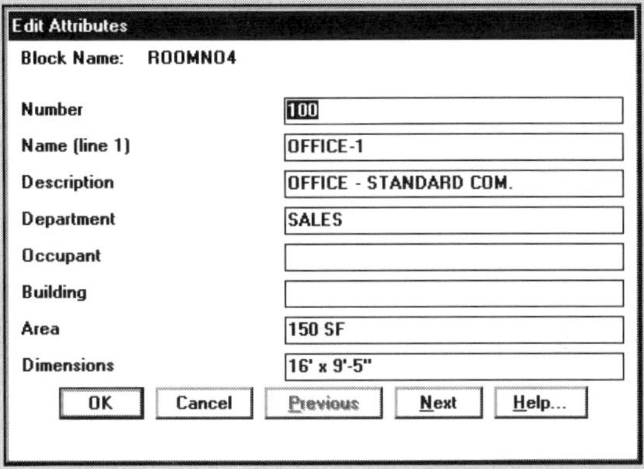

Step 8: Choose the "OK" button to continue.

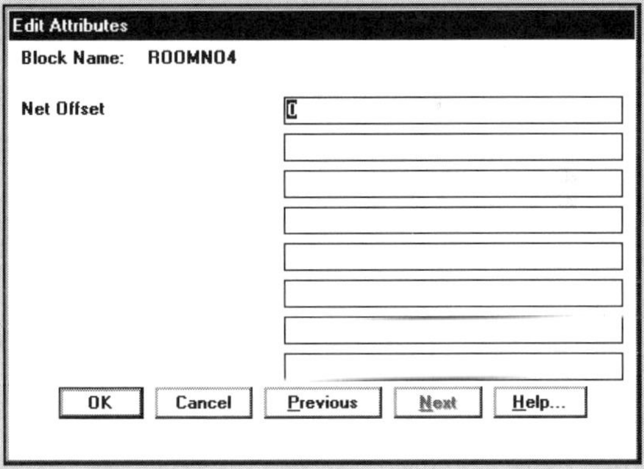

Note:

The offset is 0. This means the program does not require an offset to calculate the Gross Area.

Step 9: Create another space just like the first; snap to the bottom right corner of the first space.

Step 10: Enter the coordinate **@16′,0** for the edge point.

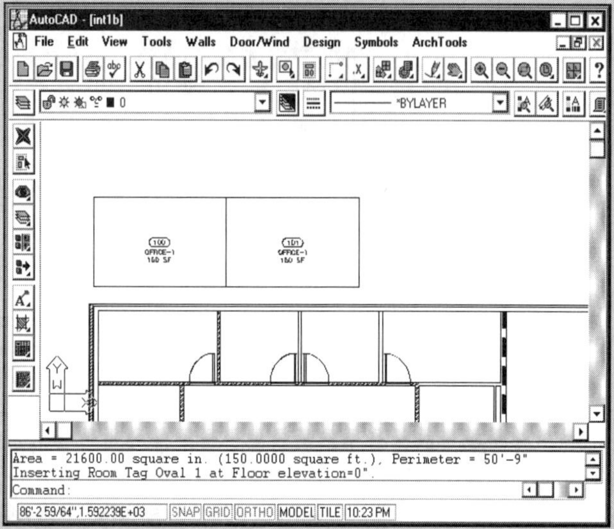

Step 11: Create another space similar to the first two but this time use "Net Area" and specify a **4 7/8″** wall width.

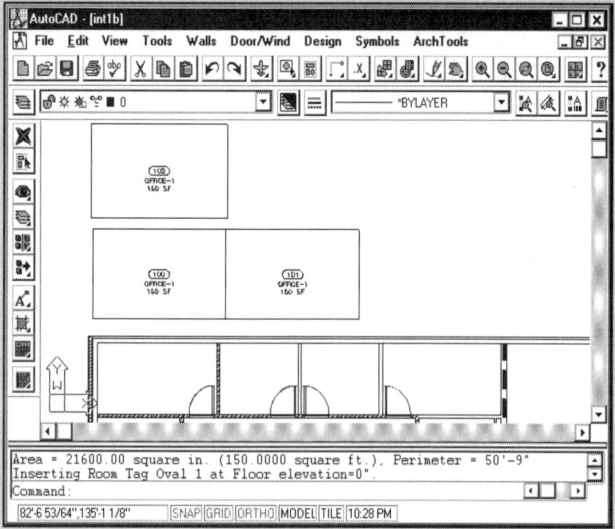

This is the intended wall width for converting to walls.

Note:

The wall width during conversion to walls is controlled by the final wall style selected, not by this setting.

Step 12: Use the "Next" button to check the Offset; verify that is shows half the intended wall width.

Step 13: Place one more boundary using the same settings; snap to the bottom right corner of the previous space.

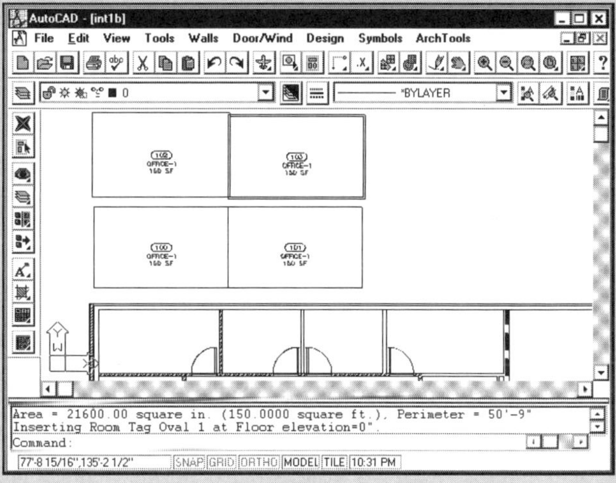

Note:

The last two spaces overlap even though you used an object snap. This overlap results from the boundary being offset by one half of the wall thickness to accommodate the wall thickness and find net area.

Step 14: Move the last space to line up with the first using the move keyboard macro.

Note:

The reported areas in the last two labels are the same as the first two, but the boundaries are offset outwards to adjust for half the wall width. The boundaries are still centerlines, but the listed areas are now Net rather than Gross.

Step 15: Convert all four areas to Control Lines with the [Convert Spaces to Control Lines] command.

Step 16: Convert the control lines to walls with the [Convert Control Lines to Walls] command.

Step 17: Set the wall style to **AB_CENTER** and set a wall width of **4 7/8**.

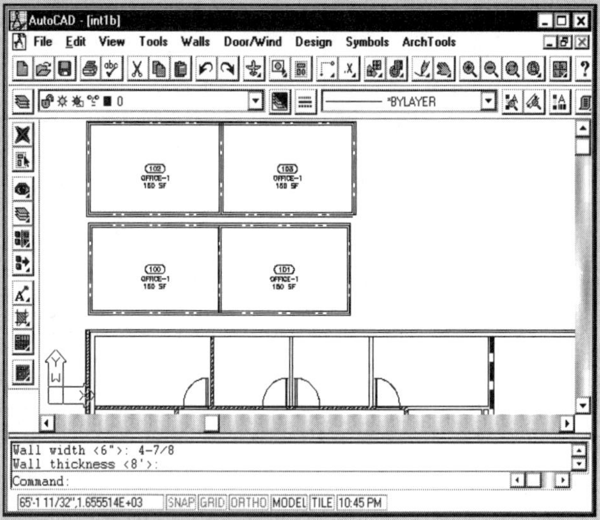

Note:

You must specify the actual wall width again when you set the wall style.

Step 18: Use the AutoCAD [Area] command to verify that the net area of space number 103 matches the label.

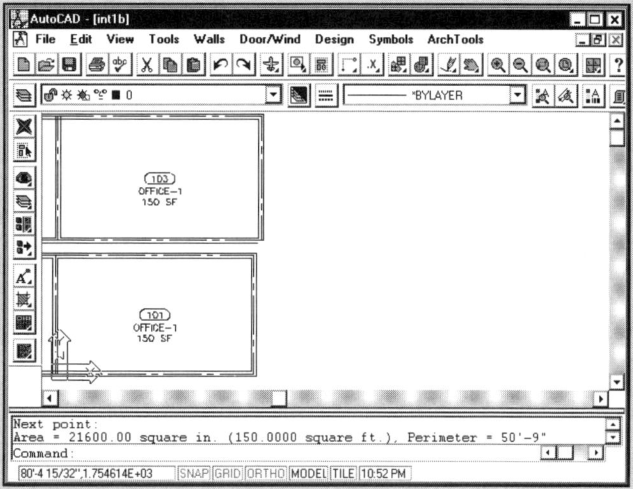

Step 19: Compare this to the area of space 101.

Find Boundary

Use the "Find Boundary" option to place room labels where walls have already been created with *Auto-Architect.*

- ✔ The "Find Boundary" option finds the inside perimeter of a room (either with or without doors and windows) and places a tag showing the area that it finds.
    - ✗ Because the area inside the wall perimeter is the same as net area, you can use this option to find Net Area without making any adjustment for wall width.
    - ✗ The "Find Boundary" option ignores door swing arcs when it determines the room perimeter.
- ✔ If you compare the "Draw Boundary" and "Find Boundary" options, you will find:

- ✗ The "Draw Boundary" option finds gross area without adjusting for wall width and offsets inwards to find Net area.
- ✗ The "Find Boundary" command finds net area without adjusting for wall width and offsets outwards to find gross area.

✔ The following exercise shows how to place room labels into the top left offices.

- ✗ In the first section, you will find the Net area.
- ✗ In the second section, you will find the Gross area.

✔ The spaces that you use in this exercise already have doors inserted into them to show how *Auto-Architect* calculates area without interference from door swing arcs.

Hands-on:

Step 1: Select [Design ⇨ Spaces and Rooms ⇨ Create Spaces or Labels...] from the pull-down menu.

Step 2: Choose the "Find Boundary" option and keep "Net Area" selected. Pick "OK". If "Find Boundary" doesn't find a boundary, Zoom all, then zoom back in and try again.

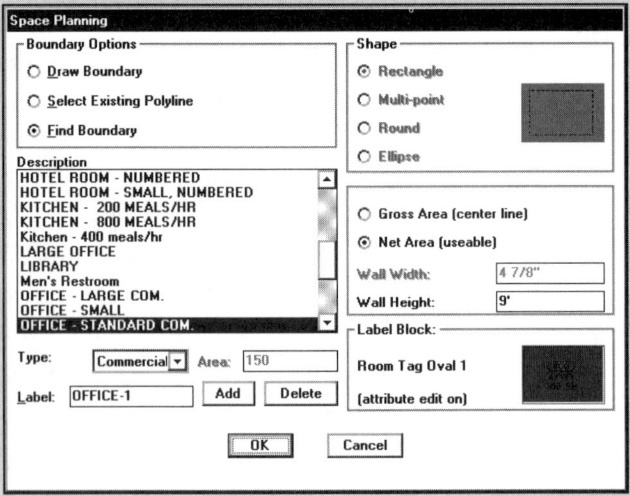

Note:

> Auto-Architect *disables both the "Wall Width" and "Area" options.* Auto-Architect *finds the area from the drawing and therefore disables the area input.* Auto-Architect *disables wall width because it does not require an offset to find net area with the "Find Boundary" option.*

Step 3: Pick points in the middle of each of the two top left offices — you can select more than one internal point.

Step 4: Choose the "Next" button to verify that the net offset is 0.

Step 5: Choose the "OK" button when you finish.

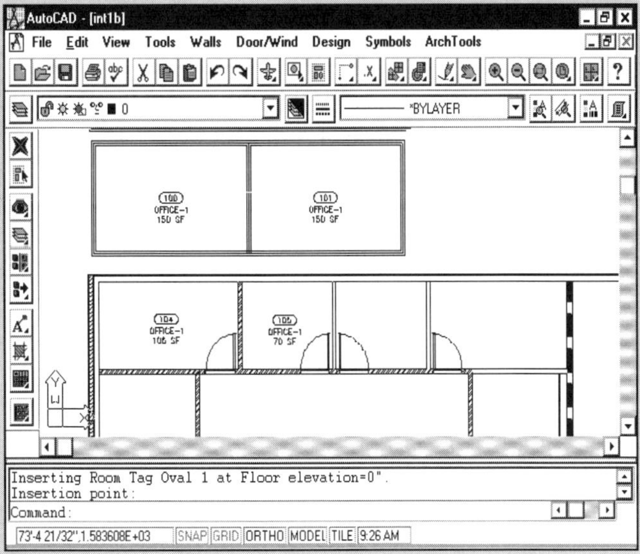

Step 6: Select [Design ⇨ Spaces and Rooms ⇨ Create Spaces or Labels...] from the pull-down menu.

Step 7: Choose the "Gross Area" option and the wall width option becomes enabled.

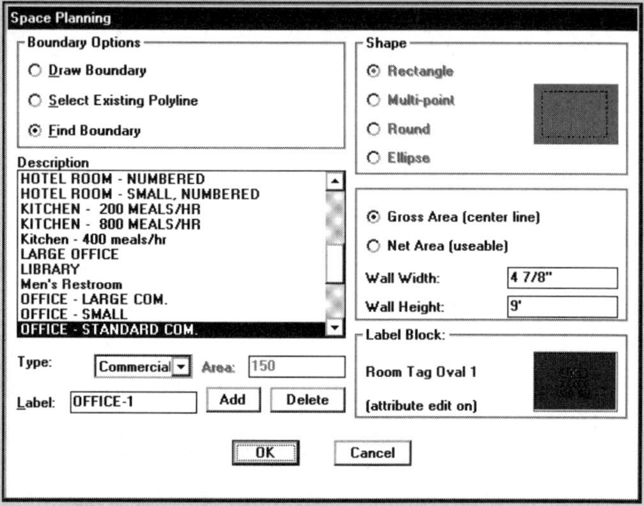

Step 8: Choose the "OK" button and pick internal points in the remaining two spaces at the top.

Step 9: Select the "Next" button during attribute entry to verify the net offset is set to minus one half the wall width.

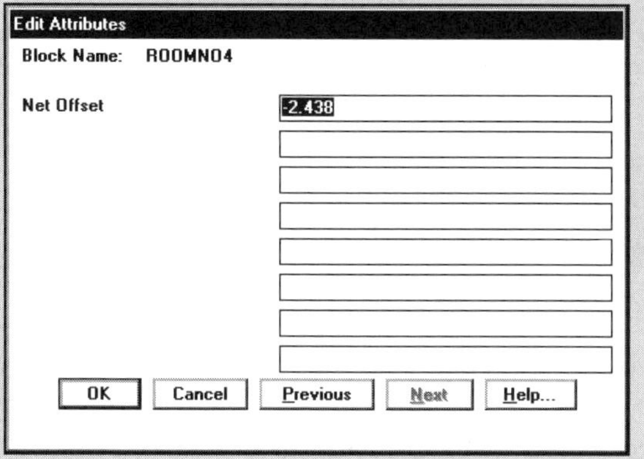

Step 10: Choose the "OK" button to continue.

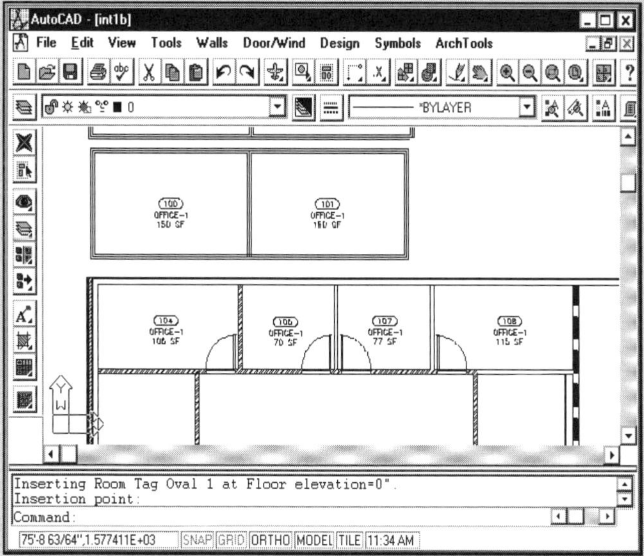

Note:

The areas in the second two offices are larger because they are showing Gross area.

Maintaining Links

Auto-Architect creates a bi-directional link between the space boundary and the label.

- ✔ *Auto-Architect* stores the data using extended entity data and entity handles.
- ✔ You will break the link if you:
  - ✗ Use AutoCAD's [Copy] or [Erase] command to edit the label or space.
  - ✗ Use the [Wblock] command to export some or all of the drawing to a separate file.
- ✔ You can fix a broken link with the [Fix Tag and Area Link...] command.

Viewing Links

You can ask *Auto-Architect* to show the relationship between space boundaries and labels.

- ✔ *Auto-Architect* shows the link as a highlighted line from the base point of the space object to the label.
- ✔ The following exercise shows how to break a link and use *Auto-Architect* to report any changes to links between spaces and labels.

Hands-on:

Step 1: Copy the top left label into the top right area.

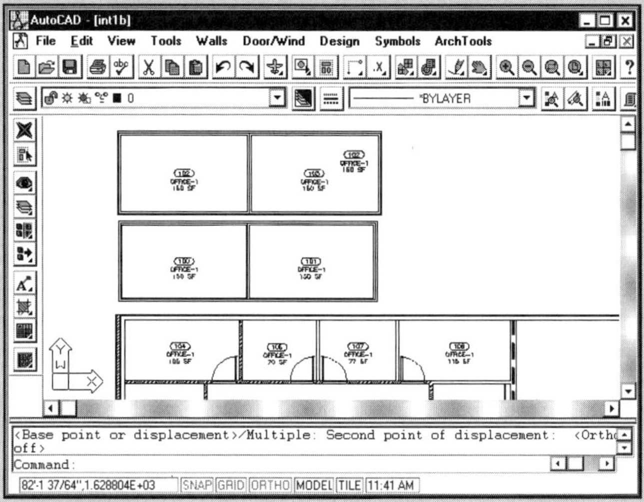

Now there are two labels in the right space. One is correct and one incorrect.

Step 2: Select [Design ⇨ Spaces and Rooms ⇨ Fix Tag and Area Link…] from the pull-down menu.

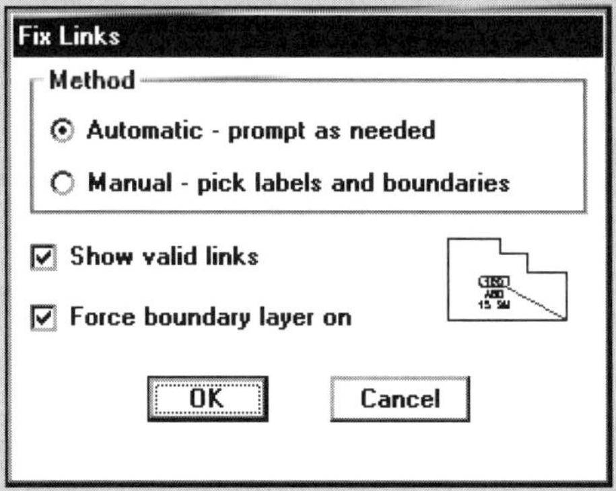

Step 3: Verify that the settings are set as shown in the previous image, then accept the program defaults.

Step 4: Notice that *Auto-Architect* draws a temporary line to show you the valid links in the drawing.

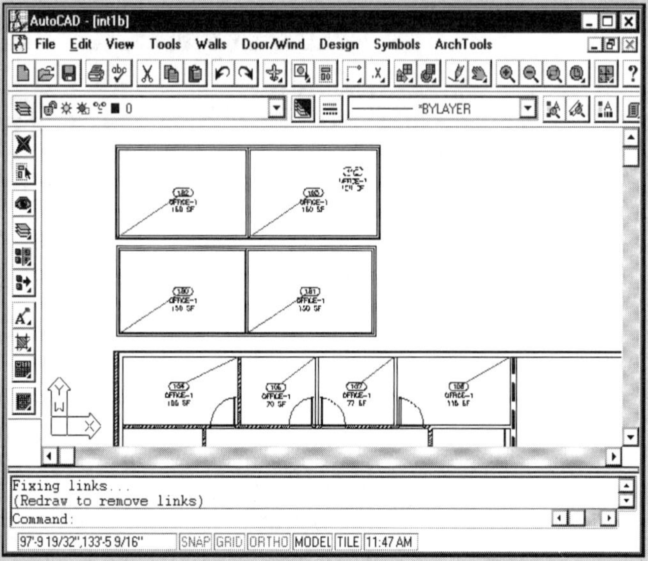

Step 5: Choose the "OK" button to accept that *Auto-Architect* found the extra label.

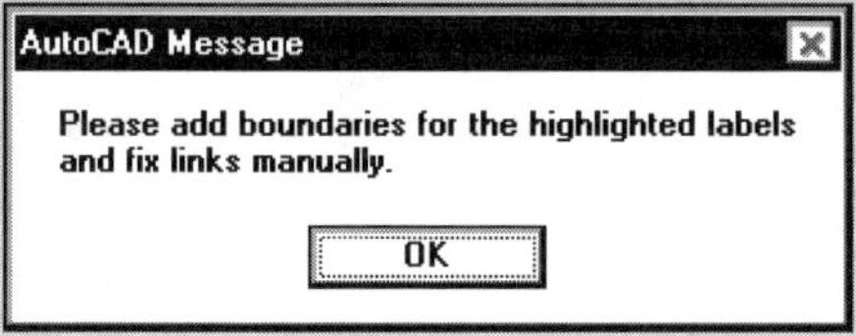

Automatic Relink of Space Objects and Labels

The next exercise shows how to link with the label that you copied.

✔ You will ask *Auto-Architect* to report on the status of links in the drawing.

- ✔ *Auto-Architect* will do the following:
  - ✗ Find the single label in the space and link the boundary to that label.
  - ✗ Since there is only one label found inside the boundary, it automatically links with that one label.

Hands-on:

Step 1: Erase the label that is still linked to the space and leave the new label that you copied.

Step 2: Select [Design ⇨ Spaces and Labels ⇨ Fix Tag and Area Link...] from the pull-down menu.

Step 3: Make sure the "Method" is set to "Automatic - prompt as needed".

Step 4: Choose "OK" to accept the defaults.

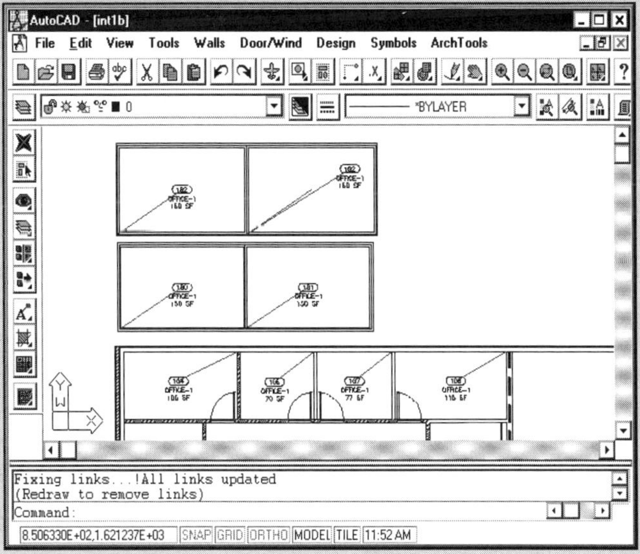

Replace Labels in Space Boundaries

The following exercise shows how to replace a label that has been erased from the drawing.

✔ You will choose the space in which to place the label and *Auto-Architect* will link all of the space boundary to the new label.

Hands-on:

Step 1: Erase the last label that you just changed.

Step 2: Start the [Fix Tag and Area Links...] command again.

Step 3: Choose "OK" to accept the program defaults.

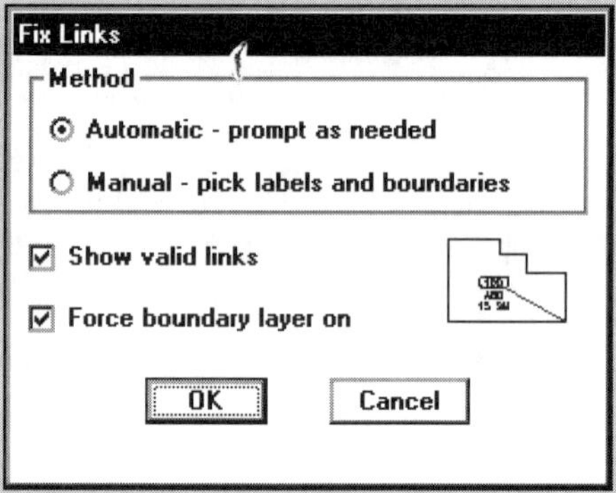

Step 4: Choose the "OK" button to accept that there is a missing tag.

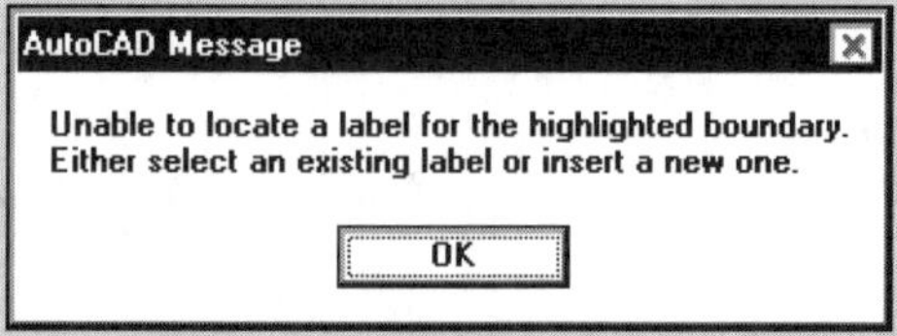

Step 5: Press <Enter> when *Auto-Architect* prompts you to select a label.

Step 6:	Pick an insertion point for the label inside the highlighted boundary.
Step 7:	Change the room number to **103**.

Adding Intelligence

Use the [Fix Tag and Area Link...] command to add intelligent links to space drawings that contain standard polyline boundaries and inserted room labels.

- ✔ This allows you to update drawings from a previous version of *Auto-Architect* or another CAD package.
- ✔ The new link stores area and offset information using attributes with the following tag names:
  - ✗ AARMAREA
  - ✗ AARMNET
    Any custom block would need to contain at least these two attributes.
- ✔ This example shows how to place a room label from the Symbol Manager inside a regular polyline and then link the label to the polyline.

Hands-on:

Step 1: Use the [RC] macro to create a closed rectangular polyline.

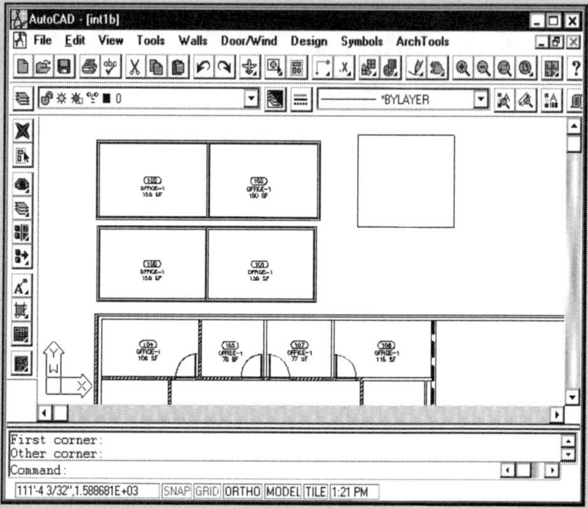

Step 2: Use the symbol manager to insert any room label.

Step 3: Look under "Annotation" and "Room Tags" to find the appropriate label.

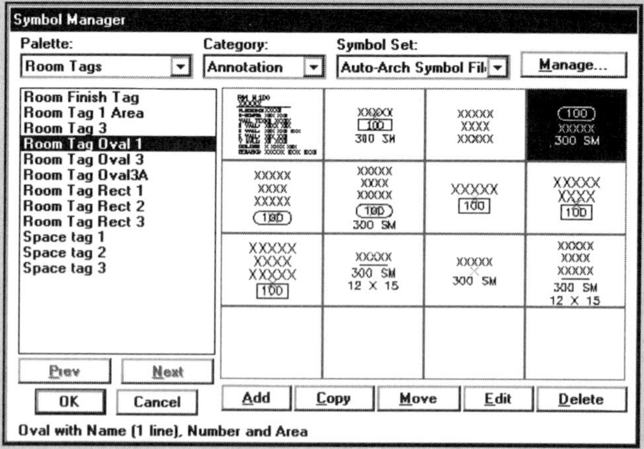

Step 4: Change the room number to **108**.

Step 5: Select [Design ⇨ Spaces and Rooms ⇨ Fix Tag and Area Link...] from the pull-down menu.

Step 6: Use the "Manual Method" option to link the label and the boundary.

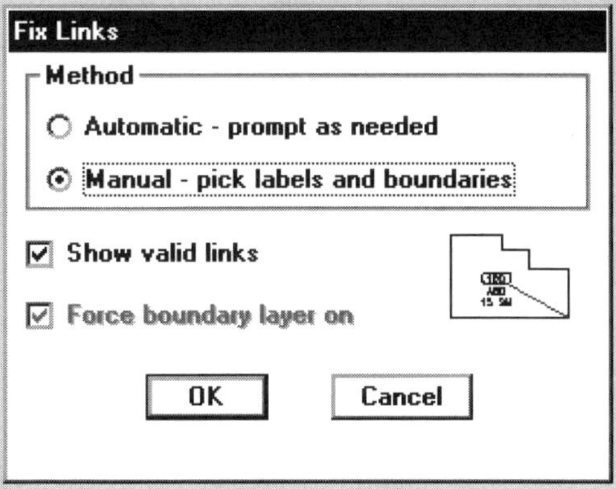

Step 7: Pick the label that you inserted.

Step 8: Pick the polyline to complete the link.

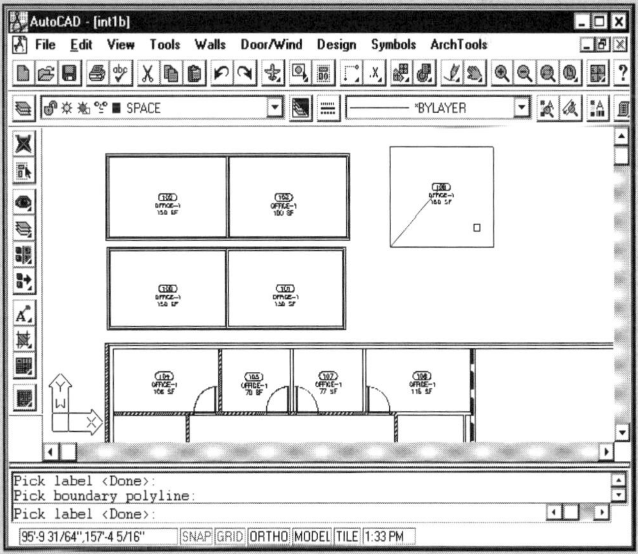

Step 9: Use the [Redraw] command to clear the link display.

Updating Areas Automatically

The link between a label and a space boundary is "intelligent."

- ✔ When you change the size of a boundary, you can update the label to show the new area value.
- ✔ *Auto-Architect* also subtracts nested areas.
  - ✗ If you move one space over another, *Auto-Architect* subtracts boundary areas from the space they are nested within.
  - ✗ A space is considered "within" another if the insertion point of the label is inside the boundary of the outer space.
  - ✗ You can nest boundaries to as many levels as you need.
  - ✗ The areas of nested boundaries subtract from outer boundaries.
- ✔ You can use this to create one large area called "Core" or "Common" around the perimeter of a building and nest all rentable areas inside.
  - ✗ *Auto-Architect* automatically calculates the non-rentable area.
- ✔ This following exercise demonstrates the usefulness of intelligent links when you edit the drawing.
  - ✗ This example subtracts a gross area from a net area.
  - ✗ Although it is possible to mix gross and net area, it is confusing and may cause difficulties in actual practice.

Hands-on:

Step 1: Use the [ST] macro to stretch the last boundary.

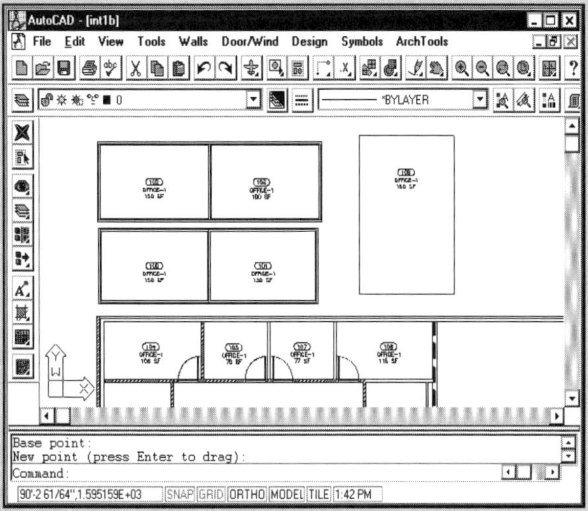

Step 2: Select [Design ⇨ Spaces and Rooms ⇨ Copy Space] from the pull-down menu.

Step 3: Select the label in space 106 and copy it to the new space.

Step 4: Change the room number to **109**.

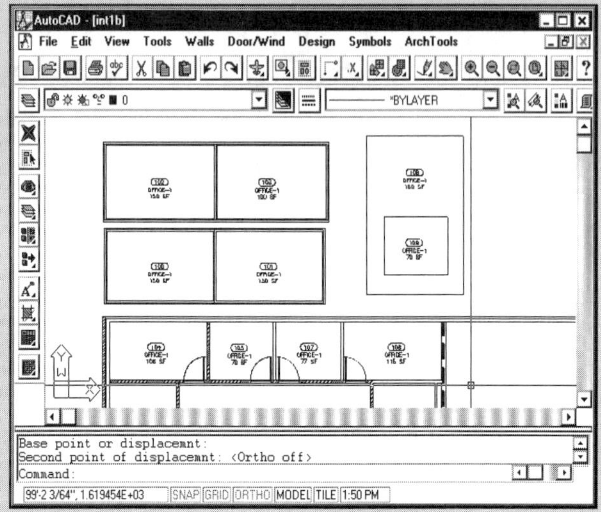

Step 5: Select [Design ⇨ Spaces and Rooms ⇨ Update Areas] from the pull-down menu.

Step 6: Press <Enter> to accept all areas.

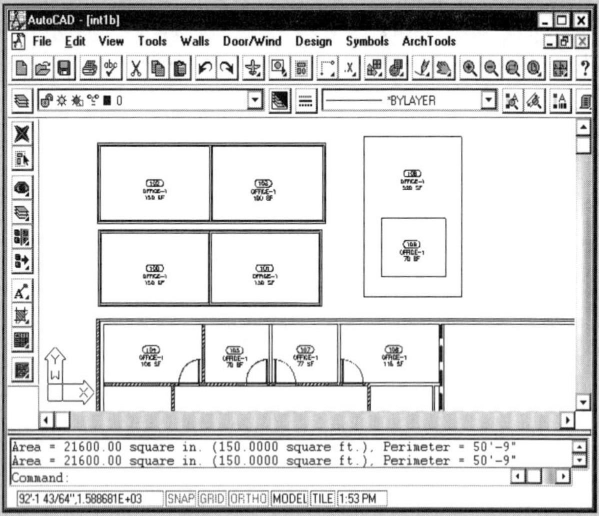

Note that the area in Room 108 has been reduced.

Chapter 2

Insert Columns

Objectives

To place columns on an existing building grid and draw walls that automatically clean up column enclosures, you should be able to:

- ✔ Insert exterior wall columns.
- ✔ Insert interior wall columns.
- ✔ Draw exterior walls with column enclosures.
- ✔ Draw interior walls with column enclosures.

Introduction

This chapter shows how to place columns on an existing building grid and draw walls that automatically clean up at the column enclosures. After you complete the first exercise, you will see how *Auto-Architect* can place columns by reading the grid lines and finding the intersection points. Use this to start placing columns, although you will have to remove some of the columns and replace them with different interior column sizes and orientations. The next exercises will show you how to do that.

When you specify the columns in the first exercise, notice that *Auto-Architect* also lets you configure the footings and enclosures for the columns. In later exercises, you will see how the [Wall] commands will tie into these enclosures to create pilasters.

Insert Columns

There are a few tips that will help you place columns onto an existing building grid and tie walls into the column enclosures that *Auto-Architect* generates for you.

- ✔ The building grid on which you want to place columns must exist in the current drawing before you start the [Place Columns...] command.
  - ✗ The building grid must consist of simple lines for the [Place Columns...] command to work.
  - ✗ You cannot use a block or external reference.
- ✔ The column enclosure height must be the same as the wall height for the clean-up routine to work.

The following examples show you how to place exterior columns with 10′ high enclosures and interior columns with 8′ high enclosures.

- ✔ You will use two placement methods:

  - ✗ Place at grid intersections
  - ✗ Select location

- ✔ You can control the orientation of each column individually with the "Select Location" method.
- ✔ The [Place Columns...] command displays a continuously updated image of the column, footing, and enclosure.

Exterior Columns

Your first step for placing columns is to place exterior columns.

- ✔ Softdesk places the exterior columns that you specify at all grid intersections.
  - ✗ You will erase the columns at interior grid points later on.
- ✔ This example shows how to place columns at all grid locations.

Hands-on:

Step 1:	Open the drawing *\sdskproj\workshop\dwg \colgrid.dwg*.
Step 2:	Select [Design ⇨ Columns and Grids ⇨ Place Columns] from the pull-down menu.
Step 3:	Verify that the placement method is set to "Place at Grid Intersections."

Step 4: Verify that "Draw Enclosure" is checked on and that "Enclosure Height" is set at 10'.

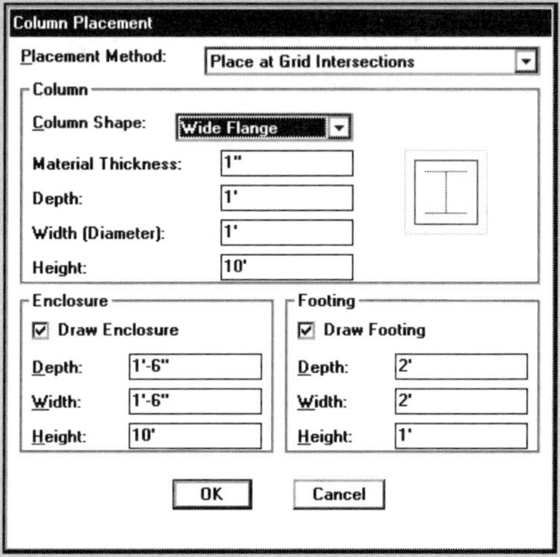

Step 5: Choose the "OK" button.

Step 6: Select a grid line when prompted to do so.

Step 7: Verify that *Auto-Architect* highlights only gridlines — use “Add” or “Remove” if necessary.

Step 8: Press <Enter> to end the command.

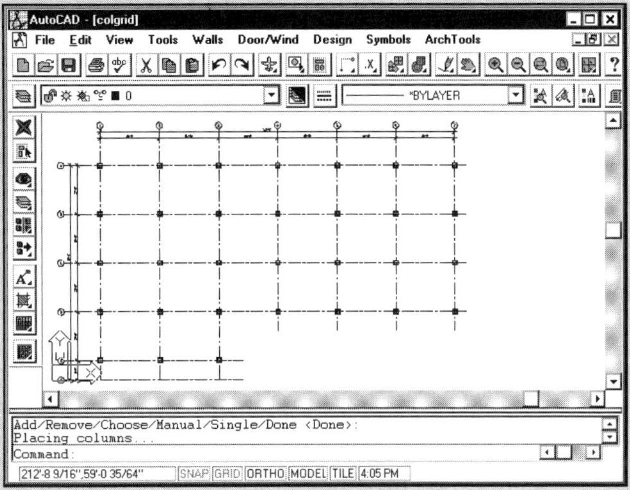

Interior Columns

The exterior columns currently appear at all grid points.

- ✔ You must erase columns at interior grid locations before you insert new interior columns.
- ✔ This following example shows how to place columns by selecting locations.

Hands-on:

Step 1: Erase all columns at locations B2-C6 and also at D2; leave all columns along the perimeter.

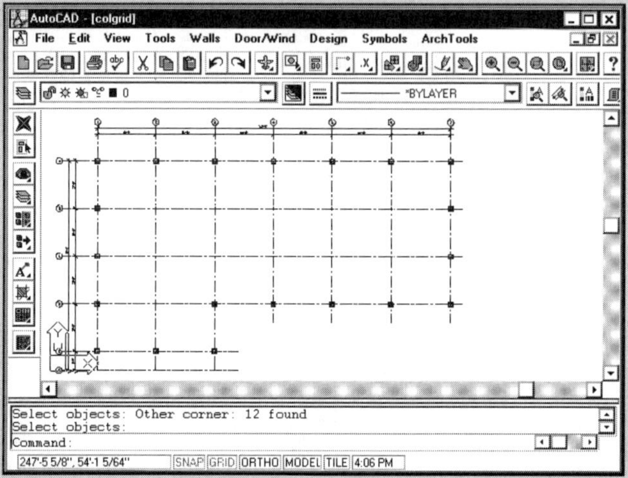

Step 2: Restart the [Place Column...] command.

Step 3: Change the placement method to "Select Location".

Step 4: Change the enclosure height to **8'**.

Step 5: Choose the "OK" button to continue.

Step 6: Use the osnap INTersection to choose column location B2.

Step 7: Type **C** to activate the copy option.

Step 8: Use osnap INTersection to copy the column to intersections C2 and D2.

Step 9: Press <Enter> at the "Copy objects:" prompt to return to the options prompt.

Step 10: Type **R** to activate the rotate option.

Step 11:	Enter **90** for the rotation angle.
Step 12:	Type **C** to activate the copy option.
Step 13:	Copy the last column to each remaining interior location.
Step 14:	Use the rotate option to rotate the columns as you see fit.
Step 15:	Press <Enter> to end the command.

Draw Walls

The column enclosures placed by the [Place Column...] command are Softdesk wall objects.

- ✔ You can use the [Wall] command to draw walls up to the column enclosure.
  - ✗ The Softdesk program will clean up the intersection of new walls and column enclosures if the wall height and enclosure heights match.

Exterior Walls

The following example shows you how to draw walls between columns.

- ✔ The first part shows you how to create exterior walls that merge with the column enclosures to create pilasters on the inside of an exterior wall.

Hands-on:

Step 1: Turn off all footing layers ("FOOT*") to make it easier to select columns with object snaps.

Step 2: Zoom in to the area in grid bays E1-C3.

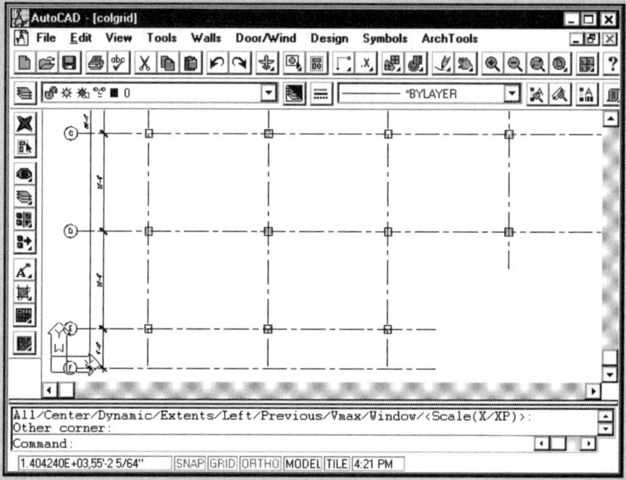

Step 3: Type **W2** at the command prompt to use the AB_SIDE wall style.

Step 4: Enter **12** for wall width and **10′** for wall thickness.

Step 5: Use an osnap to pick the lower-right corner of the column enclosure at E1.

Step 6: Use an osnap to pick the lower-left corner of the column enclosure at E2.

Step 7: Pick a point above the grid line to indicate the side.

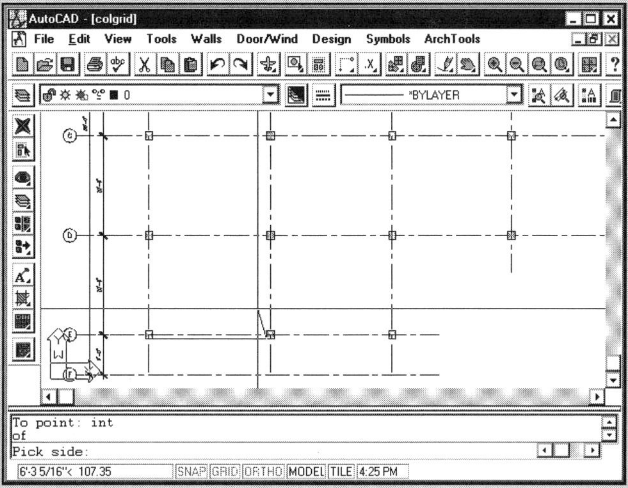

Step 8: Press <Enter> to end the wall command.

Step 9: Draw additional walls from E2-E3 and E3-D3.

Interior Walls

In the last example, the wall clean-up routine created a smooth exterior wall face and leaves the pilasters around the columns on the interior of the building.

- ✔ The next example shows how to create an interior wall between two columns.
- ✔ The wall will intersect with the column enclosure and clean up the lines to create correct wall intersections.

Hands-on:

Step 1: Type **W1** at the command prompt to use the AB_CENTER wall style.

Step 2: Enter **8** for wall width and **8'** for wall thickness.

Step 3: Use an osnap to choose the lower midpoint of the column enclosure at D2.

Step 4: Use an osnap to choose the upper midpoint of the column enclosure at E2.

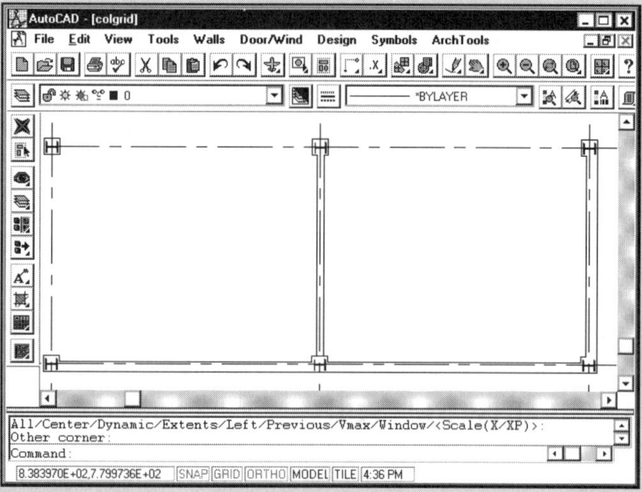

Step 5: Press <Enter> to end the [Wall] command.

Note:

Notice that the wall has cleaned up with the column enclosure at D2, where the height matches, but not at E2 where it does not match.

Chapter 3

Advanced Wall Features

Objectives

To solve complex design problems with wall styles, you should be able to:

- ✔ Create wall styles with the pick and draw options.
- ✔ Create extruded architectural elements with a wall style.
- ✔ Organize elements in a wall style using groups and priorities.
- ✔ Use lines and faces in a wall style.
- ✔ Define variable values in a wall style.

Introduction

This chapter shows you how to take complete control of the wall features in *Auto-Architect*. In the first part of this chapter, you will see how to define wall styles by choosing existing lines or wall objects on a drawing, or by creating new features in the drawing. The following section shows how to create a complex wall style, which leads into examples of using groups, priorities, and caps in a wall style for creating three-dimensional models, improving two dimensional drawing, and correcting wall styles. The final portion of this chapter shows how to solve design problems using wall routines — from tips for using lines and faces in a wall style to placing windows in walls that you extend to a roof.

As you complete this chapter, notice that *Auto-Architect* recognizes that separate elements are recognized as part of the same wall, rather than just a bunch of lines and faces. Wall styles define the combination of lines and faces into wall objects. Not only does the use of wall styles make it easy to define walls, but they are valuable tools when you need to make changes to your design. You should carefully review all of the settings available to you in the wall library and make sure that you are using wall layers and settings to your best advantage.

Wall Style Options

A common method for creating a wall style is to enter offset values for each element in the style. This "numeric" method is tedious for walls with complex cross-sections.

- ✔ The "Pick and Draw" option of the [Wall Styles...] command allows you to define wall styles graphically.
  - ✗ Use the "Pick" option to select existing objects on the drawing and read the information from those objects into a wall style.
  - ✗ Use the "Draw" option to draw objects in the controlled environment and have the features of your drawing read into a wall style.

The Pick Option

Use the "Pick" option to define a wall style by selecting objects in a drawing.

- ✔ You can choose lines, faces, polylines, and hatch patterns.
- ✔ You can also regenerate an existing wall drawn with the [Wall] command, but which does not have a style definition.
  - ✗ This allows you to restore a wall style that you may have accidentally deleted from the project file.
  - ✗ You can also read wall styles from drawings that you receive without an accompanying wall style file and add them to your project file.
- ✔ You can choose any lines and faces to define a wall style with the pick option.
  - ✗ You can choose only those hatch (wall poche) patterns and polylines that were created as part of a wall style.
- ✔ Lines and faces must be parallel for inclusion in a wall style.
  - ✗ The lines and faces may have different lengths and end alignments.

The following example shows how to create a wall style by drawing the wall with regular objects and then using the pick option to create a style.

- ✔ Your first step is to draw the wall elements — you can use AutoCAD commands to draw and copy elements to create the wall.
- ✔ Next, you define the wall style by picking the elements on the drawing — make sure you follow the sequence for picking the elements.
- ✔ Finally, you can test the new wall style.

Hands-on

Step 1: Open existing drawing *c:\sdskproj\workshop \dwg\int1b.dwg*.

Step 2: Zoom into the top left corner of the building.

Step 3: Set the layer WALL to be current.

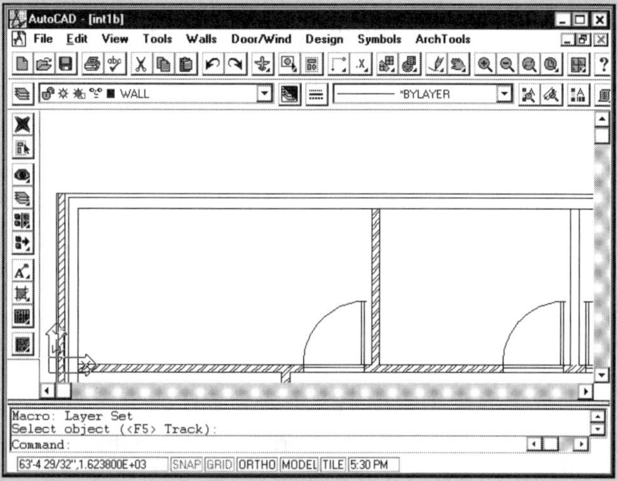

Step 4: Turn ortho on.

Step 5: Draw a horizontal line on the screen.

Step 6: Change the thickness of the line to **10′**.

Step 7: Copy the line up **6″** in the Y direction.

Step 8: Set the layer **WALL3D** to be current.

Step 9: Use the [FA] macro to draw a face parallel to the lines — place the face above your existing lines.

Step 10: Use the [Tools ⇨ Edit ⇨ Change ⇨ Change Elevation] command to change the elevation of the face to **10′**.

Step 11: Copy an existing hatch pattern in the drawing to sit between the two new lines.

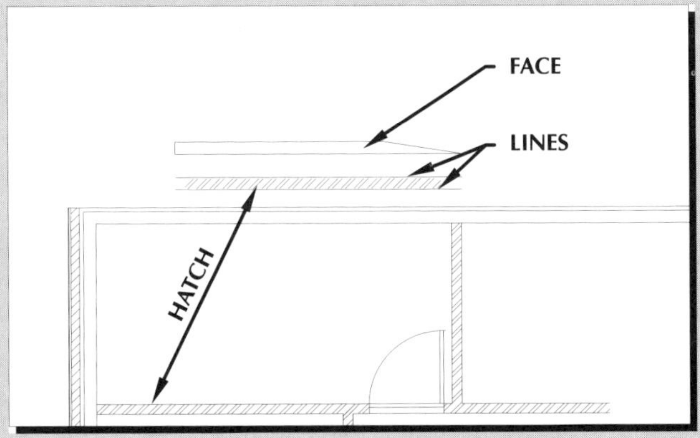

Step 12: Select [Walls ⇨ Wall Library...] from the pull-down menu.

Note:

The last object that you pick determines the "Working Point" of the wall. If you use a crossing box to select the objects, the last object that you drew (the face in this case) becomes the "Working Point". The thickness of the line is taken from the lines you create in the drawing.

Step 13: Select the “Pick<” button from the Wall Style dialog box.

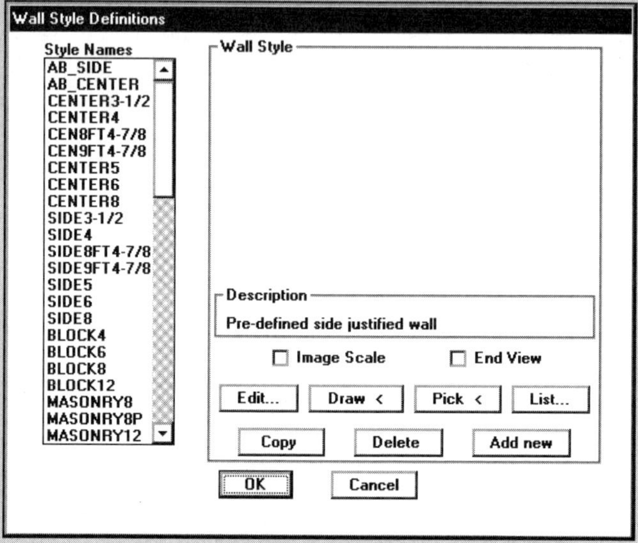

Step 14: Select the new objects individually in such an order that the outside line nearest the building is the last object.

Step 15: Press <Enter> to return to the wall dialog box.

Step 16: Enter a new name and description for the wall style.

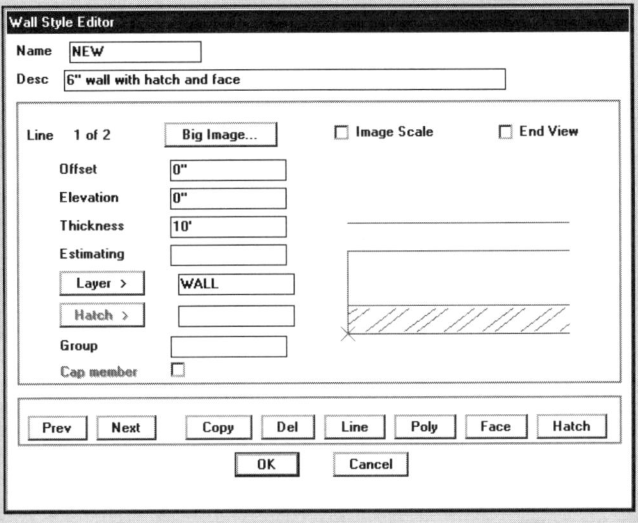

Step 17: Choose the "OK" button.

Step 18: Toggle both "Image Scale" and "End View" on to see the wall style in section.

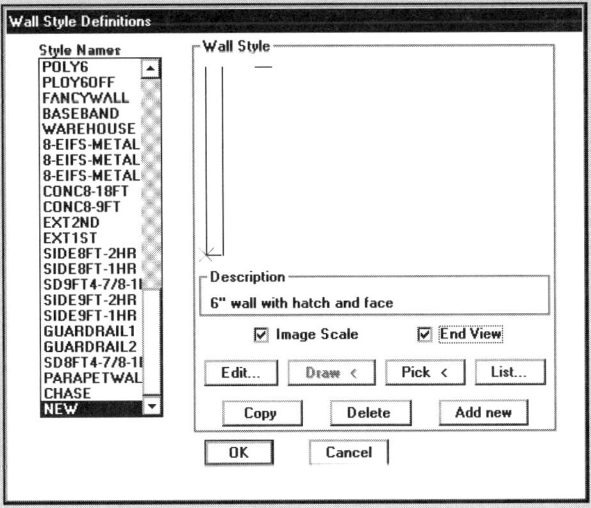

Step 19: Choose the "OK" button on the Wall Style Definitions dialog box.

Step 20: Draw several segments with the wall style — start at a point even with the line nearest the building.

Step 21: Select a point above the start point on the screen to show *Auto-Architect* which side to place the wall.

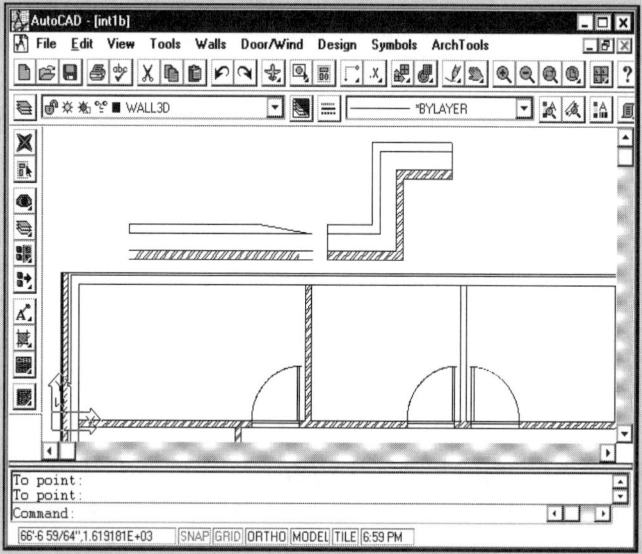

The following example shows how to make simple changes to an existing wall style using the pick option to select objects on the drawing.

- ✔ You can change a wall with regular AutoCAD commands and then read all of the wall information back into the wall library.
- ✔ Make sure your layers are set correctly before you define wall styles with this method.

Hands-on:

Step 1: Zoom in on the upper-left corner room on the plan.

Step 2: Copy a line on the lower side of an existing wall to a position below the wall.

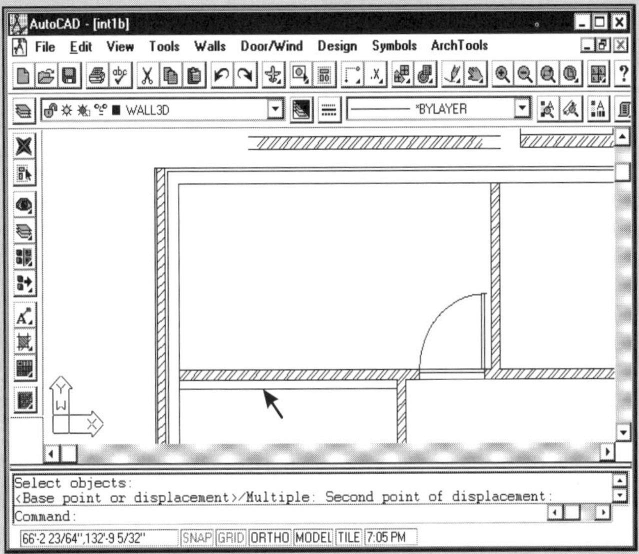

Step 3: Select [Walls ⇨ Wall Library...] from the pull-down menu.

Step 4: Select the "Pick<" button from the Wall Style dialog box.

Step 5: Select the modified wall segment with a crossing box.

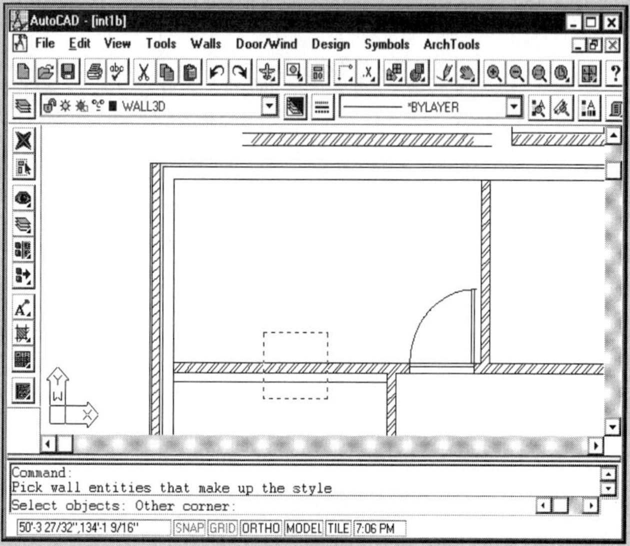

Note:

The working point in this case comes from the wall data found in the drawing instead of using the most recently copied line. Auto-Architect *finds the name from the drawing instead of using the style named "picked."*

Step 6: Change the name to MODIFIED and description to "Modified wall".

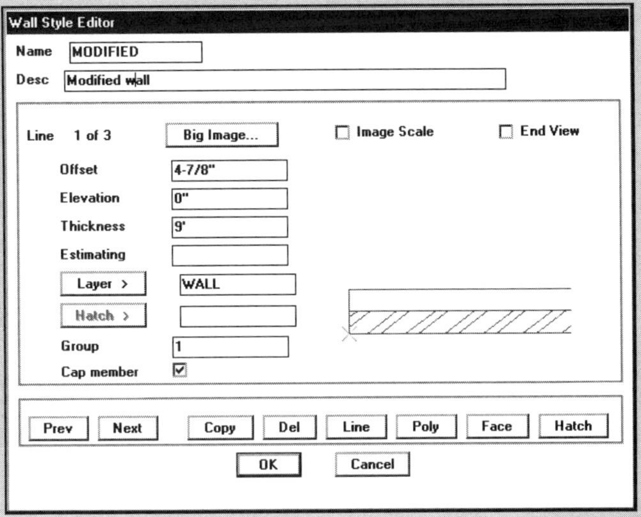

Step 7: Choose the "OK" button to continue.

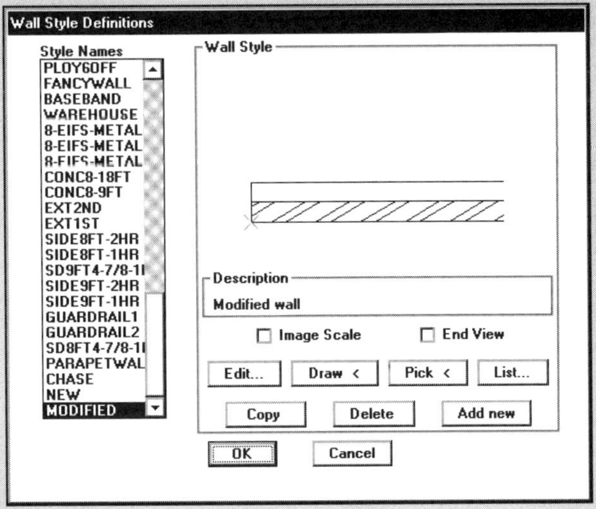

Step 8: Draw several wall segments with the "Modified" style.

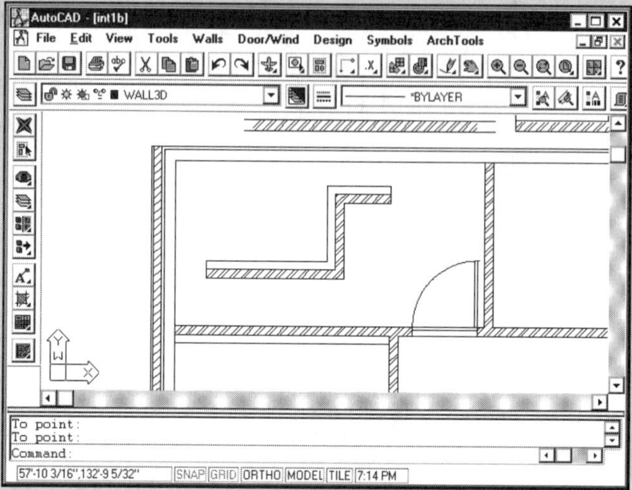

The following example shows how to use the pick option to read a style definition from the drawing if you accidentally delete the style.

- ✔ In the first part of this exercise, you will erase a wall style that you created.
- ✔ Make sure that the wall style is removed from the library.

Hands-on:

Step 1: Select [Walls ⇨ Walls Library...] from the pull-down menu.

Step 2: Select the style called "MODIFIED" from the list and select the "Delete" button.

Step 3: Choose the "OK" button to delete the style.

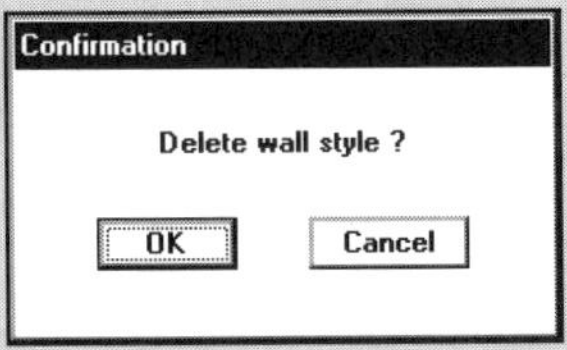

Step 4: Choose the "Pick<" button again and pick all objects along one segment of the previously drawn "MODIFIED" wall.

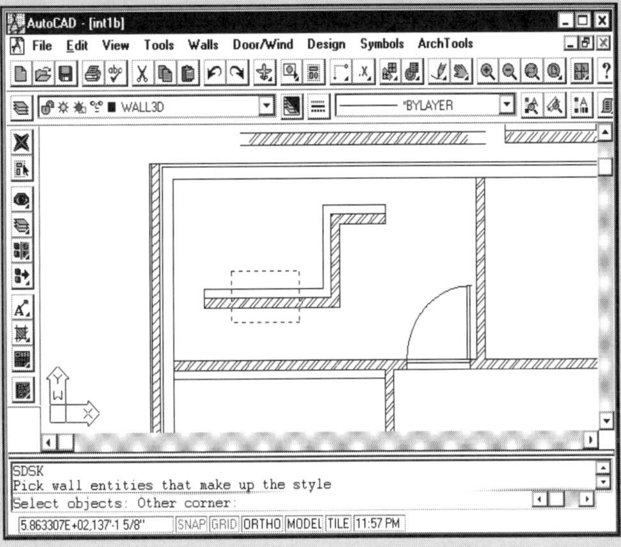

Step 5: Press <Enter> after selecting the wall and enter a new description.

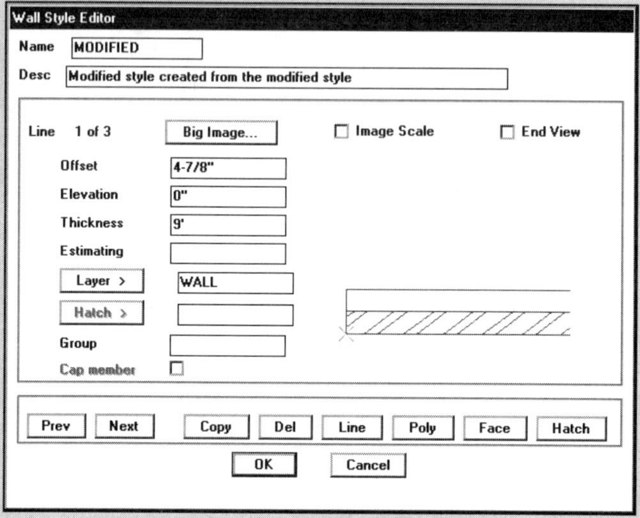

Step 6: Choose the "OK" button and verify that the style is now back on the bottom of the wall style list.

Step 7: Draw some wall segments with the restored style.

The Draw Option

The "Draw" option allows you to define a wall style by drawing the wall.

- ✔ You can work in a section view to help you define complex wall styles.
- ✔ In a section view, faces appear as simple "lines."
  - ✗ The "lines" represent planes which extend perpendicular to the screen surface.
- ✔ You can use lines to create only vertical elements.
  - ✗ You can use faces for vertical as well as horizontal and sloped elements.
- ✔ Before you define a wall style with the "Draw" option, you should enable the side screen menu.

  - ✗ This gives you full access to all draw options.
- ✔ The first step to draw a wall style is to place an automatically generated square drawing area.
  - ✗ *Auto-Architect* asks you to locate the square and removes the square when you are done.
- ✔ Three-dimensional features are for renderings only.
- ✔ Put all three-dimensional features on a 3D layer.
  - ✗ Use a 3D layer for any objects that you may need to turn off when working in a plan.

The following example shows you how to

- ✔ Access the "Draw" options.
- ✔ Place the drawing square.
- ✔ Control plan and section view of the wall style.

Hands-on:

Step 1: Select [File ⇨ Configure ⇨ Preferences...] from the pull-down menu.

Step 2: Choose the "System" tab and then choose the "Screen Menu" toggle in the Preferences dialog box.

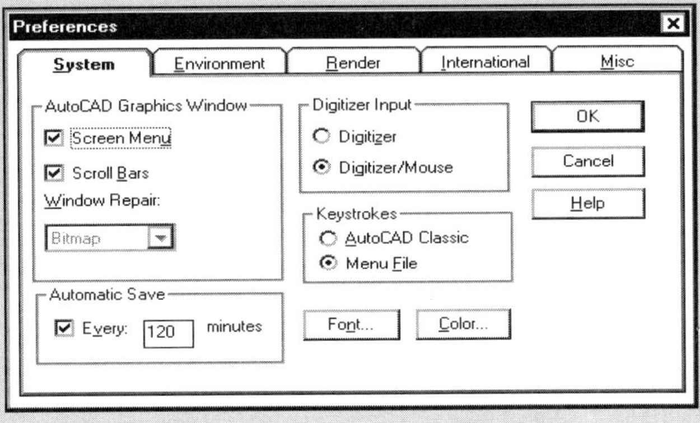

Step 3: Choose the "OK" button to exit the dialog box.

Step 4: Change to the world coordinate system if you are not already there.

Step 5: Select [Walls ⇨ Wall Library...] from the pull-down menu.

Step 6: Choose the NEW style you just created and select the "Draw <" button.

Step 7: Pick a point to locate the style definition box.

Step 8: Use a transparent zoom command to find an empty area for the box if necessary.

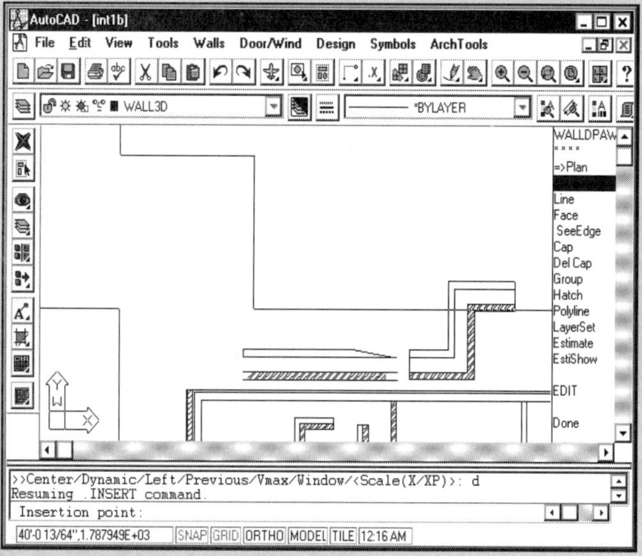

Step 9: Choose options to add lines, faces, and other elements from the side-screen menu.

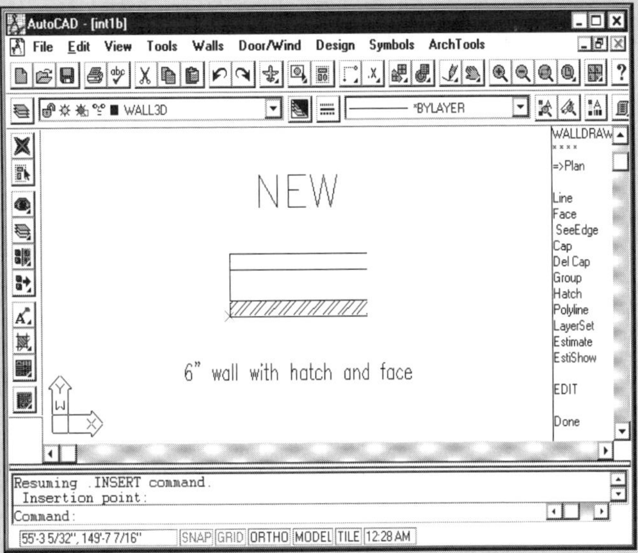

Step 10: Choose "DelCap" and select the cap on the left end — this will avoid confusion as you draw the wall style in section.

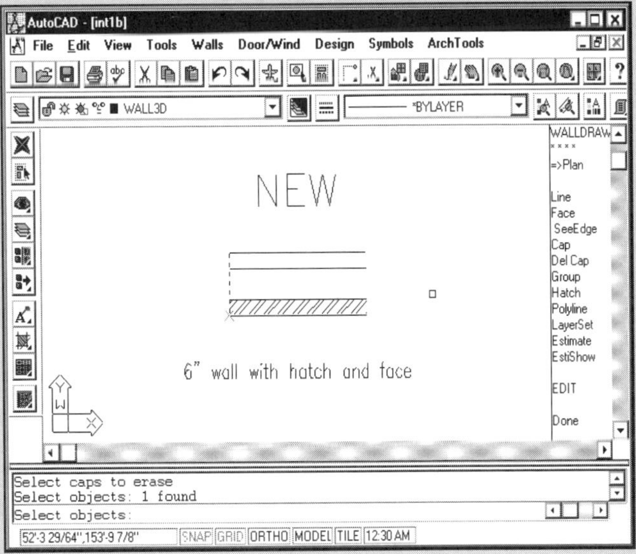

Note:

The face has invisible edges on both the left and right ends. Any horizontal face (parallel to the floor) has invisible edges on the ends to avoid excess miter lines when you view it in plan.

Step 11: Select "SeeEdge" from the side-screen menu to toggle visibility of the invisible face edges.

Step 12: Select "=>Plan" from the side-screen menu to switch from plan to a section view.

Step 13: Use the [Zoom] and [Pan] command if necessary to see the entire wall style in section.

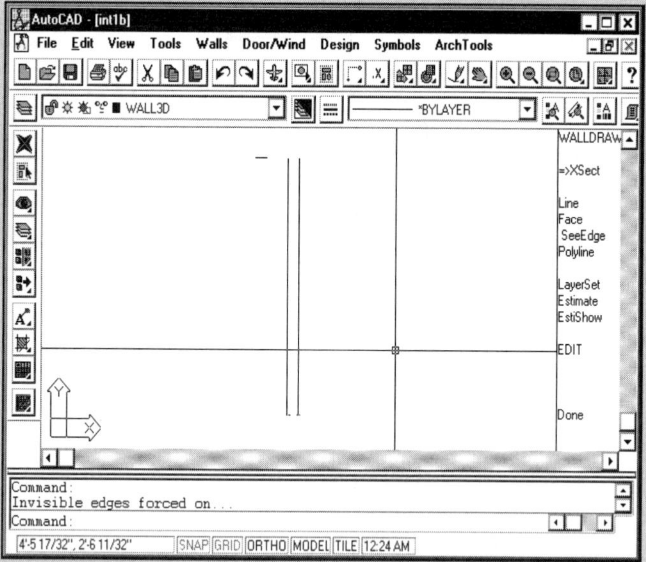

When the last example is complete, the face appears as a horizontal line to the left of the top of the lines.

✔ This example asks you to move this face with the move macro and object snap and then add a fancy molding to the wall.

Hands-on:

Step 1: Choose "LayerSet" from the side-screen menu and set to the WALL3D layer current.

Step 2: Use the [Mo] macro and object snaps to move the existing face onto the top of the wall.

Step 3: Use the [Co] macro and object snaps to copy the top face to the bottom of the wall.

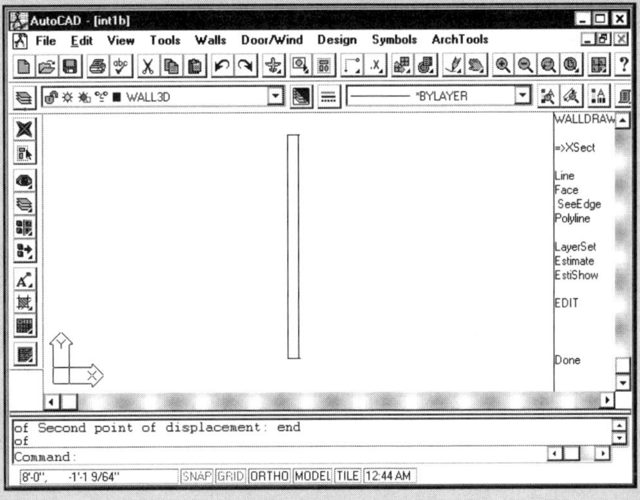

Step 4: Choose "Face" from the side-screen menu.

Step 5: Use an osnap and pick the top right of the wall to define the first point of the face.

Step 6: Pick a second point horizontally to the right.

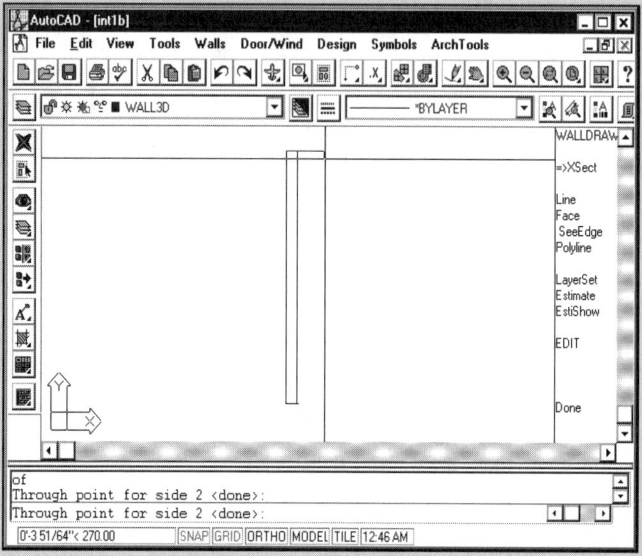

Step 7: Enter several more points to draw the molding outline.

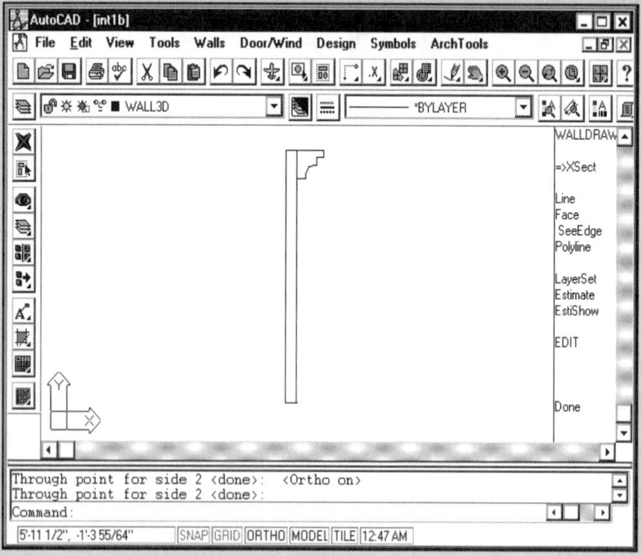

Step 8: Select "Done" from the side-screen.

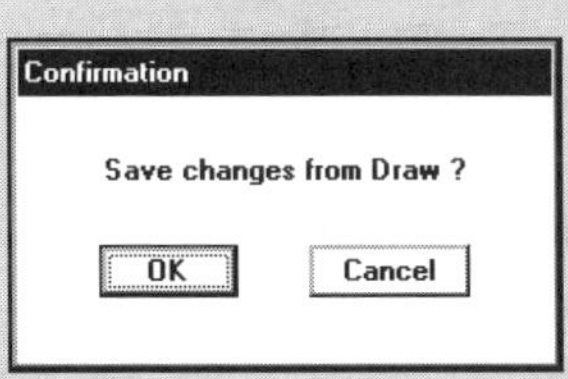

Step 9: Press the "OK" button to save changes.

Step 10: Choose the "Image Scale" and "End View" toggle to display the wall style in a section view.

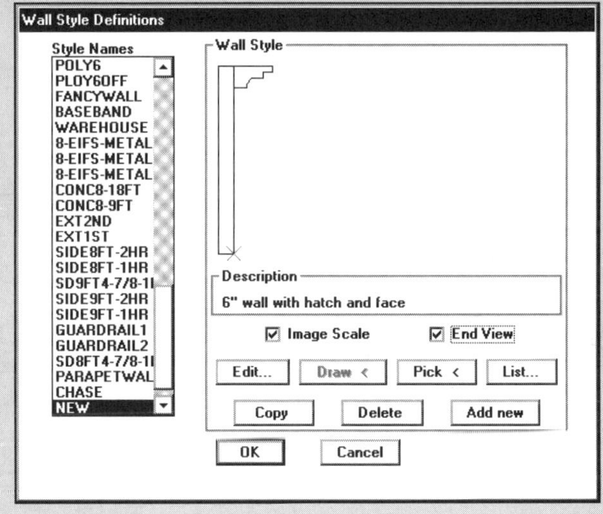

Step 11: Press the "OK" button and use the style to draw several segments.

Step 12: Create an arc segment by selecting the "=>Line" toggle from the side-screen menu.

Step 13: Use the "CE" option to create the arc and pick "=> Arc" from the side-screen menu to toggle back to straight lines.

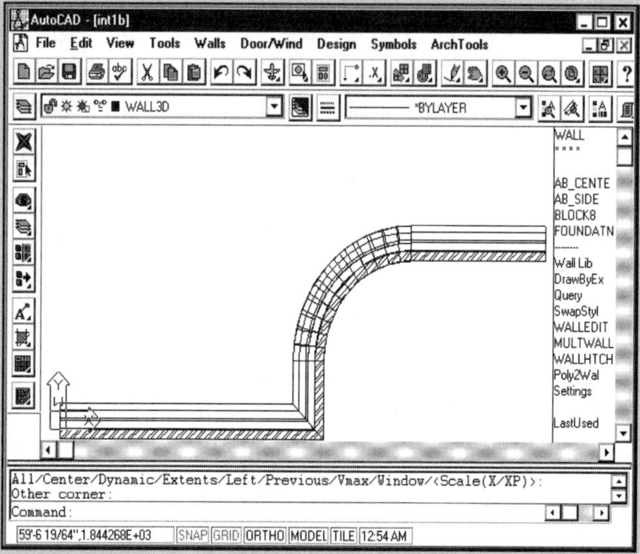

Step 14: Choose [View ⇨ Presentation ⇨ Eye Position] from the pull-down menu.

Step 15: Choose a target and eye position to view the wall in three dimensions.

Step 16: Use the [Hide] command to complete the view.

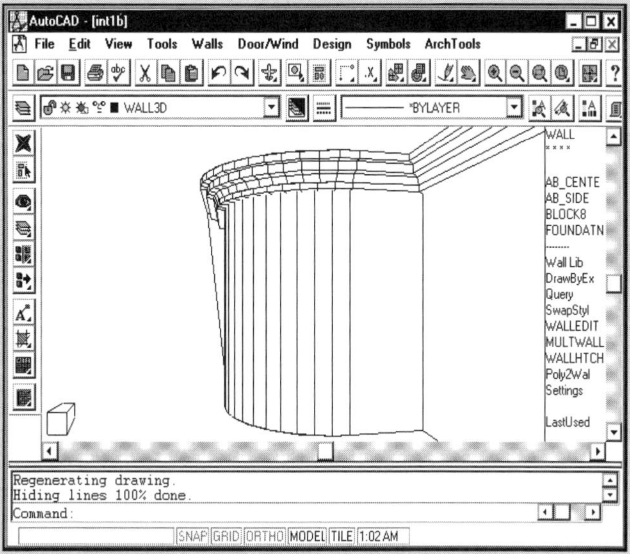

Step 17: Return to a plan view.

Step 18: Turn wall layers on and freeze 3D layers to see the 2D representation for floor and ceiling plans.

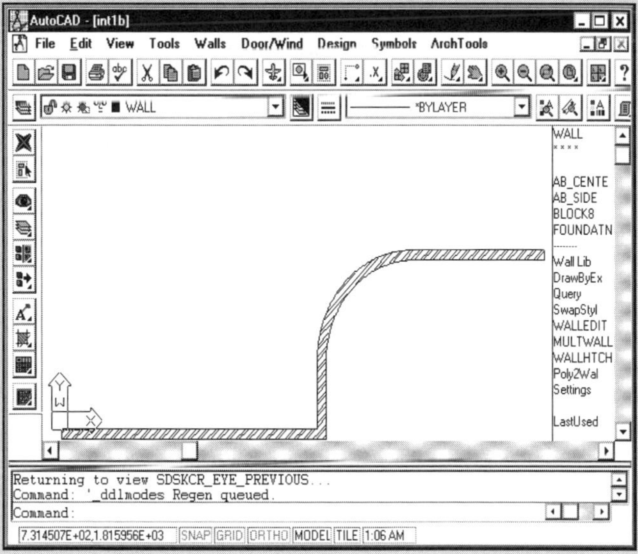

Mirroring a Wall Style

A wall style may appear mirrored in the style library when you finish the "Draw" option.

✔ The following example shows how to mirror the wall style back to the orientation in which you drew it.

Hands-on:

Step 1: Select [Walls ⇨ Wall Library...] from the pull-down menu.

Step 2: Choose the "NEW" style to mirror.

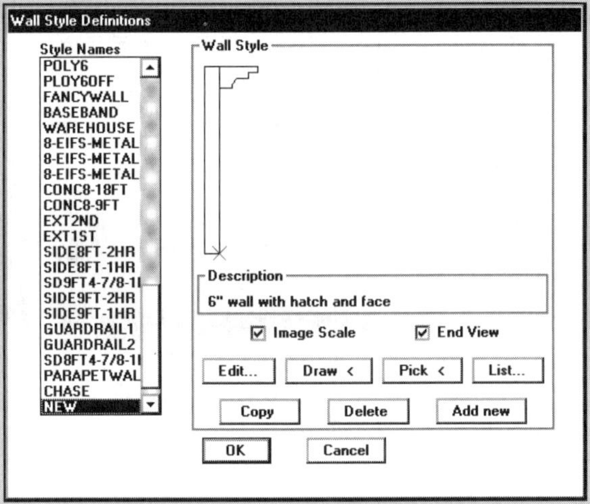

Step 3: Choose the "Draw" button.

Step 4: Pick a point to place the style definition box.

Step 5: Choose "Done" from the side-screen menu to end the command without changing the style definition.

Step 6: Choose "OK" to save the changes from draw.

Step 7: Choose the "Image Scale" and "End View" toggles to see the results of the change.

Complex Wall Styles

A wall style is not limited to simple wall definitions.

- ✔ You can use a wall style to create any extruded architectural element.

The following example shows how to create a wall and roof assembly with a single wall style.

- ✔ In the first part of this example, you will define the elements within the wall style.
- ✔ A following example shows how to place the elements in the wall style on the correct layers and test the wall style.

Hands-on:

Step 1:	Create a new drawing called *cwalls.dwg.*
Step 2:	Load *Auto-Architect* — choose the **WORKSHOP** project.
Step 3:	Choose "OK" to accept the default sheet settings.
Step 4:	Select [Walls ⇨ Wall Library...] from the pull-down menu.
Step 5:	Choose the **CENTER4** wall style, pick Copy, and rename it to **MYWALL**.
Step 6:	Pick the "OK" button.
Step 7:	Choose the "Draw" button.

Step 8: Use the [ET] macro to change the style name to **CUPOLA** and the description to **Cupola Assembly**. Be sure to use all capitals for title.

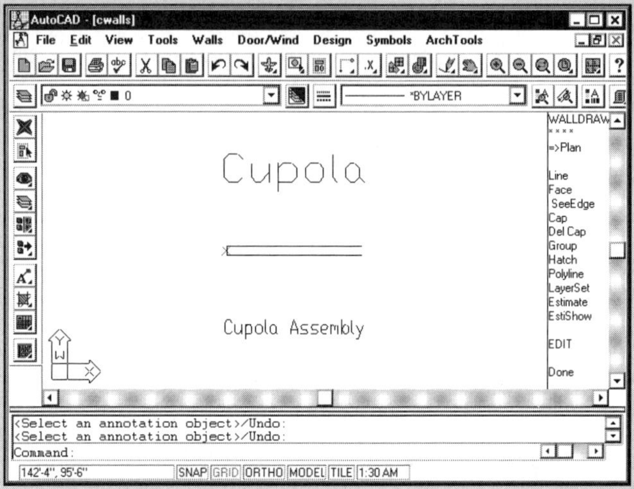

Step 9: Switch to a section view.

Step 10: Draw a Face from the top middle of the style over to the right.

Step 11: Enter the coordinate **@10'6,-52.5** to define a slope of 5/12.

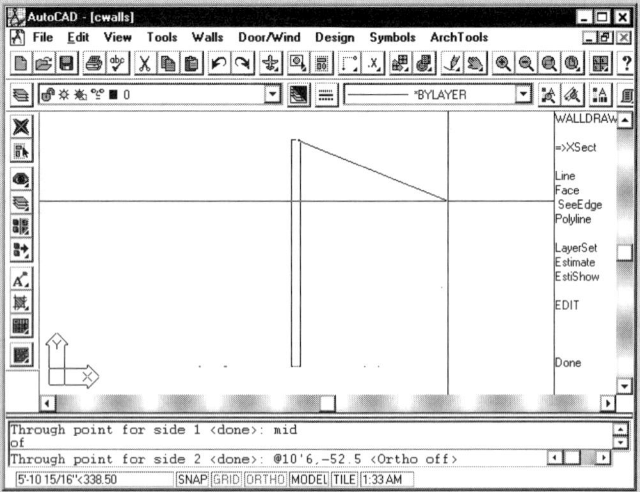

Step 12: Use the [Zoom All] command to view all of the new face if necessary.

Step 13: Continue drawing faces — enter **@0,-8** for the fascia, **@-6,0** for the soffit, and **@0,-5′** for the wall.

Step 14: Copy the last face **6″** to the left to form the inside wall surface.

Step 15: Erase the original wall style objects.

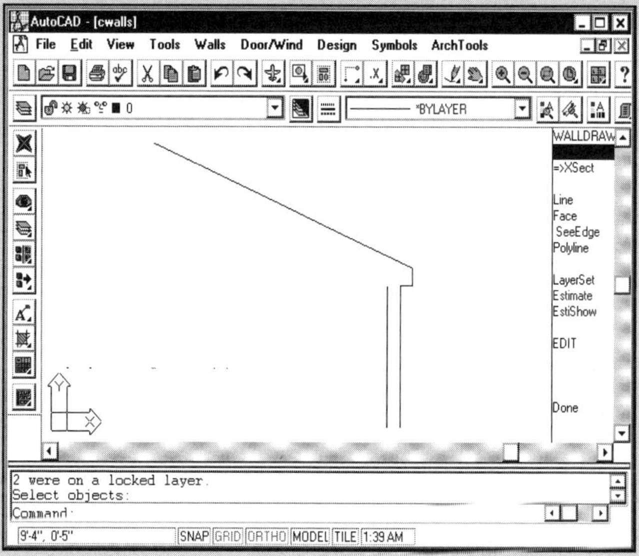

Step 16: Use the mirror macro to form the other side of the wall style.

Step 17: Select "Done" from the side-screen menu and accept the changes.

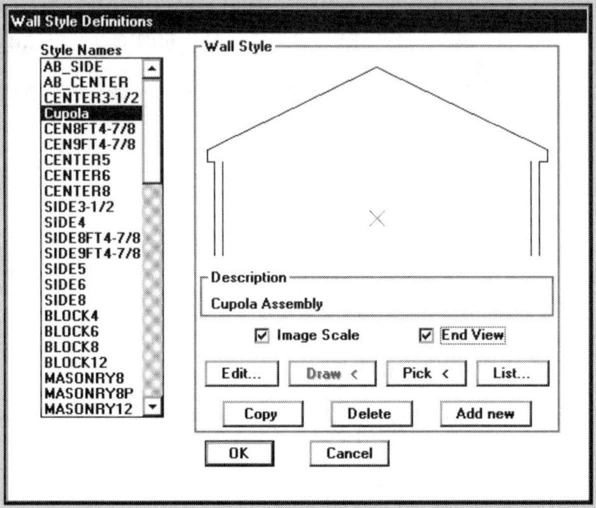

The following example shows how to change the layer of elements in a wall style.

✔ Check the layers used for the different elements in the Cupola style as follows:

✗ ROOF3D	Sloped Roof face
✗ ROOFSOF	Fascia and Soffit
✗ WALL	Wall

Hands-on:

Step 1: Select the "Edit" button and make sure the "Image Scale" and "End View" toggles are on.

Step 2: Select the "Next" button repeatedly to highlight the sloped roof face.

Step 3: Select the "Layer>" button and select "Roof faces 3D" from the list of descriptions.

Step 4: Choose the "OK" button.

Note:

The program copies the corresponding layer key "ROOF3D" into the wall style file.

Step 5: Select "Next" to highlight the fascia.

Step 6: Select the "Layer>" button and then "Roof fascia & soffit 3D".

Step 7: Select "Next" to highlight the soffit.

Step 8: Enter the layer key **ROOFSOF** in the edit field to the right of the "Layer>" button

Step 9: Assign the layer key **WALL** to the next two wall lines.

Step 10: Repeat the above steps for the other side of the cupola and choose the "OK" button.

Step 11: Draw several segments of the CUPOLA style and view the results in 3D.

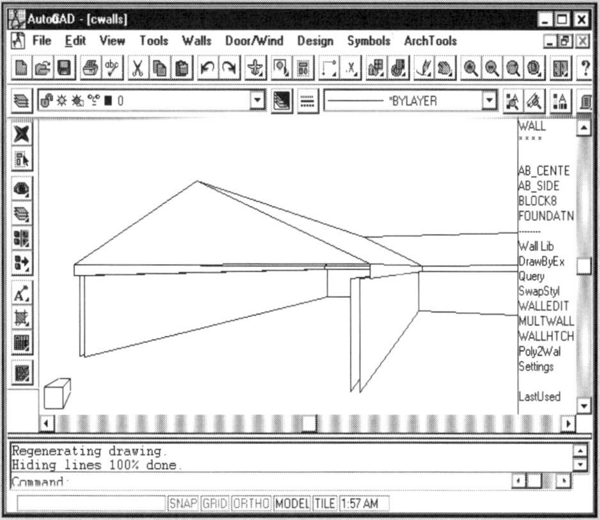

Groups, Priorities, and Caps

You can organize the elements in a wall style into groups and priorities.

- ✔ Use groups in a wall style to control which lines to cap and how those lines match with other lines at a wall intersection.
  - ✗ You can control how *Auto-Architect* places caps between the end points of lines that you group together.
  - ✗ A line group in a wall style will match up with the same wall group when you intersect another wall of the same style.
- ✔ You must assign a priority number when you create a group.
  - ✗ A lower group number indicates a higher priority.
  - ✗ Groups with high priority cut through lower priority groups at tee intersections.
- ✔ Priorities are relative and operate inside a wall style.
  - ✗ Groups and priorities do not affect the intersection of walls with different styles.
- ✔ You can place several elements in a group.
  - ✗ You can define only one cap per group.
  - ✗ A cap runs between two elements in the group.
  - ✗ You must define a cap in every group, even if there is only one item in the group.

Groups and Caps

The following example shows how to use groups and caps for a three-dimensional wall style — in this case to improve the CUPOLA wall style from the last exercise.

- ✔ The CUPOLA style does not have caps across the end.

- ✔ You may want to extend the roof over the end of the wall.
- ✔ The two outermost lines should be capped.
- ✔ The inner walls should be capped as well but with a six-inch gap between the inner and outer caps.

Hands-on:

Step 1: Change to a plan view of the drawing.

Step 2: Select [Walls ⇨ Wall Library...] from the pull-down menu.

Step 3: Select the **CUPOLA** style and choose the "Edit..." button.

Step 4: Choose the "Image Scale" and "End View" toggles.

Step 5: Choose the "Next" button to highlight the outer most wall face.

Step 6: Enter **1** for the "Group" value.

Step 7: Press <Enter> and turn on the "Cap member" toggle.

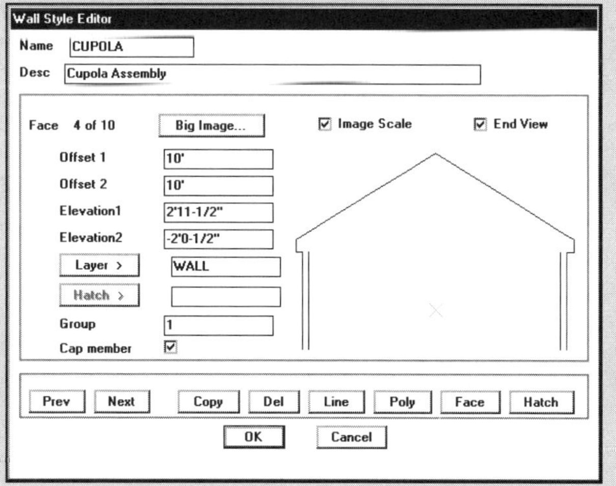

Step 8: Highlight the inner vertical wall on the right side.

Step 9: Select the "Next" button and set the "Group" number to **2**.

Step 10: Press <Enter> and turn on the "Cap member" toggle.

Note:

You must press <Enter> after entering a group value to enable the cap toggle.

Step 11: Select the "Next" button until the inner wall on the left side of the style is highlighted.

Step 12: Enter **2** for the "Group" number and turn on the "Cap member" toggle.

Step 13: Select the "Next" button to highlight the outer wall on the left side of the wall style.

Step 14: Enter **1** for the "Group" number and turn on the "Cap member" toggle.

Step 15: Set all elements on the ROOFSOF layer to group 3.

Step 16: Turn on the "Cap" member toggle for the vertical ROOFSOF face on the left and right sides of the wall style.

Step 17: Set both faces on the ROOF3D layer to group 4 and turn on the "Cap" member toggles.

Step 18: Choose the "Next" button to cycle through all elements and verify that groups and cap toggles are set properly.

Step 19: Select the "Next" button to display the cap for group 2.

Step 20: Notice that the ends of the cap are highlighted.

Step 21: Enter an offset of **-6** to recess this end cap from the cap for group 1.

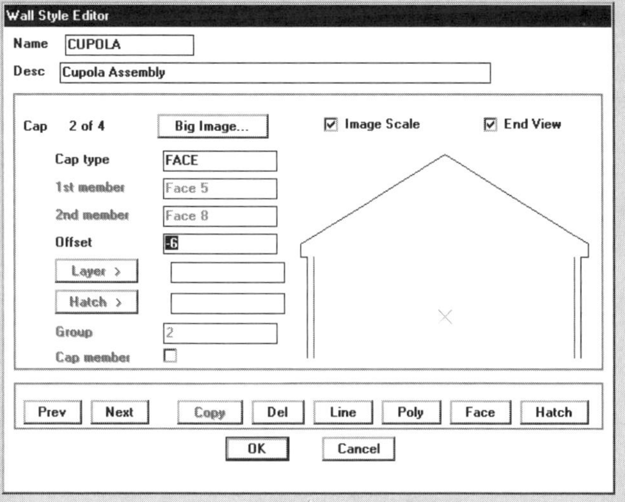

Step 22: Turn off the "End view" toggle to see the results in plan view.

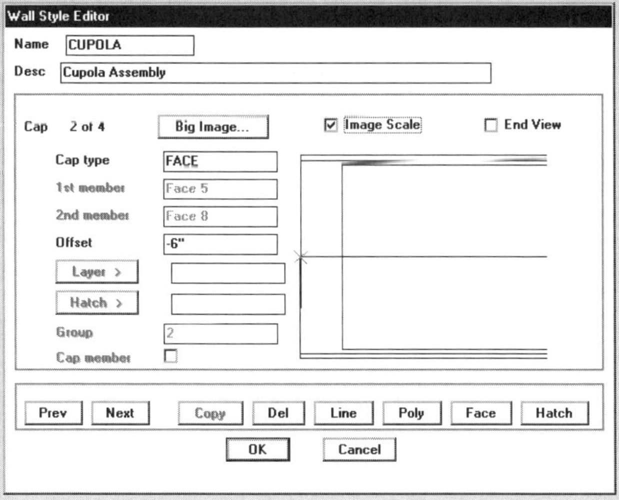

Step 23: Adjust the offsets for the group 3 and group 4 caps to be **6″**.

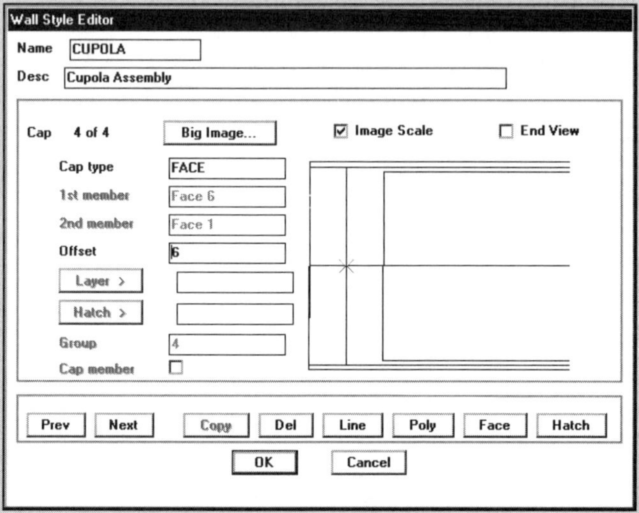

Step 24: Choose "OK" to exit from the dialog boxes.

Step 25: Draw several segments with the improved CUPOLA style.

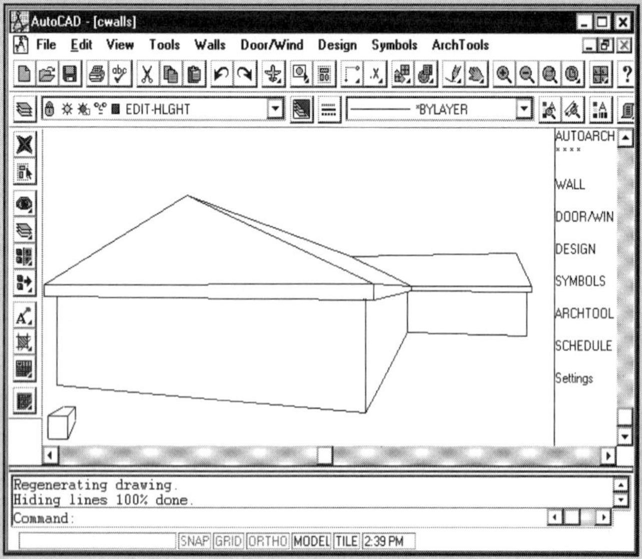

Note:

If you want to remove a cap from a wall style, delete the cap using the "Next" and "Delete" buttons rather than turning off the Cap.

Priorities for Intersections

The following exercise shows how to use priorities to improve the creation of a Tee intersection of walls.

- ✔ You will create a new wall style and see how it performs before and after you define groups in the style.
- ✔ The first part of this exercise directs you to create a wall style that will result in a intersection error.
- ✔ The following exercise shows how to correct the error.

Hands-on:

Step 1:	Create a new drawing called *twalls.dwg*.
Step 2:	Load *Auto-Architect* and use the WORKSHOP project.
Step 3:	Set drawing scale to 1/2"=1'0" — accept all other setup defaults.
Step 4:	Select [Walls ⇨ Wall Library...] from the pull-down menu.
Step 5:	Choose the **CENTER6** wall style.
Step 6:	Select the style "Copy" button and rename the style to **CLINE**.
Step 7:	Add "with centerline" to the description.

Step 8: Select the element Copy button and change the offset of this third line to 0, the thickness to 0, and the layer to WALLCL.

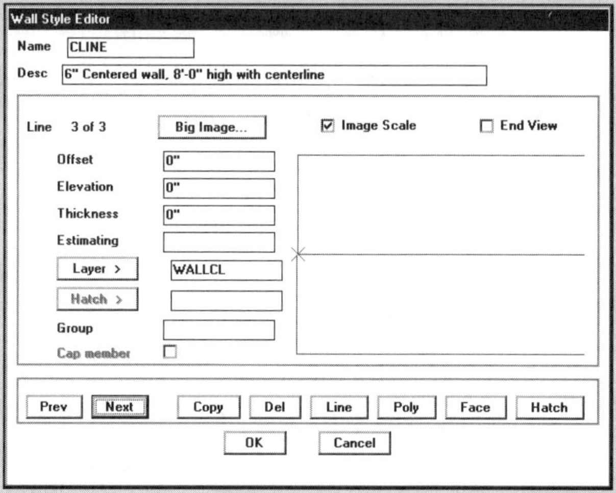

Step 9: Choose the "OK" button twice and draw some segments with the style — pick the last wall point back on itself to form a Tee intersection.

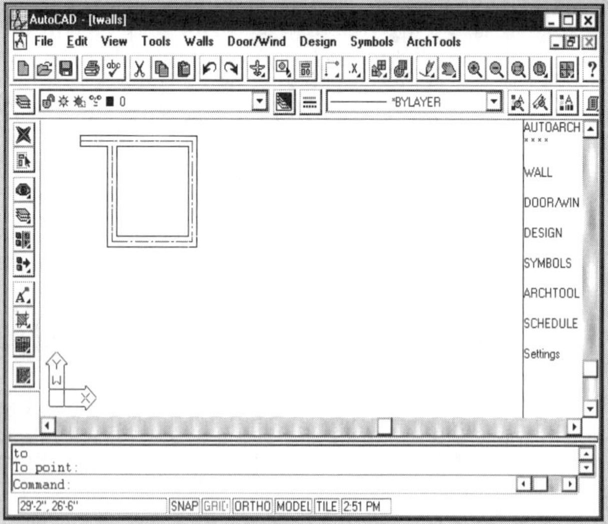

The centerlines do not join at the Tee intersection.

- ✔ All lines in the last segment stop at the outermost line of the first segment.
  - ✗ You can set a higher group priority if you want the centerline to extend through the outer wall lines to meet up with the other centerline.
- ✔ The following example shows how to define a group for the centerline and test the results of by creating a Tee intersection.

Hands-on:

Step 1: Select [Walls ⇨ Wall Library...] from the pull-down menu.

Step 2: Choose the **CLINE** wall style and then choose the "Edit" button.

Step 3: Choose the "Next" button and set the outer lines to group 2 and the centerline to group 1.

Step 4: Turn on the "Cap member" toggle for all three elements.

Step 5: Test the new wall style.

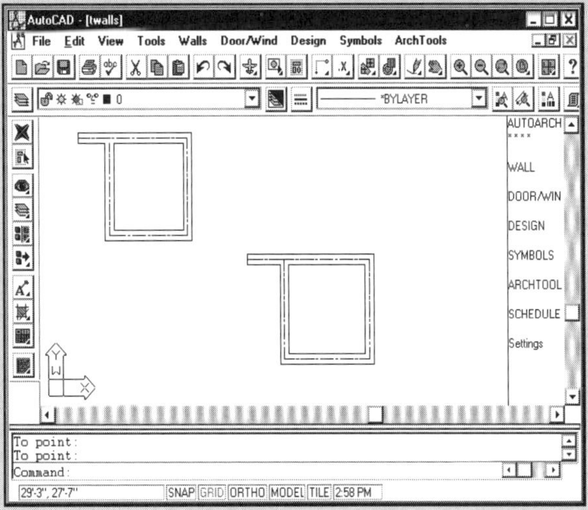

Notice that the centerline in group 1 must have the "Cap member" toggle on, making it cap with itself.

- ✔ There must be at least one cap member in each group to make the group work properly.

Analyzing and Correcting a Wall Style

The following exercise shows how to correct a problem in a wall style by using a group.

- ✔ The first step is to analyze the wall style by drawing a wall with that style.
  - ✗ In this case, the error appears only when you hide a three-dimensional view of a footing wall.
  - ✗ The top of the end surface does not hide — the bottom inside line of the footing appears.
- ✔ You can then assess the problem and change groups within the wall style.
  - ✗ In this case, you must include the top surface of the footing with the same group as the sides of the footing.

Hands-on:

Step 1:	Create a new drawing called *acwalls.dwg*.
Step 2:	Load *Auto-Architect* and use the WORKSHOP project.
Step 3:	Set the drawing scale to `1/2"=1'0"`.
Step 4:	Select [Wall ⇨ Wall Library...] from the pull-down menu and highlight the style **FOUNDATN8**.
Step 5:	Draw several segments with the style.
Step 6:	Select [View ⇨ View ⇨ View Presets...] from the pull-down menu and choose the "South West Isometric" view.

Step 7: Hide the view.

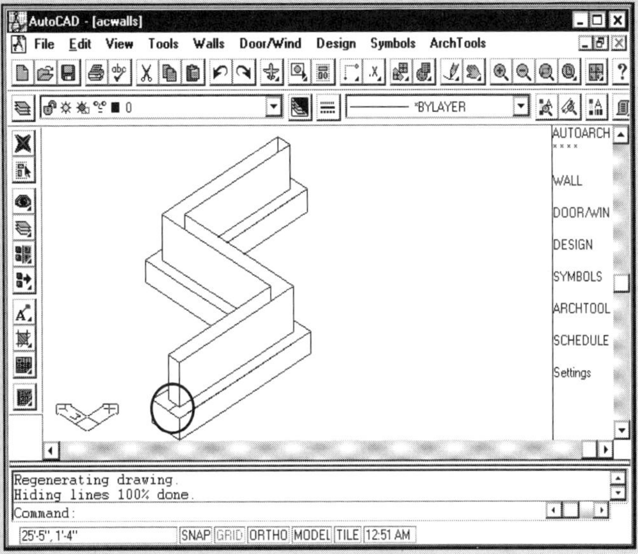

This example shows that the horizontal top face of the footing is not following along with the sides of the footing.

- ✔ This leaves a small gap at the first and last segments of the wall.
  - ✗ You can fix this with a group.
- ✔ You must figure out which group contains the sides of the footing and ensure the top face is in the same group.

Hands-on:

Step 1: Select [Walls ⇨ Wall Library...] from the pull-down menu.

Step 2: Choose the **FOUNDATN8** style and then choose the "Edit" button.

Step 3: Turn the "Image Scale" and "End View" toggles on.

Step 4: Use the "Next" button to verify the group number for the footing sides is 2.

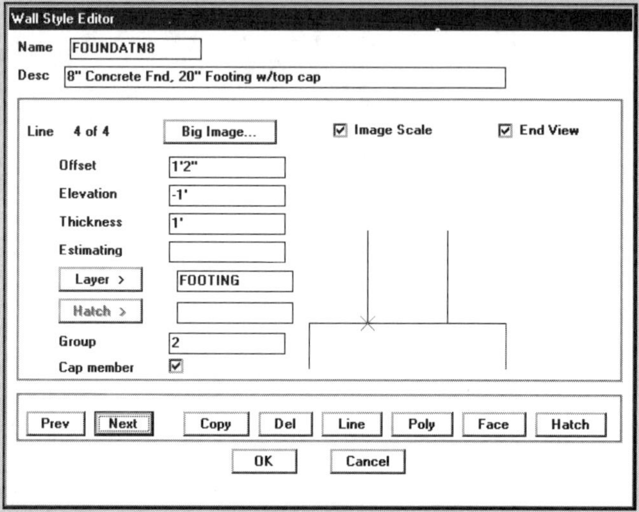

Step 5: Use the "Next" button again to highlight the horizontal face on the FOOTING3D layer.

Step 6: Set the "Group" to **2**.

Step 7: Select "OK" to exit the dialog box.

Step 8: Cancel the command instead of drawing wall segments.

Step 9: Select [Walls ⇨ Swap Wall Styles] from the pull-down menu.

Step 10: Select the old wall segments of FOUNDATN8 to update them in the new style.

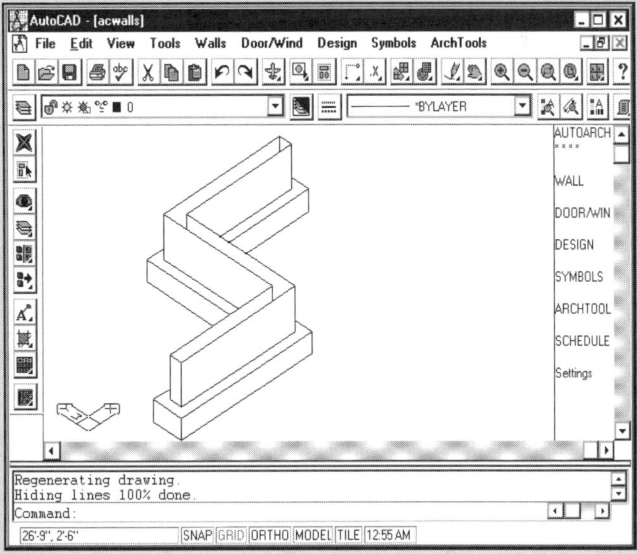

Using Lines and Faces

You must decide whether to use lines or faces when you create a wall style.

- ✔ You must use faces for any non-vertical element.
- ✔ You can use lines or faces for vertical elements.
- ✔ Use lines if you do not expect to do much design work in 3D.
  - ✗ Drawing files are smaller if you use lines.
  - ✗ You can edit lines with the standard AutoCAD [Trim] and [Extend] commands.
- ✔ Use faces if you plan to do any work in 3D.
  - ✗ You can edit faces with the wall edit commands, [Stretch] command, or grips.

- ✗ Vertical lines do not appear above and below door and window openings if you use faces in the wall style.

Variable Values in Wall Styles

You can replace the fixed values in a wall style definition with variable values.

- ✔ This allows you to draw walls with different sizes using the same wall style.
- ✔ You create variables by placing a question mark (?) in any wall style data field that accepts a numeric entry.
  - ✗ When you use the wall style, *Auto-Architect* will prompt you to enter a variable value.
- ✔ You should use only one or two variables in a style.
  - ✗ Using too many variables makes the wall style cumbersome and confusing to use.

The following example shows how to add variable values to an existing wall style.

Hands-on:

Step 1:	Create a new drawing called *vwall.dwg*
Step 2:	Start *Auto-Architect* and choose the WORKSHOP project.
Step 3:	Set the drawing scale to 1/2"=1'0".
Step 4:	Choose [View ⇨ View ⇨ View Presets] from the pull-down menu.
Step 5:	Choose SOUTH EAST ISOMETRIC from the list.
Step 6:	Choose "OK" to continue.
Step 7:	Select [Walls ⇨ Wall Library] from the pull-down menu.

Step 8: Choose the CLINE style.

Step 9: Choose the "Edit" button.

Step 10: Replace the 8′ thickness for line 1 with a question mark.

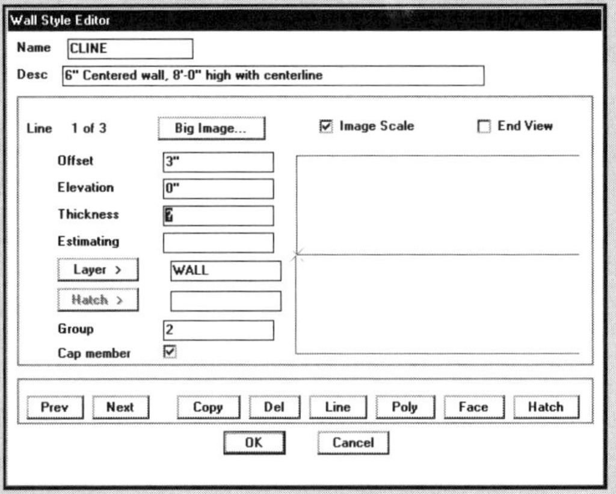

Step 11: Select the "OK" button.

Step 12: Enter **4′** for the wall 1 thickness.

Step 13: Draw several segments with the style.

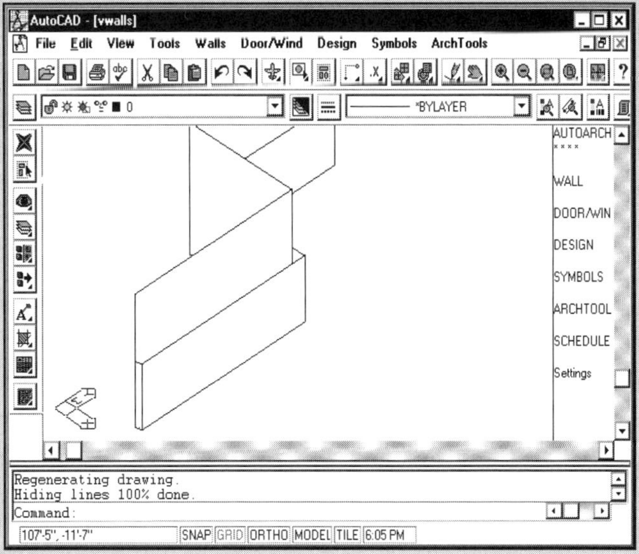

Presetting Wall Justification

If you consistently define and use side-justified walls, you will not have to specify the exterior side of the wall when you place doors and windows.

- ✔ When viewing a wall style in the Wall Style Definitions dialog box, the working point should be at the bottom of the definition drawing.
  - ✗ The inside of the wall should be towards the top of image box in the library dialog definition drawing.
  - ✗ The offset side point should be towards the interior of the building when drawing the wall.
  - ✗ You can make it easier to draw a wall by distinguishing the interior or exterior of a wall with a veneer or other unique material feature in the wall style.
- ✔ The following example clarifies the directional sense inherent in walls.
  - ✗ The example style includes brick veneer on the exterior with thicker concrete block on the interior.

Hands-on:

Step 1: Create a new drawings called *jwalls.dwg*.

Step 2: Start *Auto-Architect* and choose the WORKSHOP project.

Step 3: Set the drawings scale to 1/2″=1′-0″.

Step 4: Select [Walls ⇨ Wall Library...] from the pull-down menu.

Step 5: Choose the MASONRY12P wall style.

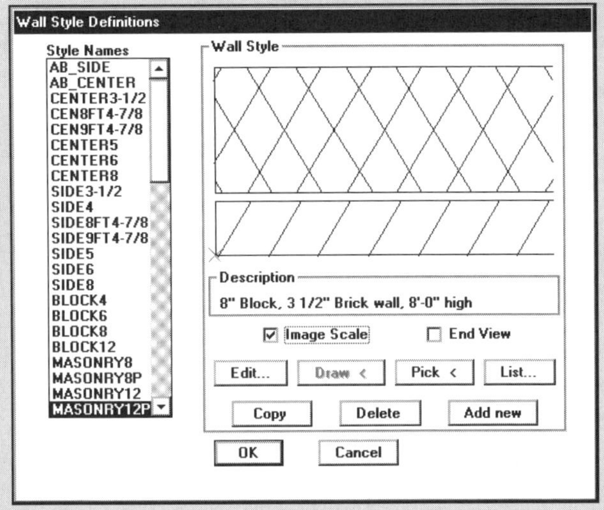

Step 6: Draw several wall segments using this style.

Step 7: Select [Door/Wind ⇨ Door/Window Settings] from the pull-down menu.

Step 8: Turn off the "Prompt for exterior side during insertion" toggle.

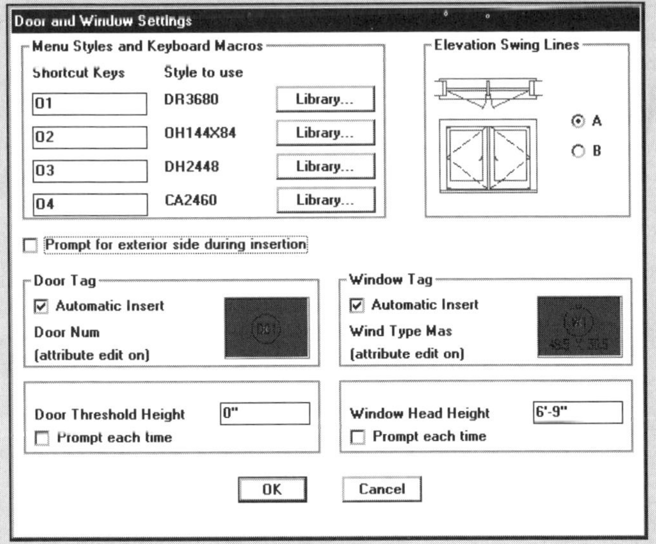

Step 9: Select [Door/Wind ⇨ Library...] from the pull-down menu.

Step 10: Highlight and insert the window style FM3624 anywhere on the wall segment.

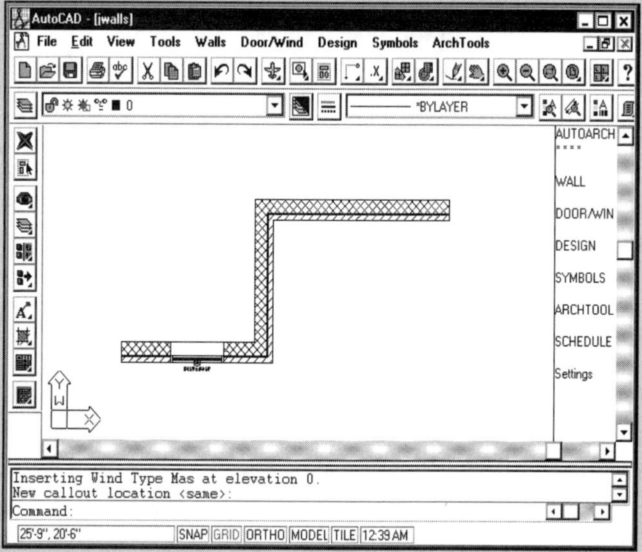

✔ This window style is defined to mount flush with the exterior.

Walls to Roof

Use the [Wall to Roof] command to extend walls to a roof when creating a 3D model.

✔ The routine creates faces on the WALL3D layer above the existing wall elements.

✗ The faces have invisible bottom edges where they meet the top of the wall.

✔ The more wall and roof faces you select, the longer *Auto-Architect* takes to calculate the walls.

✗ *Auto-Architect* checks every wall with every roof face.

✗ *Auto-Architect* takes additional time to merge adjacent faces together to reduce the file size.

In the following example, you will extend interior office partitions to the roof surface.

✔ At the end of the exercise, make sure you save your work.

✔ You will need these changes for a later exercise.

Hands-on:

Step 1: Open the existing drawing *c:\sdskproj\workshop \dwg\office.dwg.*

Step 2: Make sure that *Auto-Architect* is loaded.

Step 3: Select [Walls ⇨ Wall Edit ⇨ Extend Walls to Roof] from the pull-down menu.

Step 4: Select a wall line on an interior office partition — *Auto-Architect* finds all similar wall lines.

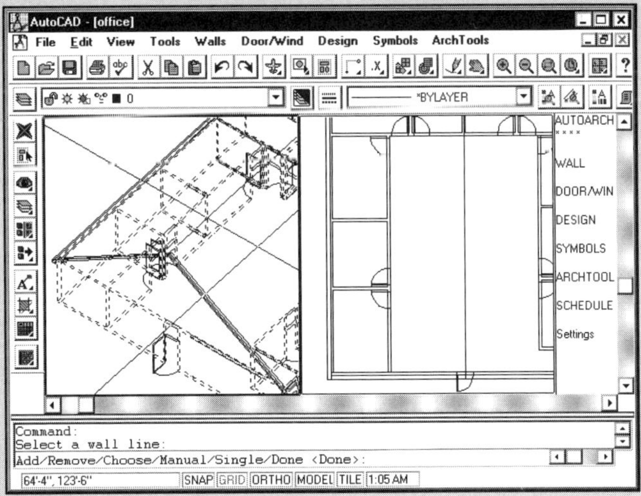

Step 5: Enter "M" to use the manual option.

Step 6: Select the interior walls running vertically on the right viewport — use a crossing windows.

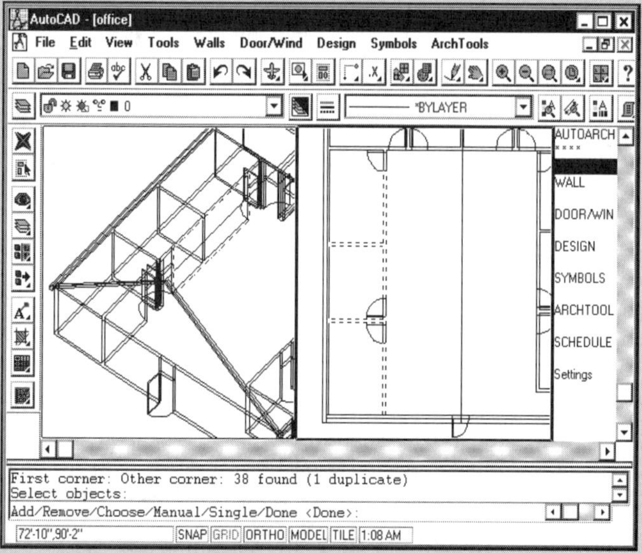

Step 7: Press <Enter> to continue.

Note:

Auto-Architect *removed the headers above the doors from the selection set because they do not match the first line you selected.*

Step 8: Type **A** to add objects and select the headers with crossing windows.

Step 9: Enter **No** when *Auto-Architect* prompts “Change Layer to match first object”.

Step 10: Press <Enter> to continue.

Step 11: Pick a point along the roof ridge when *Auto-Architect* prompts “Select a roof face”.

Step 12: Press <Enter> to continue.

Step 13: Wait while *Auto-Architect* calculates the faces between the walls and the roof.

Step 14: Use the [Zoom] command to examine the added faces.

Step 15: Save as a new drawing title ExtWalls.

Step 16: Erase the roof faces and use the [Hide] command to create the view shown below.

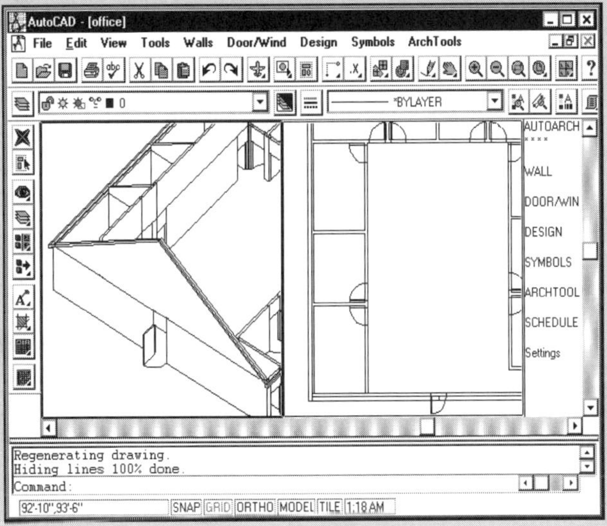

Step 17: Save the drawing.

Swap Wall Styles

You can convert a wall drawn with one wall style to a different wall style before or after inserting doors and windows.

✔ The following example shows how to display centerlines in existing walls that did not include centerlines in the preliminary design.

✗ Do not save the changes that you make to the drawing in this exercise.

✗ You will want to return to the previously saved version of this drawing after this exercise.

Hands-on:

Step 1: Turn off the roof layers ROOF, ROOFSOF and 3DROOF.

Step 2: Use the [Zoom Extents] command in the left and right viewports.

Step 3: Select [Walls ⇨ Swap Wall Styles] from the pull-down menu.

Step 4: Select the entire plan.

Step 5: Remove the triangular walls at the eaves by selecting them in the 3D viewport.

Step 6: Switch back to the plan viewport and press <Enter> to end the selection process.

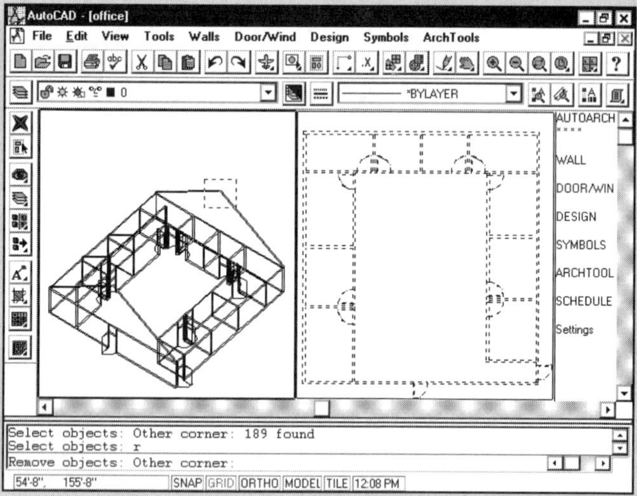

Step 7: Select the wall style CLINE and then choose the EDIT button.

Step 8: Change wall height (line thickness) of the outer lines to **10′**.

Step 9: Save the modified style.

Step 10: Choose the "OK" button to swap styles.

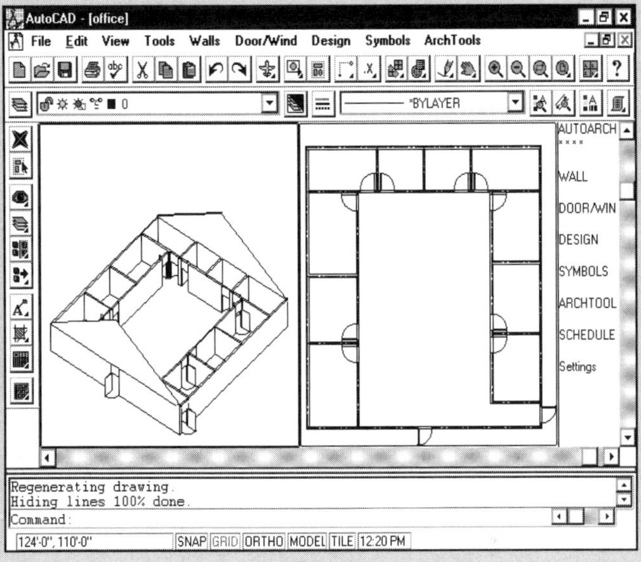

✔ Notice that *Auto-Architect* recreates all door breaks.

- ✗ Use this process to change wall widths or internal complexity.
- ✗ If new walls are significantly different in overall width, you may need to perform some manual clean-up.
- ✗ You can replace a wall style with a different style or a modified version of itself.

✔ You can use a wide polyline instead of a simple centerline.

- ✗ Use this for applications such as assigning different fire ratings on layers with unique linetypes.

Insert Windows into Extended Walls

You can insert a window into the 3D faces that the [Extend Walls] or [Roof Generator] commands create.

- ✔ The windows may be entirely inside the new faces or overlap the original walls and the 3D faces.
- ✔ For windows insertion to work in an extended wall, make sure that two parallel faces exist.
  - ✗ You may have to create a second face using the [Copy] command.
- ✔ In the first step of this exercise, make sure that you discard the changes you made in the previous exercise.
  - ✗ Reopen the *office* drawing to return to the version of the file with the extended office partitions.

Hands-on:

Step 1:	Select [File ⇨ Open...] from the pull-down menu.
Step 2:	Discard changes to the drawing.
Step 3:	Open the drawing file *c:\sdskproj\workshop\dwg \office.dwg*.
Step 4:	Select [Door/Wind ⇨ Door/Window Settings...] from the pull-down menu.
Step 5:	Verify that the "Prompt each time" toggle under "Window Head Height" is turned on.
Step 6:	Pick "OK".
Step 7:	Select [Door/Wind ⇨ Library...] from the pull-down menu.
Step 8:	Choose the DH2448 window style and then choose "OK".
Step 9:	Enter **12'** when the "Head height" prompt appears.

Step 10: Use the plan viewport on the right to pick a point on the office wall that runs vertically as shown.

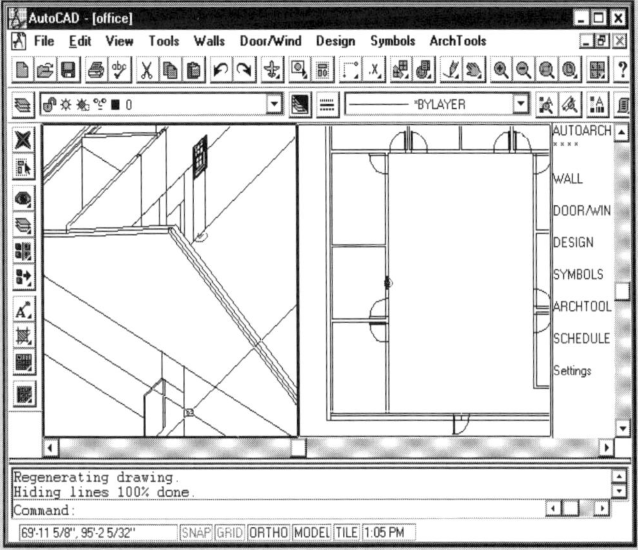

Step 11: Repeat the window placement and pick a point on the front wall with a head height of 12'.

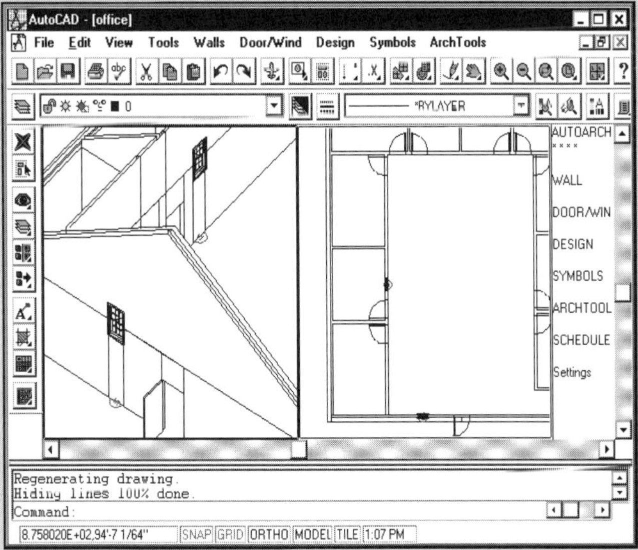

Chapter 4

Doors and Windows

Objectives

To use advanced window and door style features, you should be able to:

- ✔ Control advanced windows and door style settings.
- ✔ Place quick windows and doors for and swap them with full style windows and doors.
- ✔ Change windows and doors with query/edit or style swap.
- ✔ Create window and door assemblies, including bow and bay windows.
- ✔ Generate window and door schedules.

Introduction

This chapter presents detailed tips and shows you time-saving procedures for placing doors and windows with *Auto-Architect*. The first portion of this chapter gives you tips for door and window settings and shows you how to take full advantage of quick doors and windows as well as style library doors and windows. The next section shows how to build assemblies of windows and doors, describes the internal structure of library doors and windows, and shows how to build bay windows. The final section gives you the recommended method for placing door and window tags during a project and shows how to generate customized door and window schedules.

As you complete these exercises, you should notice the sophistication of the *Auto-Architect* door and window database. To really master the skills for using door and window functions in *Auto-Architect*, you must be able to use the power of that database to full advantage. Make sure that you understand what *Auto-Architect* is doing for you as you complete each step in the exercises. Think about how you can benefit from the power of the database and begin to consider how you will apply this power to your own specific projects.

Window and Door Style Settings

Most of the settings for window and door styles are covered in the *Softdesk Architecture 1 Certified Courseware*.

- ✔ The information in this section shows you advanced tips and examples to give you complete control over window and door settings in *Auto-Architect*.

Depth

You should always set the frame depth to the actual manufactured frame dimension.

- ✔ Do NOT increase it to match the wall width.

- ✔ *Auto-Architect* adds an extension jamb to fill any gap between the interior edge of the frame and the interior casing when you work in 3D.
- ✔ *Auto-Architect* draws the frame without the extension jambs when you work in 2D.
    - ✗ This applies to both doors and windows.

Casing

Casing options are available for doors with standard frames and all windows except fixed metal type.

- ✔ The casing width and trim width values determine how far the window sill extends past the edge of the opening in both 2D and 3D.
    - ✗ If you turn either toggle off, the corresponding sill does not extend past the edges of the opening.
- ✔ If the offset position of the frame from the exterior of the wall is not 0, exterior casing is not available.
    - ✗ The sill will not extend past the edges of the opening.

The following example shows you where to find the casing and trim settings.

Hands-on:

Step 1:	Open the drawing *\sdskproj\workshop\dwg \int1.dwg* and zoom to the upper-left corner.
Step 2:	Select [Door/Wind ⇨ Library...] from the pull-down menu.
Step 3:	Select CA2448 from the style list.
Step 4:	Pick the "Edit" button.

Step 5:	Pick the "Casing..." button.
Step 6:	Verify that the "Apply Exterior Casing" and the "Apply Interior Casing" toggles are both turned on.
Step 7:	Choose the "Cancel" button — remain in the Edit Window Style dialog box.

Rough Opening and Masonry Opening

There are entries for rough opening width and height and for masonry opening width and height in the User Supplied Data dialog box.

- ✔ Enter opening sizes here for use in labels and schedules.
  - ✗ *Auto-Architect* does not use these values to create the wall opening.
- ✔ The width and height of your window style is the overall size of the frame.
  - ✗ Each frame usually has a rough opening size and a masonry opening size the manufacturer specifies.
  - ✗ One or the other is actually used, depending on the type of construction.
  - ✗ Because *Auto-Architect* has no way to determine sizes, you must enter them manually if you need to use them.
- ✔ Any change in height, width, or unit type requires you to change these opening sizes.
  - ✗ *Auto-Architect* cannot know how much to change the manufacturer values if you change the window frame sizes.
  - ✗ You must enter the changes yourself.
  - ✗ To safeguard against incorrect information on a drawing, *Auto-Architect* sets the manufacturer values to 0 when you change the width and height.
  - ✗ This makes the error very obvious to detect and reduces the chances of erroneous data on a drawing.

- ✔ *Auto-Architect* automatically supplies the opening information to the corresponding item in a window tag.
    - ✗ *Auto-Architect* determines which opening sizes (rough or masonry) to use in labels by the window tag that you choose.
    - ✗ Some windows tags, such as Wind Type Rgh, include the rough opening; others, such as Wind Type Mas, include the masonry opening.
- ✔ The rough and masonry opening settings apply to doors, assemblies, and windows.

The following example shows where to find the user specified window data settings.

Hands-on:

Step 1: Choose the "Data" button on the Edit Window Style dialog box.

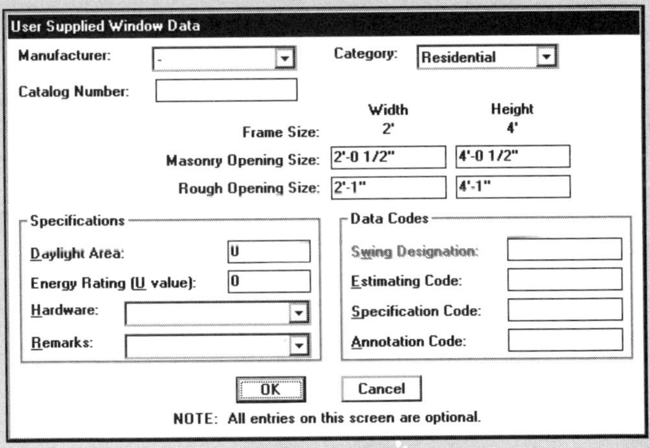

Step 2: Choose the "Cancel" button to exit from all dialog boxes.

Default Style Names

Whenever you change the type, width, or height of a door or window, *Auto-Architect* updates the name and description to reflect the change.

- ✔ *Auto-Architect* assigns a short code to each door and window type.
  - ✗ Examples of this code include DR for a hinged door and 2-DR for a double-hinged door.
- ✔ Edit the *ab.dfm* file in the *sdskprot\softdesk\ab* directory to change the default descriptions and codes.
  - ✗ Search for the [ABWindoorTypes] section in the file to find the door and window codes.

```
[ABWindoorTypes]
; Do not change key names on left
; Code,Description,Default style name prefix
MET=Fixed Metal Frame,FM
AWNG=Awning,AW
CAS=Casement,CA
DBLH=Double Hung,DH
```

- ✔ The first item in each line before the equals sign is a key name.
  - ✗ Do NOT change the key names.
- ✔ The second item between the equals sign and the comma is the description.
- ✔ The last item following the comma is the code.
  - ✗ You can edit these items with any ASCII text editor such as the Edit program in DOS or Notepad in Windows.

- ✔ You should change descriptions and codes at the very beginning of a project.
  - ✗ Otherwise, since each drawing in the project will have its own *dwgname.dfm* file in *sdskproj\projname \dwg* directory, you would need to edit each of these files.
  - ✗ You will also have to edit existing style names because *Auto-Architect* will not update them automatically.

Quick vs. Style Library Doors

This section shows you how to use quick doors and windows for initial design and then swap them with full-style doors and windows.

- ✔ You can also swap style library doors and windows for other style objects.
  - ✗ You can convert a quick door or window to any style library door, window, or assembly.
  - ✗ You can convert a style library door, window, or assembly to any other style library window, door, or assembly.

Quick doors and windows are rudimentary compared with doors and windows from the style library.

- ✔ The following table compares features of quick doors and windows to style library doors and windows.

Comparison of Quick vs. Full-Style Doors and Windows

Feature	Quick	Full Style
Size	You enter a size when you insert quick doors and windows.	All dimensions are preset in a door and window style.
Detail	Quick doors and windows work in both 2D and 3D, but are generic and contain less detail.	Full-style objects have enough parameters to represent a particular manufacturers model in 2D and 3D.
Functionality	You can use quick objects for final designs and drawings, or you can use them in for initial design and convert them to full-style doors, windows, or assemblies.	The full-style objects include construction details for hardware, casing, and trim in 3D, which makes them useful for realistic renderings and animation.

The following example directs you to place quick doors which you will swap for style library doors in the following exercise.

Hands-on:

Step 1: Open the drawing *\sdskproj\workshop\dwg \int1.dwg* and zoom to the upper-left corner.

Step 2: Select [Door/Wind ⇨ Quick Doors and Windows] from the pull-down menu.

Step 3: Set values to create a 3′ single door.

Step 4: Choose the "OK" button to exit.

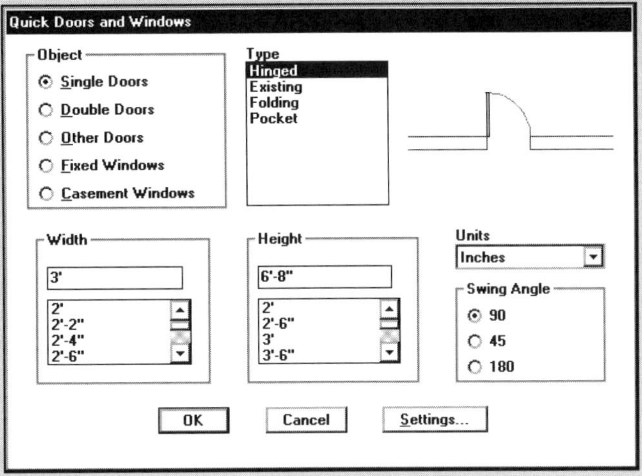

Step 5: Use the "Auto" placement method to place a door at locations A and B as shown below.

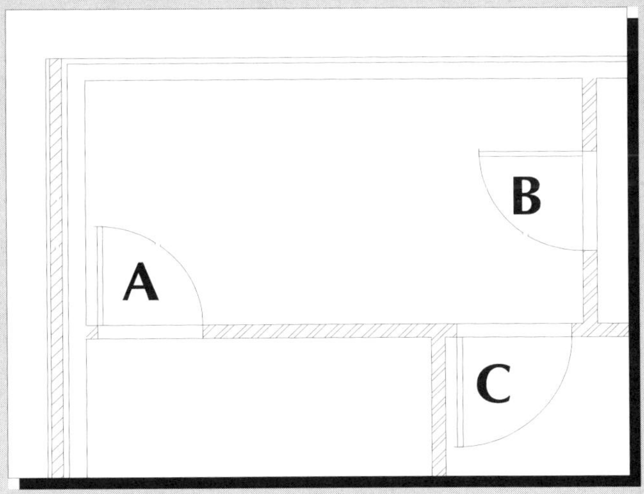

Step 6: Press <Enter> to end the command.

Step 7:	Press <Enter> to repeat the command.
Step 8:	Type **S** to select from library.
Step 9:	Select a width of **3'4"** and choose the "OK" button.
Step 10:	Place a door in the corner at location C.

Change Door Style

You are now ready to swap the quick doors for style library doors.

- ✔ You can use the same size and type of door or you may swap to a completely different door.

The following exercise directs you to define a different door size and type.

- ✔ You will edit style DOOR1 and make it a double door.
- ✔ You will restore it to a single door in the next exercise.

Hands-on:

Step 1:	Select [Door/Wind ⇨ Library] from the pull-down menu.
Step 2:	Highlight DOOR1 and pick the "Edit" button in the Select Window or Door Style dialog box.
Step 3:	Change Door from Single to Double.

Step 4: Change the name from the new default name back to DOOR1.

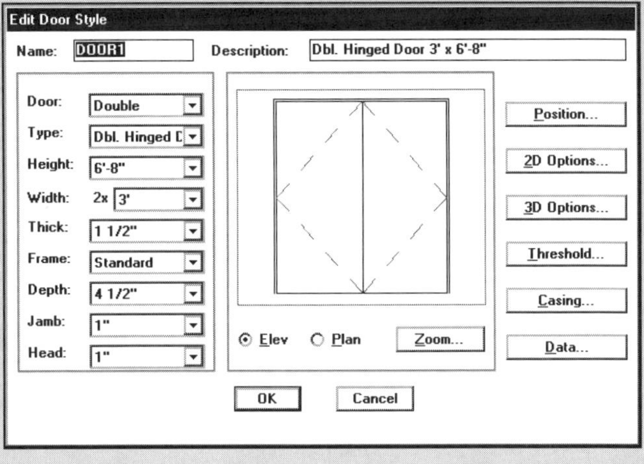

Step 5: Choose the "OK" button to save style then choose the "OK" button again to confirm the style name.

Step 6: Choose the "Cancel" button to exit the dialog box without inserting anything.

Swap Doors

When you select a door to swap, *Auto-Architect* will find all other doors with the same type and size.

✔ *Auto-Architect* does not find matching doors on other levels of a multi-level drawing.

✔ *Auto-Architect* reports the number of doors it finds, the description, and the size.

```
"Found 2 DR1H90 -- Width: 3', Height: 6'-8".
```

✗ Use this to help you decide which library style you want to swap to.

✔ You can unselect some of the highlighted doors.

Hands-on:

Step 1: Select [Door/Wind ⇨ Swap Doors and Windows] from the pull-down menu.

Step 2: Select the first door that you placed in the drawing.

Step 3: Press <Enter> to end the selection process.

Step 4: Choose the "OK" button to accept DOOR1, which is highlighted in the Select Window or Door Style dialog box.

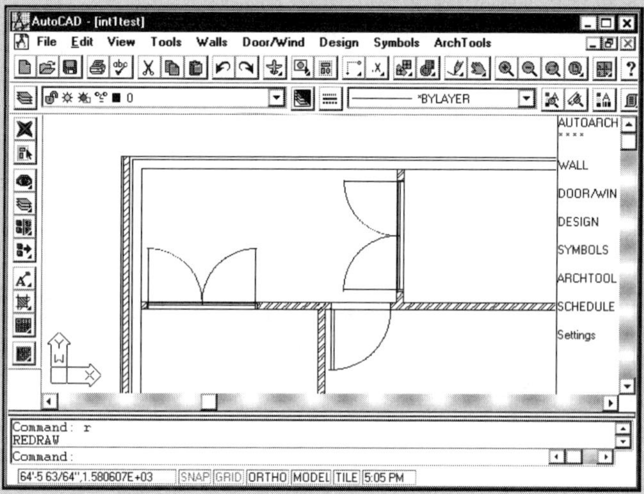

Auto-Architect proceeds to replace both quick doors with double doors.

- ✔ The first door retains its original distance from the corner to the edge.
  - ✗ The second door retains its center location.
- ✔ The third door (location C) does not change because it is a different size.

Query/Edit vs. Style Swap

You have two choices to change the style of doors you have been placed on a drawing.

- ✔ You can swap style library doors or windows from one style to another, or:
- ✔ You can revise the style definition.

Revise the style if you want to make the same minor change for all doors or windows of a particular style.

- ✔ Use the Query/Edit command for this change.

This exercise shows how to revise doors on a drawing by changing the style definition.

Hands-on:

Step 1:	Select [Door/Wind ⇨ Query/Edit] from the pull-down menu.
Step 2:	Pick either door A or B from the previous exercise.
Step 3:	Change the "Door:" to "Single" in the Query/Edit Window Object dialog box.

Note:

This time the name does not automatically change. This is because you are working with an existing object of that name.

Step 4: Pick "Data" and enter the Rough Opening Width and Masonry Opening Width.

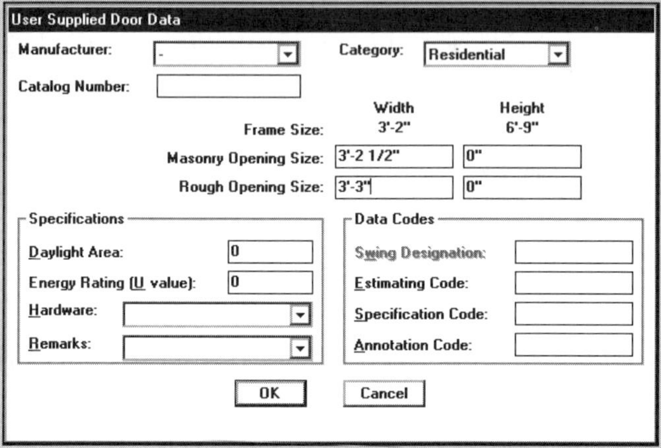

Step 5: Choose the "OK" button to continue.

Step 6: Choose the "OK" button to save the style changes and update the existing objects.

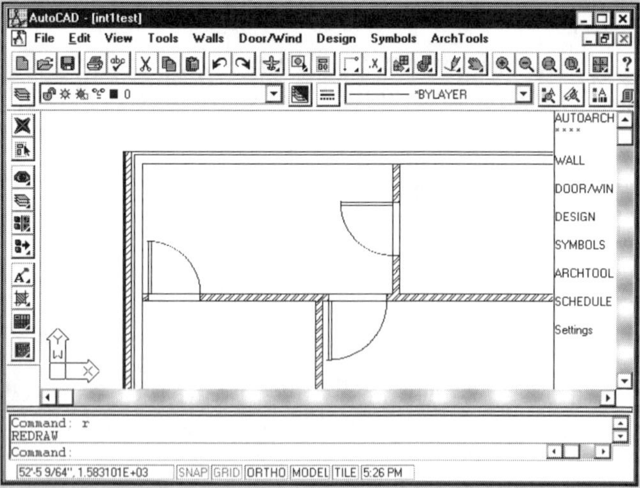

Auto-Architect redefines all objects of "DOOR1".

- ✔ *Auto-Architect* re-creates the wall opening for each object of this style to reflect the new overall size.
  - ✗ If there are "DOOR1" objects on other levels of a multi-level drawing, *Auto-Architect* updates the door openings on each level.
  - ✗ If your changes do not affect the overall size, *Auto-Architect* redefines all objects of the style without affecting the wall openings.
- ✔ If you anticipate changes to the size or type of unit in a drawing, use generic style names like the one in this exercise.
  - ✗ If you revise the style CA2448 to be a 3′ wide double hung unit, it can cause confusion later on.
  - ✗ You can make subtle changes to a style such as CA2448 (sash sizes, mullion pattern, etc.), which do not conflict with the style name.

Door and Window Assemblies

The following example shows advanced features of door and window assemblies.

- ✔ In the following examples, you will see how to:
  - ✗ Create a vertically stacked assembly consisting of three fixed metal frame units with opaque glass spandrel units at the top and bottom.
  - ✗ Expand this assembly into a store-front assembly.
  - ✗ Create an assembly using both doors and windows.

Define a Window Unit

- ✔ Your first task is to create two fixed metal frame units in an assembly.

Hands-on:

Step 1: Open the drawing *\sdskproj\workshop\dwg\int1.dwg* and zoom to the upper-left corner.

Step 2: Select [Door/Wind ⇨ Library] from the pull-down menu.

Step 3: Set "Objects:" filter to "Windows".

Step 4: Highlight FM3672 in the "Style Names" list and pick the "Edit" button.

Step 5: Change the width to **4'** using the "*OTHER*" option in the width list.

Step 6: Choose the "OK" button to save to the new default name FM4872.

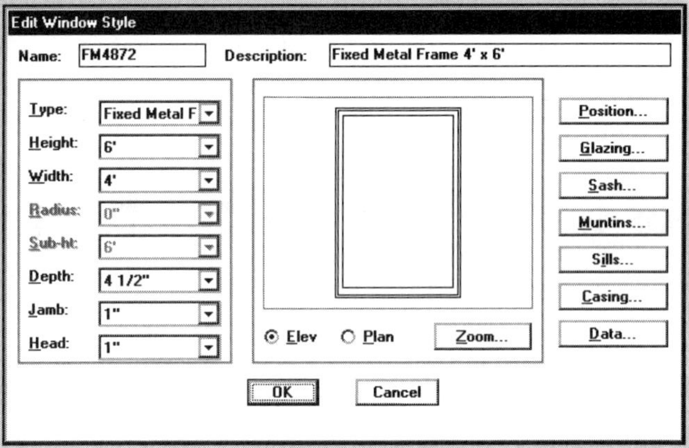

Step 7: Pick the "Edit" button to change style FM4872.

Step 8: Change "Height:" to **2'**.

Step 9: Pick "Glazing" and change "Glazing Type" to "Special" (opaque glass).

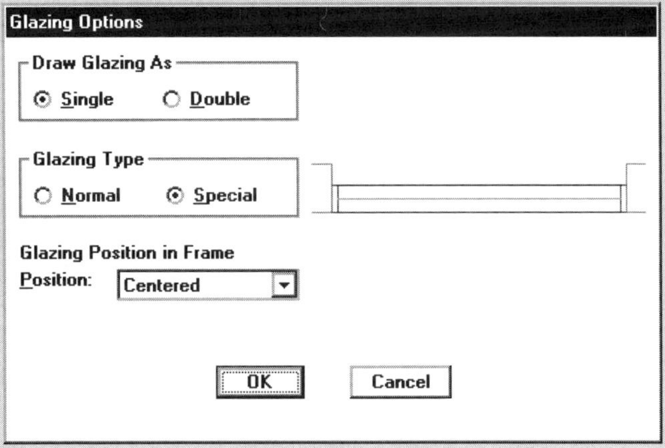

Step 10: Choose the "OK" button.

Step 11: Add "– Spandrel Unit" to the default description and add "-SPAND" to the default name.

Step 12: Choose the "OK" button to save the style.

Define an Assembly

You have created the Fixed Metal Frame units.

- ✔ The following exercise shows how to create the assembly.
  - ✗ You will select FM4824-SPAND as the first unit of the assembly.
  - ✗ Grips will appear on each corner and midpoint of this unit to indicate placement points for attaching other units.
  - ✗ These grips also show the "current" unit you are working on — The Copy, Move and Delete options affect only the current unit.

✔ The "Mull Space" settings will appear disabled.

- ✗ When you join metal frame units in an assembly, they share a common frame member.
- ✗ No spacing adjustment is possible.

Hands-on:

Step 1: Make sure that FM4824-SPAND is highlighted and pick the "Create Assembly" button.

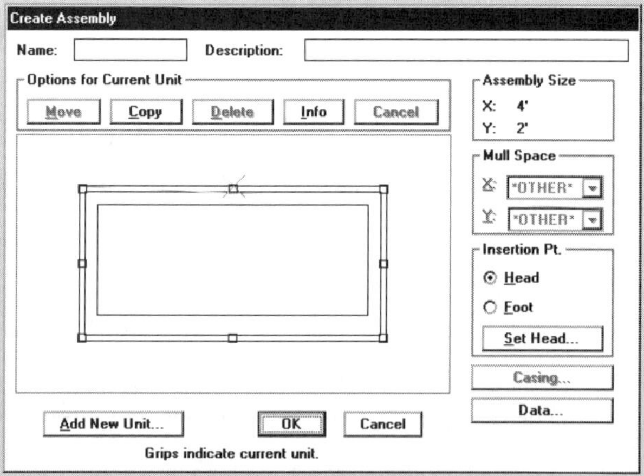

Step 2: Pick "Info" to see identification and other information on the current unit — you cannot check the glazing type here.

Step 3: Choose the "OK" button to continue.

Step 4: Pick the "Add New Unit..." button.

Step 5: Set the "Objects:" filter to "Windows".

Note:

There are now fewer windows to choose from in the first step. You can join metal frame units only to other metal frame units with the same jamb size. Auto-Architect *displays only matching units by filtering out all other units.*

Step 6: Highlight FM4872 and choose the "OK" button.

Step 7: Pick the "Move" button from "Options for Current Unit".

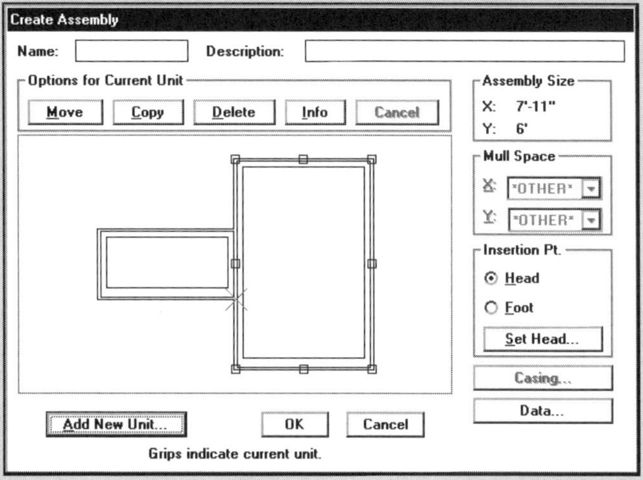

Step 8: Select the bottom center grip to be the base point.

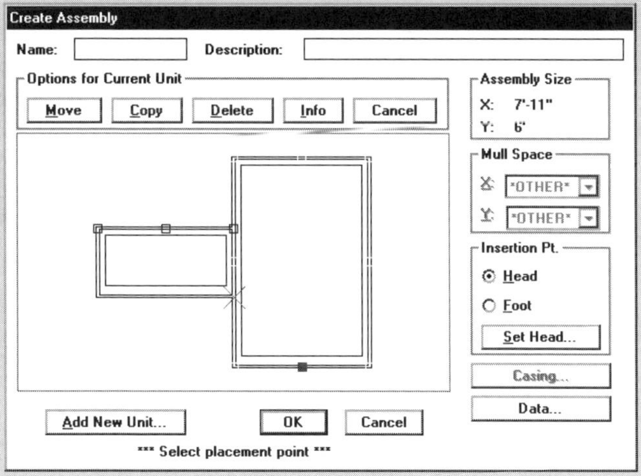

Step 9: Select the center grip that appears on the top of the first unit as the placement point.

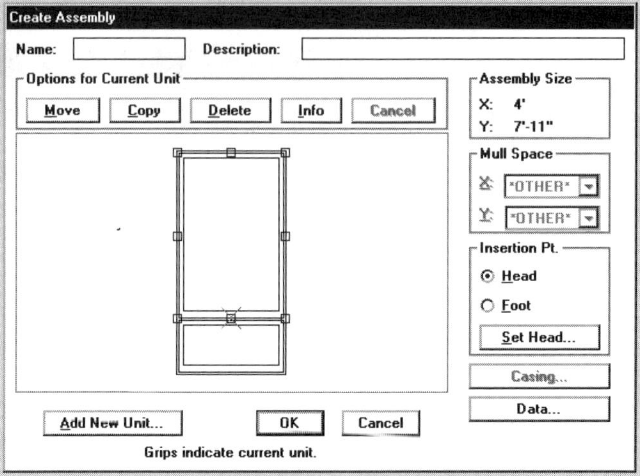

Note:

The overall assembly height appears as 7′11″, even though you placed a 6′ high unit on a 2′ high unit. Auto-Architect *knows the joining frame member of metal frame units is shared in common and sets the correct height.*

Step 10: Pick a point anywhere inside the bottom unit to make it the current unit.

Step 11: Pick the "Copy" button from "Options for Current Unit".

Step 12: Select the bottom center grip as the base point and then the center grip at the top of the assembly as the placement point.

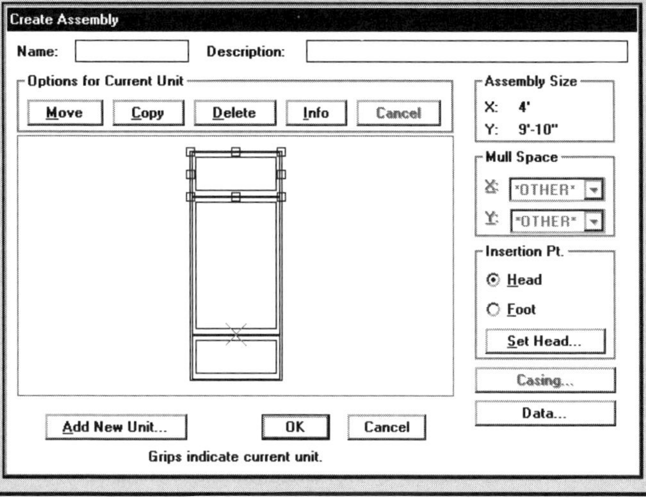

Locate Insertion Point

The assembly is now complete, but the insertion point (indicated by the green "X") is not in practical location.

- ✔ The following exercise shows how to adjust the insertion point of an assembly.
- ✔ You can choose between a head or foot insertion.
  - ✗ A head insertion point is useful for typical wood windows you normally place with a top of window elevation.
  - ✗ A foot insertion point is more practical for a metal frame assembly store-front or curtain-wall, which you normally place at the floor or some specified distance above the floor.

Hands-on:

Step 1: Pick "Set Head" from the "Insertion Pt." portion of the dialog box.

Step 2: Select any of the three grips at the top of the middle unit to see the head insertion options.

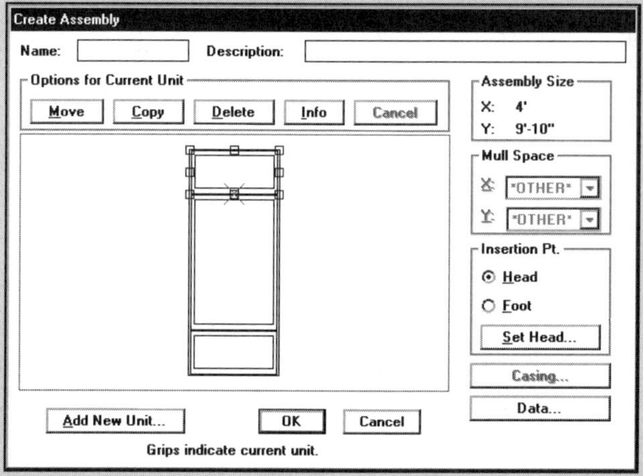

Step 3: Pick the "Foot" radio button in the "Insertion Pt." portion of the dialog box and choose an insertion point.

Step 4: Enter **STOREFRONT1** for the style name and **4′ x 9′10″ Metal Frame** for the description.

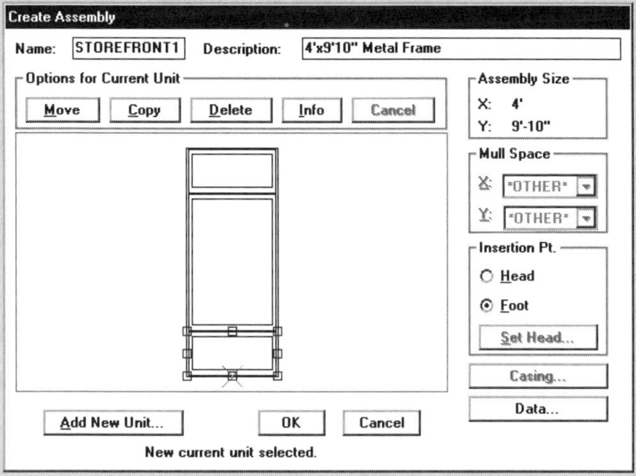

Step 5: Choose the "OK" button to exit this dialog.

Step 6: Choose the "OK" button to save the assembly.

Create New Assembly from Existing Assembly

You can use this new assembly on its own or as part of a curtain wall.

- ✔ You can also edit it to provide the beginning of a larger storefront assembly.

The following exercise shows how to create a storefront assembly using your existing assembly.

Hands-on:

Step 1: Set the "Objects:" filter to "Assemblies" in the Select Window or Door Style dialog box.

Step 2: Highlight STOREFRONT1 and choose the "Edit" button.

Step 3: Copy the current unit from the bottom left grip to the bottom right grip.

Step 4: Copy the new current unit from the bottom left grip to the grip at the bottom of the assembly.

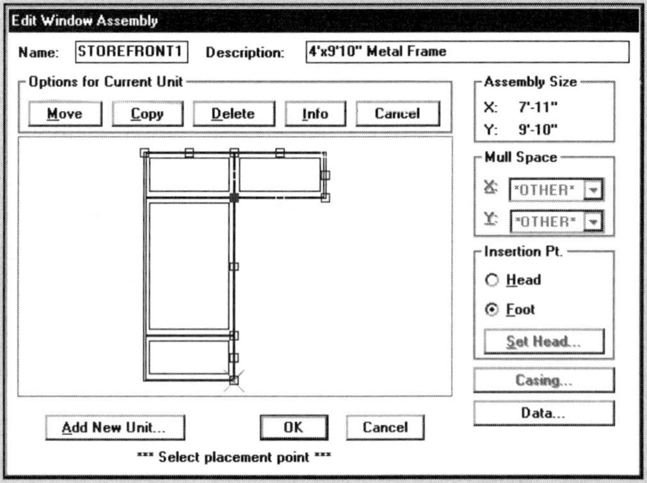

Step 5: Pick inside the large unit to make it current.

Step 6: Copy this unit from the left center grip to the center grip at the right of the unit.

Step 7: Pick the "Add New Unit..." button.

Step 8: Highlight FM1872 and choose the "OK" button.

Step 9: Move it down to align with the other 6′ high units.

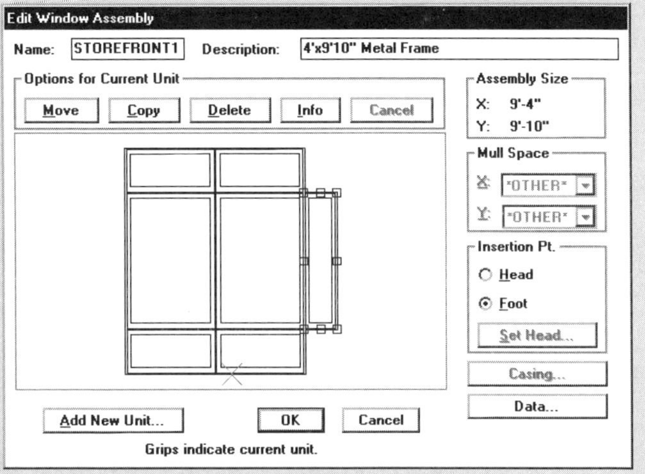

Step 10: Copy this unit to the left side.

Step 11: Change the style name to **STOREFRONT2** and the description to **10′-9″ x 9′-10″ Storefront**.

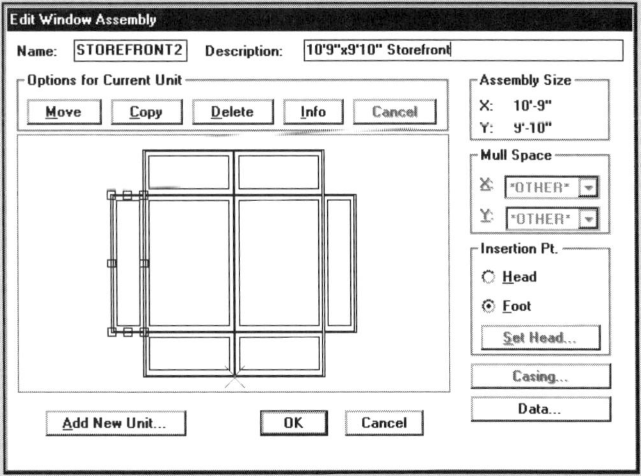

Step 12: Choose the "OK" button to continue.

Step 13: Choose the "OK" button to save the assembly.

Create an Assembly with a Door

When an assembly contains doors and windows, you should start with the door as the first unit, add the sidelights next, and the transoms last.

- ✔ This helps prevent creating a confusing casing condition at the bottom of the assembly.
- ✔ When you create an assembly with a door, the insertion point is automatically set to "Foot".
    - ✗ Head insertion is not applicable to doors or any assembly that has a door in it.

Define Sidelights and Transom Units

The following example shows how to create a residential entry assembly with a door, sidelights, and transom windows.

- ✔ You can use the door DR3680-EXT1 from the style library.
- ✔ You need to create the sidelight and transom units.
    - ✗ Choose 2′ wide sidelights and 1′-4″ high transoms.
- ✔ You need to determine how high the sidelights should be and how wide the door transom should be.
    - ✗ The door is 36″ x 80″ with 1″ jambs and head.
    - ✗ This makes the frame size 38″ x 81″.
    - ✗ Because window sizes are set according to their frame dimensions, the height of the sidelight must be 81″ (6′-9″) and the width of the door transom must be 38″ (3′-2″).
    - ✗ Doors are specified by the size of the swinging or moving element.
    - ✗ Windows are specified by the outer dimension of the frame.

Hands-on:

Step 1: Select [Door/Wind ⇨ Library] from the pull-down menu.

Step 2: Set the "Objects:" filter to "Windows" and the "Category" filter to "Residential".

Step 3: Highlight FX2460 from the "Style Names" list and choose the "Edit" button.

Step 4: Change "Height:" to **6′-9″** using the "*OTHER*" option in the width list.

Step 5: Choose the "OK" button to save to the new default name FX2481.

Step 6: Highlight FX2481 and choose the "Edit" button.

Step 7: Change "Height:" to **1′-4″**.

Step 8: Pick the "Sills" button.

Step 9: Change the "(A) Overall Thickness:" to **1″**.

Step 10: Choose "Flush Sill" for the "Exterior" and "Picture Frame" for the Interior.

Step 11: Choose the "OK" button.

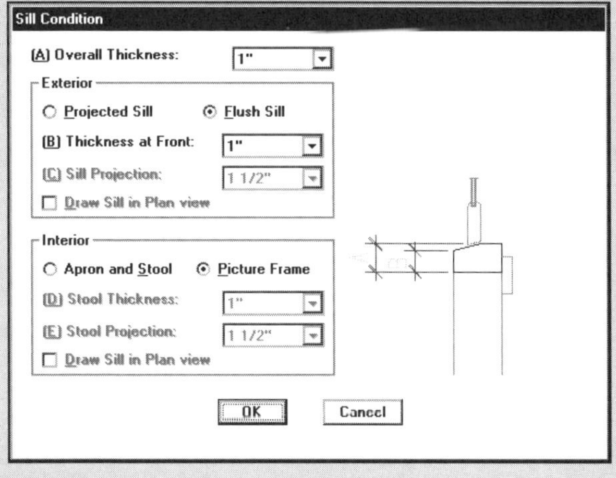

Step 12: Choose the "OK" button to continue.

Step 13:	Choose the "OK" button to save the new default name FX2416.
Step 14:	Highlight FX2416 and choose the "Edit" button.
Step 15:	Change the "Width:" to **3'-2"** and save the style with the new default name FX3816.

Create the Assembly

The sidelights and transom units are now complete.

- ✔ The next stage is to create an assembly.
- ✔ When the Create Assembly dialog box appears, an advisory message may tell you to "Set Mullion Spacing, if desired, while there is only one unit present."
  - ✗ This advisory message only appears the first time you begin an assembly of standard frame units.
  - ✗ You cannot change mullion spacing after joining units together.
- ✔ If you use this assembly in a load-bearing wall, you will require stud pockets between the units.
  - ✗ You can provide this by setting the "X Mullion Spacing".
  - ✗ If a large assembly requires horizontal or vertical stiffening members, you can set the spacing (X and/or Y) equal to the size of the stiffening member used.

Complete Assembly

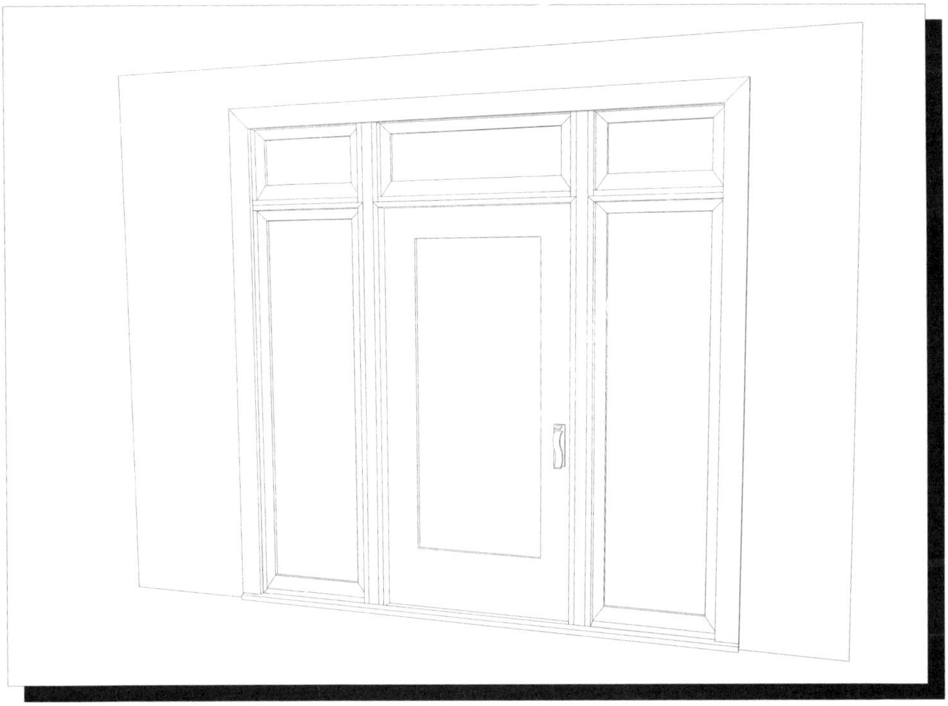

Hands-on:

Step 1: Set the "Objects:" filter to "Doors".

Step 2: Highlight DR3680-EXT1 and choose the "Create Assembly" button.

Step 3: Select the number "3 Hinge Point" for an inward swing and choose the "OK" button in the Swing Orientation dialog box.

Step 4: Choose the "OK" button to accept the advisory message.

Step 5: Pick “Info” and verify that the “Frame Width” and “Frame Height” of the door matches your calculations.

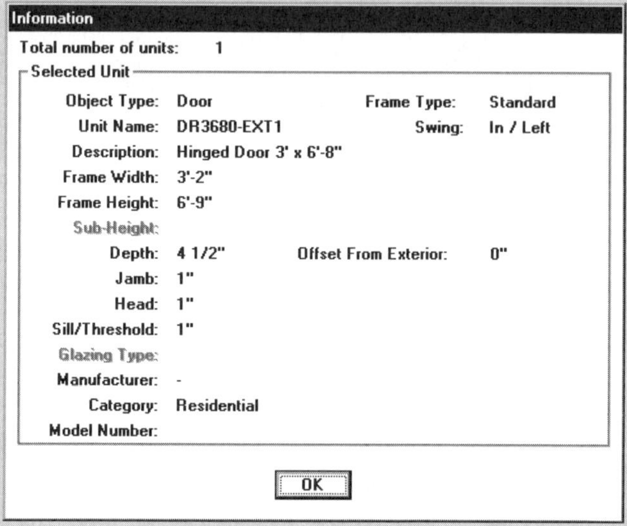

Step 6: Choose the “OK” button to continue.

Step 7: Change the “X” mullion space to ***2″*** to create stud pockets — 1½″ for the stud plus ¼″ shim space on each side. Notice that the grips change position slightly.

Step 8: Choose the “Add New Unit...” button.

Step 9: Set “Objects:” filter to “Windows.”

Step 10: Highlight FX2481 and choose the “OK” button.

Step 11: Copy this sidelight to the other side.

Step 12: Choose the “Add New Unit...” button.

Step 13: Highlight FX3816 and choose the “OK” button.

Step 14: Move the door transom to its proper location above the door.

Step 15: Choose the “Add New Unit...” button.

Step 16: Highlight FX2416 and choose the “OK” button.

Step 17: Move the sidelight transom into position and copy it to the other side.

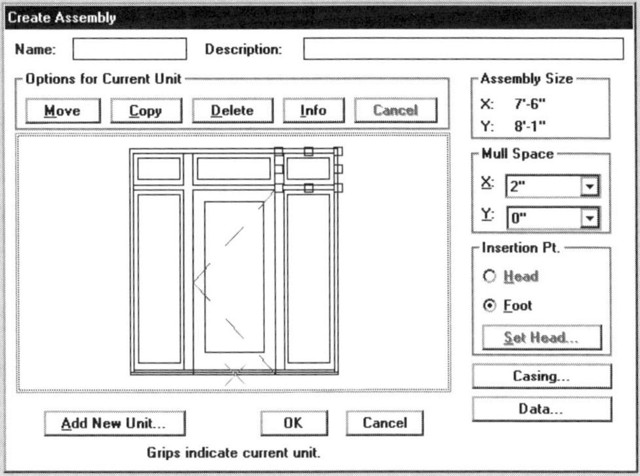

Change Casing and Trim

You can use units with different casing and trim values in the same assembly.

✔ Values from the initial unit are inherited for use by the entire assembly.

✗ You can change these values or the assembly may be changed as desired.

Hands-on:

Step 1: Pick "Casing".

Step 2: Change the Exterior Casing Width to **4″**.

Step 3: Enter "DR3680SL2T3" for the style name and "Door w/ Sidelights and Transoms" for the description.

Step 4: Choose the "OK" button to continue.

Step 5: Choose the "OK" button to save the assembly.

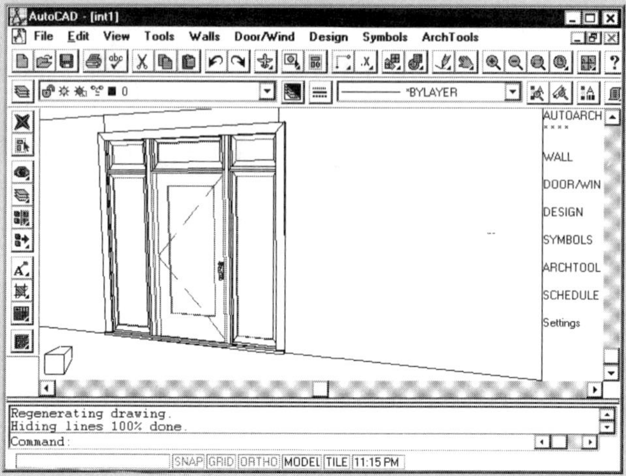

Step 6: Pick "OK" to insert the assembly into the wall.

Vertically Stacked Windows

You may find it advantageous to place two or more separate units or assemblies at different heights.

- ✔ You can place vertically stacked windows using assemblies or you can place windows separately.
- ✔ The upper units may be different sizes and you can place them directly over another unit or off to the side.

The following example shows how to place windows above existing windows in the same wall.

- ✔ You will see that by setting the correct head height, *Auto-Architect* allows you to place windows over windows in a plan view without any interference.

Hands-on:

Step 1: Remove the door assembly from the wall by using the [Door/Wind ⇨ Door/Wind Edit ⇨ Remove Door/Wind] command.

Step 2: Make the upper-left viewport current.

Step 3: Select [Door/Wind ⇨ Door/Window Settings…] from the pull-down menu.

Step 4: Verify that "Window Head Height" is set at **6′-9″**.

Step 5: Turn on the "Prompt each time" toggle under "Window Head Height".

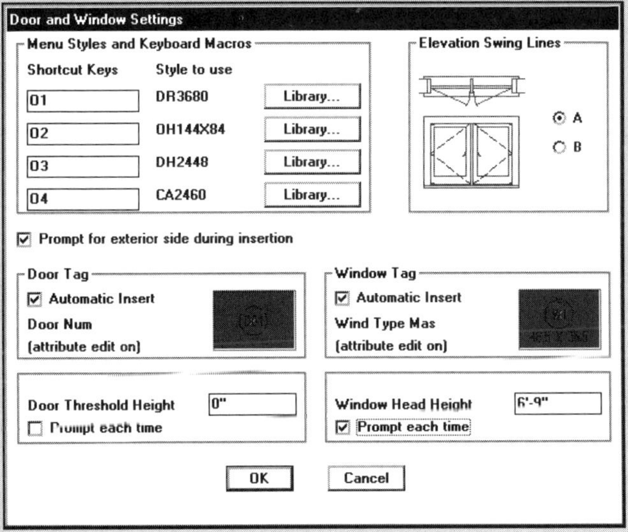

Step 6: Choose the "OK" button.

Step 7: Select [Door/Wind ⇨ Library…] from the pull-down menu.

Step 8: Highlight WINDOW1 and choose the "OK" button.

Step 9: Accept the default head height.

Step 10: Switch to the plan viewport.

Step 11: Accept the default head height.

Step 12: Use the "Auto" placement option to insert a window in the center of the wall.

Step 13: Choose the exterior side of the wall toward the bottom of the screen.

Step 14: Select [Door/Wind ⇨ 1. WINDOW1] from the pull-down menu.

Step 15: Insert two more windows centered in the wall segments at each side of the first window.

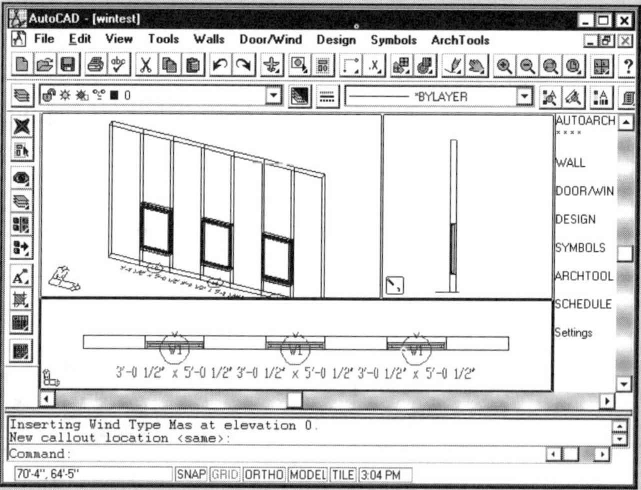

Step 16: Restart the command and enter **12'** for the head height.

Step 17: Use the same Auto placement method to insert a window at location A to place a window directly above another window.

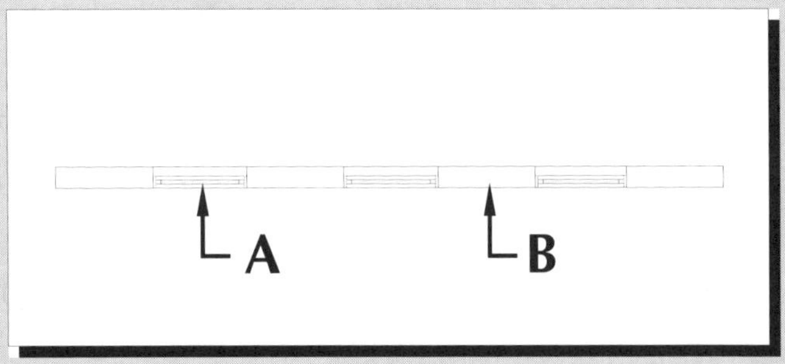

Step 18: Use the plan view to place the windows accurately.

Step 19: Restart the command and enter **12'** for the head height.

Step 20: Insert another window at location B to place a window above others in a staggered arrangement.

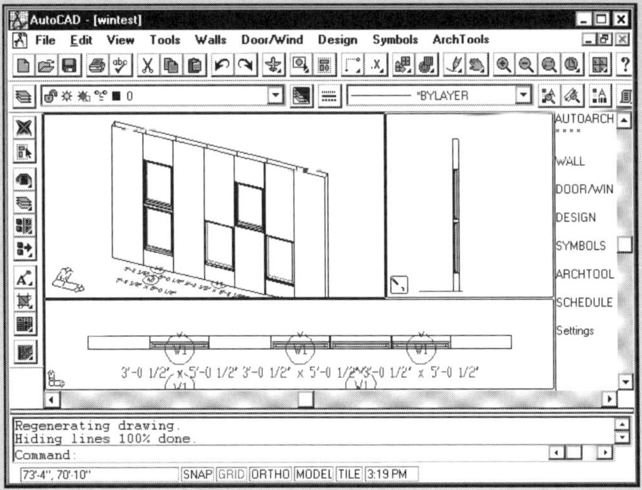

Working without Wall Exterior Prompt

You can choose a toggle in the Door/Window Settings dialog box to "Prompt for exterior side during insertion".

- ✔ This setting is normally turned on so you can establish a definite interior/exterior orientation.
- ✔ You may be able to work faster in some cases if you turn this toggle off.
  - ✗ You can turn this prompt off if the wall style has an obvious exterior and interior side (such as the MASONRY12 wall style).
  - ✗ You will have difficulties with a center-justified wall style or a simple two-line wall style where the interior/exterior may be ambiguous.
- ✔ A simple style such as AB_SIDE may allow you to achieve a stable interior/exterior condition.
  - ✗ The working side of the wall (at which you pick points while drawing the wall) is considered the exterior.
  - ✗ The other side (which is designated in response to the "Pick side" prompt of the Wall command) is the interior.
  - ✗ If you drew all walls with the working side at the exterior, you can turn the exterior side prompt off without causing any problems.

Turning off the exterior side prompt for other walls will result in limitations you may not consider acceptable.

- ✔ Some limitations you may encounter if you use quick doors and windows:
  - ✗ Quick doors and windows have no interior/exterior differences so you can disregard this orientation.
  - ✗ Your windows may be backwards if you convert quick doors or windows to style library objects.

- ✔ Some limitations you may encounter if you use style library objects that do not have any interior/exterior differences.
  - ✗ Exterior casing may be different than interior trim.
  - ✗ Casing values will affect the side extension of sills on a 2D drawing.
- ✔ You must consider if there are interior/exterior differences in the window style at this time AND if there might be changes to the style that introduce differences later on.
  - ✗ Most windows have interior/exterior differences, especially the sloping sill in 3D.
  - ✗ Fixed metal frame windows have no interior/exterior differences unless the glazing position is modified.
- ✔ You must consider if the frame depth matches the wall depth.
  - ✗ If the frame and wall depth are the same and the style has the same casing and trim on both sides, you can turn the exterior side prompt off.
- ✔ Weigh any potential problems against the convenience of working with this prompt turned off.
  - ✗ It may be beneficial to turn it off for some portions of the drawing and turn it back on for others.

Door and Window Anatomy

Each style library door, window, or assembly is a composite block made of three or more nested component blocks.

- ✔ One component block is for the exterior casing.
- ✔ Another component block is for the trim, including any extension jambs.

- ✔ Another component block is for the unit — two or more unit blocks for an assembly.
  - ✗ The unit component block for a door includes a 2D symbol block, a 3D door block, and any possible 3D hardware blocks.
- ✔ Each of these component blocks contains entities on specific layers other than layer 0.
  - ✗ You must control the component layers in the *Auto-Architect* layer settings.
  - ✗ These layers do not contain a level designation if you use levels in the drawing.
  - ✗ This allows you to use the same block on any level — *Auto-Architect* inserts the object on the OPENING layer, which is associated with a level.
- ✔ This layering scheme gives you flexibility to identify and control the visibility of various components in a door or window block.
  - ✗ In most cases, you do not have to change any window or door block layers.
  - ✗ You may need to control the layers to remove 3D components when you display a 2D drawing.
  - ✗ Turn off all *3D* layers before you plot the drawing.
- ✔ For additional layer control:
  - ✗ Use the [LL] Layer List macro to see a report of the block layer and the nested object layer.
  - ✗ Use the "Pick <" option of the [LF] Layer off macro — make sure the "Pick Nested Entities" toggle is turned on.
- ✔ The HEADER layer contains the header lines within the composite block.
  - ✗ This layer is normally on but has an INVISIBLE linetype that causes the header line to display with a dot at each end.
  - ✗ Change the linetype to CONTINUOUS to close the opening for a drawing such as a ceiling plan.

  - ✗ You can change the linetype manually and regenerate the drawing or use the [Plan Types] command.

- ✔ The unit component of a door block contains a 2D door symbol block and a 3D door block.
  - ✗ *Auto-Architect* stores 2D symbols in the directory *sdsk/ab/dwg/*.
  - ✗ You can customize these blocks to conform to office standards.

- ✔ The layer names in these drawings are layer "key" names that *Auto-Architect* needs to function.
  - ✗ Do NOT change the layer names inside the door drawings.
  - ✗ When *Auto-Architect* creates a door style block, these layer keys become the layer names chosen in the *Auto-Architect* layer settings.

- ✔ *Auto-Architect* stores the 3D components with drawing filenames DOOR3D*.DWG for single doors and DDOR3D*.DWG for double doors.
  - ✗ *Auto-Architect* stores these files in the *sdsk/ab/dwg* directory.
  - ✗ The layers in these files are also key names which should not be changed.
  - ✗ Do NOT change the layer keys.

- ✔ If you work with 3D turned off, *Auto-Architect* creates door and window blocks without 3D components.
  - ✗ Their appearance is the same as using 3D block and turning off all 3D layers.

Quick doors and windows are much simpler than style library objects.

- ✔ Each one is a single block with no nested blocks.
  - ✗ If you want to customize the files, *Auto-Architect* stores them in the directory *sdsk/ab/dwg*.

- ✔ Quick doors and windows do not contain lines on the header layer.
  - ✗ *Auto-Architect* includes the header lines as part of the opening.

Bow and Bay Windows

Using a bow window is easy. Bow windows do not use style library windows.

- ✔ Each bow window is a single block you scale to the size you want.

Bay windows do use style library windows.

- ✔ You must create the individual component windows specifically for the bay window.
  - ✗ You must not include interior trim.
- ✔ *Auto-Architect* includes individual windows for creating bay window assemblies.
  - ✗ Their names end with "-BAY".
  - ✗ You can find them by setting the "Category" filter in the style library to "Bay Window".

Define a Unit for a Bay Window

The following example shows you how to create a window style for a bay window unit before you create a bay window assembly.

Hands-on:

Step 1:	Reopen the drawing *\sdskproj\workshop\dwg\wintest.dwg* and do not save the changes.
Step 2:	Select [Door/Wind ⇨ Library] from the pull-down menu.

Step 3: Set the "Category" filter to "Bay Window".

Step 4: Highlight FX6060-BAY and choose the "Edit" button.

Step 5: Pick the "Casing..." button and make sure that the "Apply Interior Trim" toggle is off.

Step 6: Choose the "OK" button.

Step 7: Change the Height to **4'**. Notice how the style name updates to FX6048.

Step 8: Add "-BAY" to the new default name.

Step 9: Add " - No Int. Trim" to the new default description.

Step 10: Choose the "Data..." button and note that "Category:" box is still set to Bay Window.

Step 11: Enter **4'-0 1/2"** for "Masonry Opening Size - Height" and **4'-1** for "Rough Opening Side - Height".

Step 12: Choose the "OK" button to continue.

Step 13: Choose the "OK" button to save the style and to confirm the style name.

Step 14: Choose the "Cancel" button to exit the library without inserting a window.

Step 15: Select [Door/Wind ⇨ Draw Bows and Bays...] from the pull-down menu.

Step 16: Choose "Bay" near the top of the Bow and Bay Window dialog box.

Choose Units for the Bay Window Style

You must use window units defined specifically for bay windows in the bay window assembly.

- ✔ In this example:
  - ✗ The Side Style (DH2448-BAY) is a style for bay windows.
  - ✗ The Front Style (FX4848) is not for bay windows.
- ✔ You must substitute your new style for the current Bay Front window.

Hands-on:

Step 1: Pick the "Library" button to the right of the "Front Style:" setting.

Step 2: Verify that the "Category" filter is set to "Bay Windows".

Step 3: Highlight FX6048-BAY and choose the "OK" button.

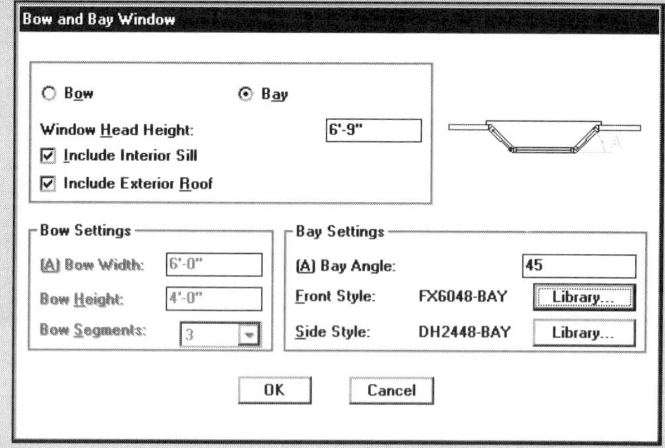

Placing a Bay Window

The height of this window matches that of the side window, as determined by the "48" size component of both style names.

- ✔ You are responsible to make sure the heights match.
  - ✗ If the heights do not match, *Auto-Architect* displays a message saying "Window heights do not match. Fill in the gaps manually".
  - ✗ *Auto-Architect* will create the bay window, but the window is not correct by common design standards.

Hands-on:

Step 1: Choose the "OK" button to insert the bay window in the drawing as shown below.

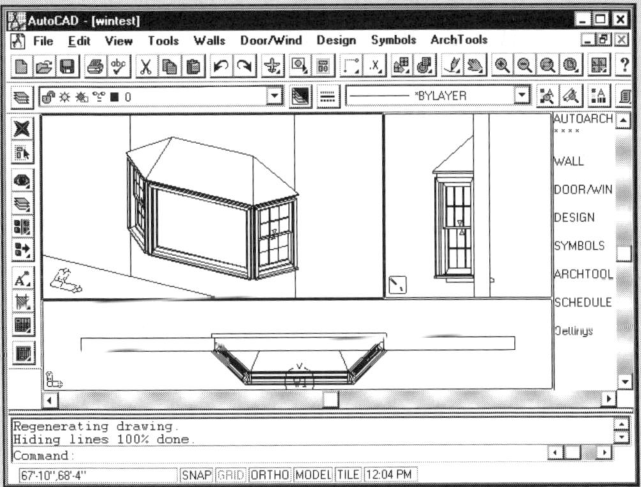

Mirror Doors and Windows

You can mirror doors and windows manually or with the [Flip] command without affecting *Auto-Architect's* internal data.

- ✔ You must mirror the window *before* placing window tags.
  - ✗ When you place a tag on the door or window, the tag obtains Right/Left hand information from the object and supplies that information to the tag block.
  - ✗ If you flip or manually mirror the object after you place the tag, *Auto-Architect* does not record the change in the tag.
  - ✗ Use the [EA] macro to update the tag if necessary.

Tags and Schedules

You should place window tags by choosing the "pick Door/Window" option under "Door/Window Tags" in the symbol manager after you place all the windows and doors.

- ✔ You should not place tags when you insert the windows and doors.
- ✔ Placing tags after you place all doors and windows has a number of advantages:
  - ✗ It is faster to insert doors and windows without the tags — you can focus on design and worry about annotation later on.
  - ✗ You can copy and mirror portions of a building with doors and windows without causing confusion in the tag numbering or "hand" (R/L) orientation of the object.
  - ✗ You have better control of the numbering order of door tags.

✗ When you place tags with the "pick Door/Window" option in the symbol manager, *Auto-Architect* obtains size and style data from the door or window and supplies it to the tag you are placing.

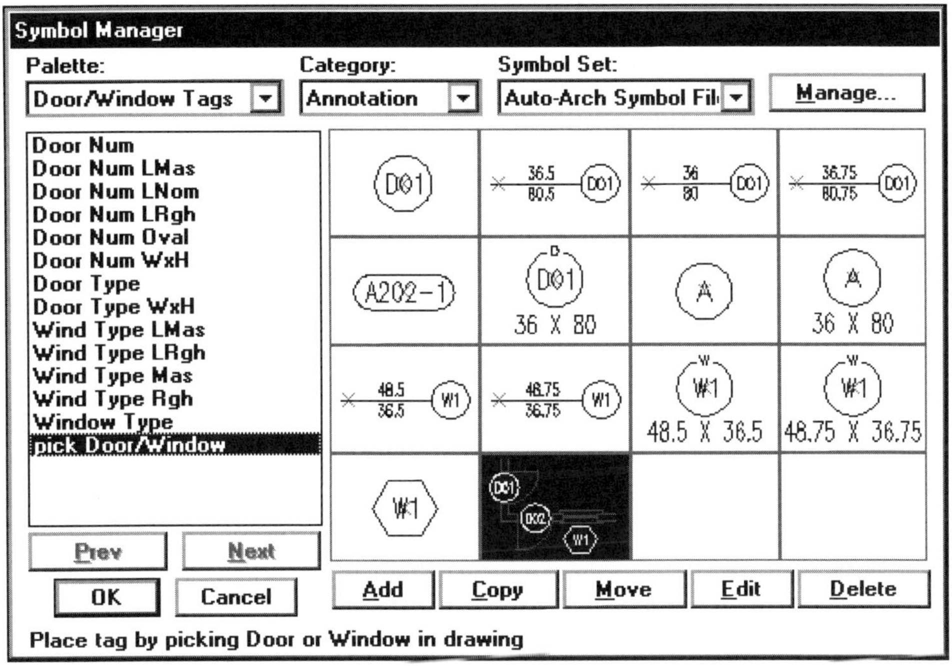

You can select which tag to use for "pick Door/Window" in the [Door/Window Settings...] command.

- ✔ *Auto-Architect* supplies a variety of tags for doors and windows.
  - ✗ There are differences in shape as well as the visibility of some attributes.
  - ✗ All the tags contain the same attributes.
- ✔ *Auto-Architect* provides the following door and window tags.

Door and Window Tags

Tag Type	Description
Door Num	This tag provides information for a door schedule. Typically used by an architectural office, this circle shape tag is commonly used in the United States. Each door is given a unique number which automatically increments when you place the tag. Each door has its own line in the schedule. Quantities are not applicable.
Door Num Lmas	Same as Door Num except that it displays masonry opening sizes on a stem line connected to the bubble.
Door Num Lnom	Same as Door Num except that it displays the nominal width and height on a stem line connected to the bubble.
Door Num Lrgh	Same as Door Num except that it displays rough opening sizes on a stem line connected to the bubble.
Door Num Oval	Same as Door Num except for an elongated bubble instead of a circle. Use this tag for a numbering scheme where each door number includes the room number and a unique door number starting with "-1" for each room. For example, "236-1".
Door Num WxH	Same as Door Num except that it displays the nominal width and height under the bubble. The graphic symbol also includes a "D" at the top of the circle, which you can use to distinguish it from a window tag. This is a visible attribute labeled "Secondary annotation".
Door Type	Similar to Door Num except that it uses an ID mark instead of a unique number. This scheme is normally used for windows. You can use quantities with this tag as explained below.
Door Type WxH	Same as Door Type except that it displays the nominal width and height under the bubble.

Tag Type	Description
Wind Type Lmas	This tag provides information for a window schedule. This tag includes an ID mark rather than a unique number. The schedule typically shows quantities of each type. The tag displays masonry opening sizes on a stem line connected to the bubble.
Wind Type Lrgh	Same as Wind Type Lmas except that it displays rough openings instead of masonry openings.
Wind Type Mas	Same as Wind Type Lmas except that it displays masonry openings under the bubble instead of on a stem. Top of bubble also includes a "W", similar to Door Num WxH.
Wind Type Lrgh	Same as Wind Type Mas except that it displays rough openings instead of masonry openings.
Window Type	Similar to Door Type except the bubble is hex shaped and it does not include any stem or sizes. This tag is commonly used in the United States for window tags.
Pick Door/Window	Use this item to place the desired tag the "smart" way. When setting which tag to use for "auto" or "smart" tag placement through [Door/Wind ⇨ Door/Window Settings...], do NOT choose this item. Choose one of the above items.

The following example shows how to adjust the door and window settings to allow you to place tags after you place windows and doors.

Hands-on:

Step 1: Reopen the drawing *\sdskproj\workshop\dwg \wintest.dwg* and discard the changes.

Step 2: Use the [VP] macro and the "SI" option to change the display to a single viewport.

Step 3: Select [Door/Wind ⇨ Door/Window Settings…] from the pull-down menu.

Step 4: Turn on the "Window Tags Automatic Insert" toggle to enable the tag selection image button.

Step 5: Pick the tag selection image button.

Step 6: Highlight "Window Type" from the list of symbols and choose the "OK" button.

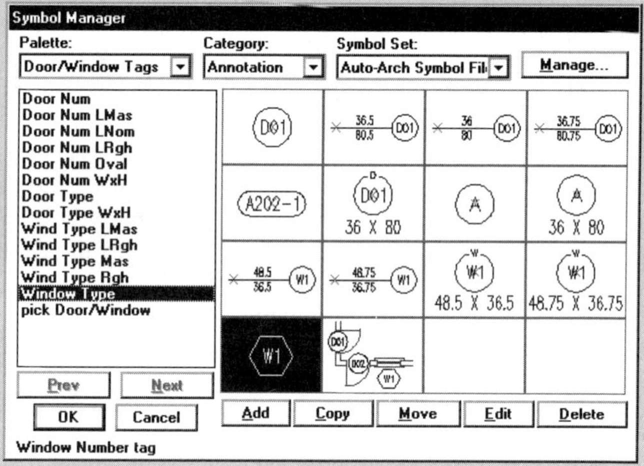

Step 7: Turn the "Window Tag Automatic Insert" toggle off.

Step 8: Choose the "OK" button.

Place Windows

The following example directs you to place windows in a wall and begin the steps to place window tags after placing the window.

✔ You should notice that the window tags do not appear when placing the window.

Hands-on:

Step 1: Select [Door/Wind ⇨ CA2460] from the pull-down menu.

Step 2: Insert five of these windows into the wall segment as shown.

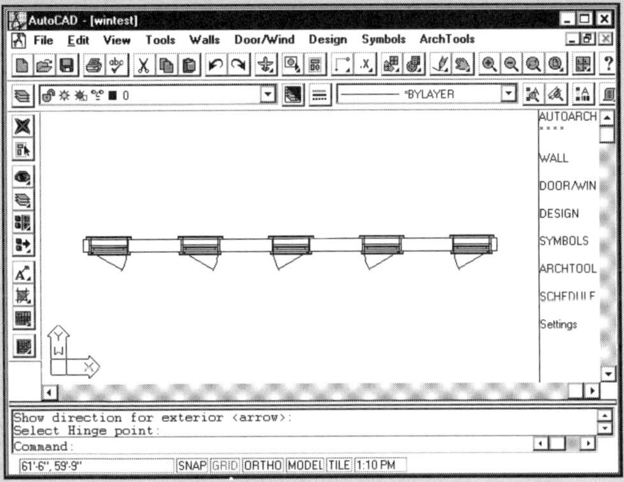

Step 3: Select [Symbols ⇨ Annotation] from the pull-down menu.

Step 4: Choose the "Door/Window Tags" palette.

Step 5: Highlight "pick Door/Window" and choose the "OK" button.

Step 6:	Pick the window farthest to the left when *Auto-Architect* prompts you to "Pick door, window, or assembly <exit>:".

Enter Attribute Information

Notice that there is no description in the Edit Attributes dialog box.

✔ Frame type, can be used for an office standard code designation for the frame configuration.

  ✗ Use frame type for an office standard code designation for the frame configuration.

  ✗ You can use these codes for hollow metal frames to denote such information as single door frame, door frame with transom, or door frame with sidelight.

✔ You can then set the frame material to be "Wood" or "Hollow Metal."

Hands-on:

Step 1:	Enter **Standard** for "Glazing type" and **Wood** for "Frame material."
Step 2:	Choose the "Next" button to view more.
Step 3:	Change the "Rough opening" height to **5′-1″**.
Step 4:	Choose the "OK" button.
Step 5:	Place the callout and then pick the next window.
Step 6:	Choose the "Next" button.

Note:

Auto-Architect *retains attribute values from one tag placement to the next if it does not find a value in the object or its style data.* Auto-Architect *does not retain any changes you make to attribute values that it obtains from the object or its style. Edit the User Data of the window style to avoid having to edit the rough opening and masonry opening for each tag.*

Step 7: Do not correct the rough opening data.

Step 8: Choose the "OK" button and place the tag.

Step 9: Press <Enter> to exit.

Step 10: Select [Door/Wind ⇨ Query/Edit] from the pull-down menu.

Step 11: Press <Enter> to check existing door and window blocks.

Step 12: Select any one of the five windows.

Note:

Notice that the height does not match the style name (CA2460) in the Query/Edit Window Object dialog box. The height of this style was changed during a previous Query/Edit. Because you cannot change the name of the style in Query/Edit, you should not make changes to a window or door style that make the descriptive name different from the actual settings in the style.

Step 13: Change "Height:" to **5'** to make the style name appropriate for the size.

Step 14: Choose the "Data..." button.

Step 15: Change the "Masonry Opening Size - Height" to **5'-0 1/2"** and "Rough Opening Size - Height" to **5'-1"**.

Step 16: Choose the "OK" button.

Step 17: Choose the "OK" button to save the changes to the style.

Step 18: Start the [EA] macro and pick the last tag that you placed on the drawing.

Step 19: Choose the "Next" button and review the changes.

Step 20: Choose "Cancel" to exit.

Step 21: Select [Symbols ⇨ Annotation] from the pull-down menu.

Step 22: Switch to the "Door/Window Tags" palette.

Step 23: Highlight "pick Door/Window" and choose the "OK" button.

Step 24: Choose the third window when *Auto-Architect* prompts you to "Pick door, window, or assembly <exit>:"

Step 25: Verify that "Standard" and "Wood" have been retained and that the opening sizes are correct in the Edit Attributes dialog box.

Step 26: Place the callout and pick the fourth window.

Step 27: Change Glazing type to "Low-E".

Step 28: Choose the "OK" button.

Step 29: Place the callout and pick the last window.

Step 30: Verify that "Low-E" has been retained.

Step 31: Choose the "OK" button.

Step 32: Place the callout and press <Enter> to exit the command.

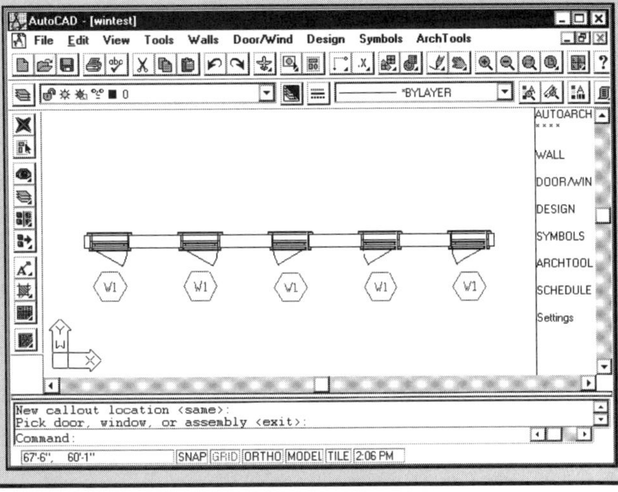

Create a Schedule Template

The tags are now ready to create a schedule.

- ✔ One way to create a window schedule is to select [ArchTools ⇨ Schedules ⇨ Window Schedule] from the pull-down menu.
  - ✗ The schedule that you create this way includes all available information.
  - ✗ This may be more than you want, so you may have to make modifications.
- ✔ For example:
  - ✗ The schedule includes masonry opening and rough opening information — you need only one or the other.
  - ✗ Making changes is not difficult; however, any changes you make to this template apply globally to all projects.
- ✔ The following example shows how to create a new template for the current project and use it to create a schedule.

Hands-on:

Step 1: Select [Tools ⇨ Schedules ⇨ Make Template] from the pull-down menu.

Step 2: Pick any one of the window tags when *Auto-Architect* prompts you to "Select a typical block."

Step 3: Choose the "OK" button to accept the default name for the template — *Auto-Architect* creates the file in the directory */sdskproj/workshop*.

Step 4: Choose the "Add Tag" button in the Attribute Report Specification dialog box.

Step 5: Select WINDNO from the "Blocks in Drawing" list in the Add Attribute dialog box.

Highlight the following items in the Tags list:

AAWIANNOT
AAWITYPE
AAWIROUGH
AAWISWG_CODE
AAWIGLASS
QTY

Note:

Including QTY causes the schedule program to place all identical objects on one line with a quantity rather than listing each object individually. All other values in the above list are attribute "tags."

Step 6: Choose the "OK" button.

Step 7: Highlight ID Mark in the Attribute Report Specification dialog box.

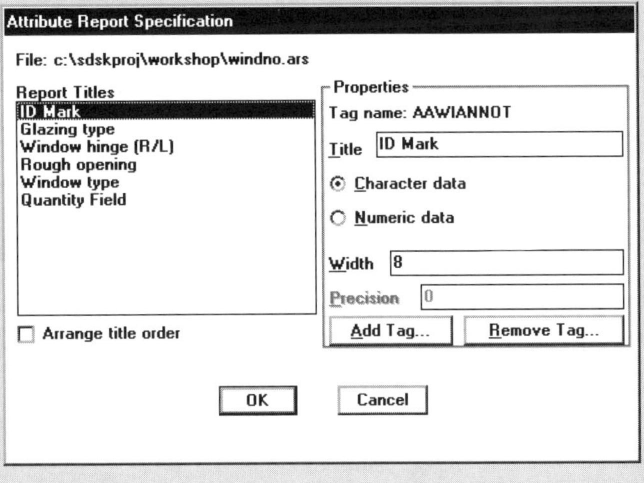

Step 8: Change each title and width as shown in the following table.

Change Title and Width

Tag name	Title	Width
AAWIANNOT	ID	12
AAWIGLASS	GLAZING	8
AAWISWG_CODE	HINGE	5
AAWIROUGH	R.O.	16
AAWITYPE	TYPE	7
QTY	QTY	3 (Also change Precision to 0)

Step 9: Turn on the “Arrange title order” toggle to disable Properties and prepare to move the titles.

Step 10: Highlight the TYPE title when *Auto-Architect* displays a message at the bottom of the dialog box to "Select title to move".

Step 11: Select ID to place TYPE to be right after ID.

Step 12: Move GLAZING to follow R.O.

Step 13: To avoid creating confusing results, make sure that QTY is the last item.

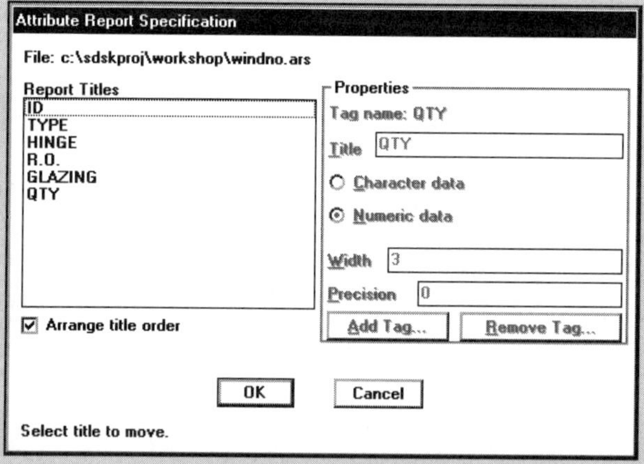

Step 14: Choose the "OK" button to complete the creation of a new template.

Create the Schedule

You can create a schedule with the new template.

Hands-on:

Step 1: Select [ArchTools ⇨ Schedules ⇨ Other Schedules] from the pull-down menu.

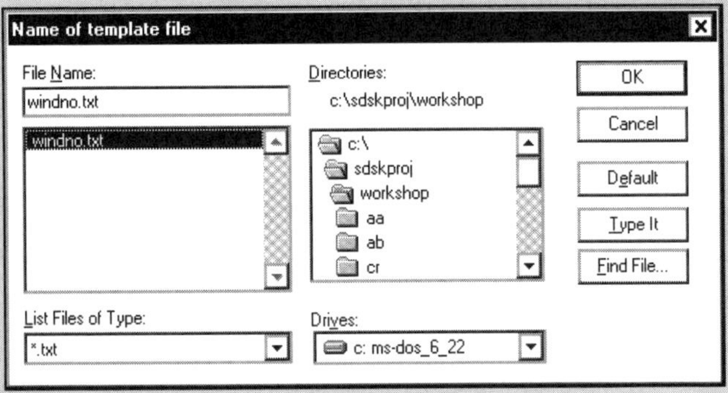

Step 2: Choose *windno.txt* and choose the "OK" button.

Step 3: Choose "OK" to accept the Attribute Report Specification in the dialog box — you can change it now or at any time prior to creating a schedule.

Step 4: Enter WINDOW SCHEDULE and press <Enter> when *Auto-Architect* prompts for the "Schedule Title".

Step 5: Choose the "OK" button to accept ID in the Sort by tag name dialog box.

Step 6: Press <Enter> when *Auto-Architect* prompts for "Output to (Drawing/Printer/Screen) <Drawing>:".

Step 7: Pick a point somewhere below the window tags when *Auto-Architect* prompts you to "Digitize start point:".

Step 8: Press <Enter> to accept the defaults for the remainder of the prompts in the command.

Step 9: Use the [Zoom Extents] command to view the schedule.

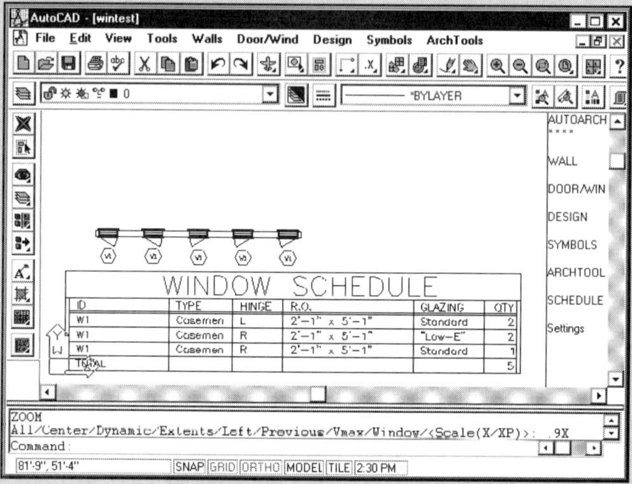

Chapter 5

Advanced Stair Design

Objectives

To solve commercial stair design and annotation problems, you should be able to:

- ✔ Design an offset stair tread transition.
- ✔ Place stair break annotations on a three-dimensional stair.

Introduction

This chapter shows you a valuable design technique for commercial stairs and solves a typical problem when annotating a stair that includes three-dimensional information.

The offset tread discussion will help you design a safer, more economical stair for commercial buildings. This technique not only helps you with stair design, but it shows the flexibility that you have with many design functions in *Auto-Architect*. In this and all other chapters, you should consider how each setting in a dialog box can help you develop the most effective solution for your specific design tasks.

Offset Tread

When you design a stair with landings, you may offset the bottom of each run by a distance equal to one tread.

- ✔ This applies most often to commercial stairs.
  - ✗ The purpose is to allow the handrail and stringers to flow smoothly with no abrupt vertical transition.
- ✔ In the following figure Part A shows a stair with no tread offset.
  - ✗ A section detail at the landing shows the vertical transition that occurs in the handrail and the stringer.
  - ✗ This "gooseneck" transition is common in residential stair railings.
  - ✗ Modern commercial stair construction avoids this transition.
- ✔ B shows a tread offset in the wrong direction.
  - ✗ Although there is no vertical transition, it now has an unnecessary horizontal transition.
- ✔ C shows a tread offset at the bottom of each run.
  - ✗ The handrails and stringers join smoothly.
- ✔ Although the figures show a U-Shaped stair, the offset tread design applies to stairs with 90° landings as well.

Offset Stair Tread Transitions

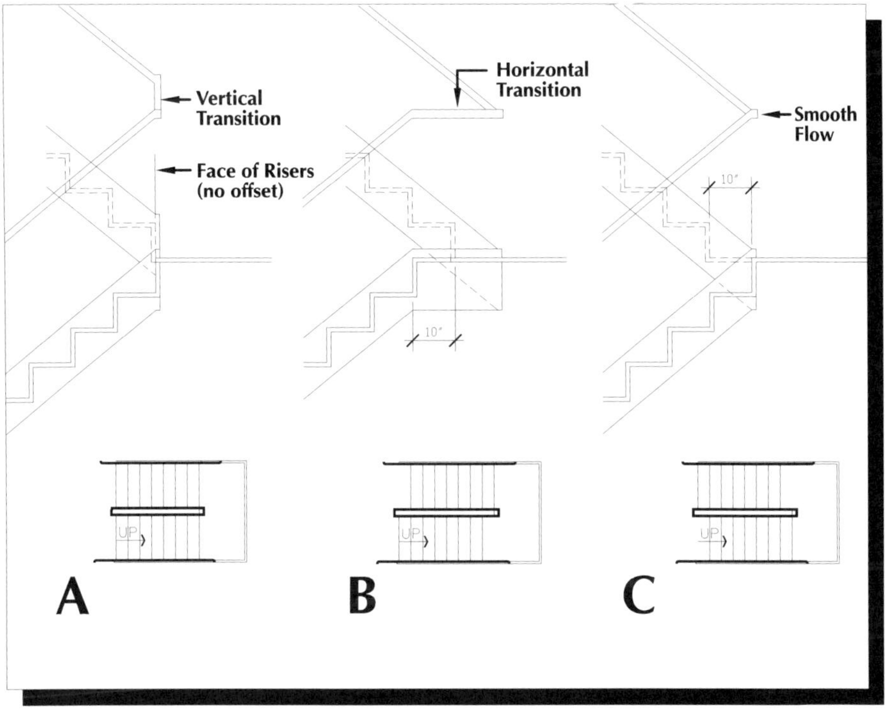

- ✔ The [U-Shaped stairs] command in *Auto-Architect* does not allow offset treads.
  - ✗ Use the [Stair Generator] or [Multi-Landing Stairs] commands to create stairs with offset treads.
- ✔ The following exercise shows how to use the [Stair Generator] to create a U-Shaped stair.

Hands-on:

Step 1:	Open the drawing *\sdskproj\workshop\dwg \stairdrw.dwg.*
Step 2:	Select [Design ⇨ Stair ⇨ Stair Settings...] from the pull-down menu.
Step 3:	Choose the "Annotation" button.

Step 4: Turn the "Number Each Tread" toggle off and exit the dialog boxes.

Step 5: Select [Design ⇨ Stairs ⇨ Stair Generator…] from the pull-down menu.

Step 6: Choose the "OK" button to accept default stair values.

Step 7: Select "Drawing Options".

Step 8: Verify that the "Handrails" toggles are turned on and that the "Continuous around landings" toggle for the right side is turned on and exit the dialog box.

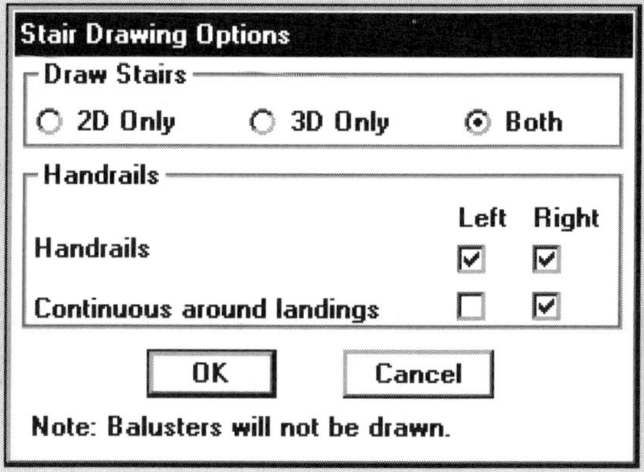

Note:

The right side is the inside edge as shown in the dialog image. You must turn the "Continuous around landings" option on for correct results.

Step 9: Choose the "U-Shaped" toggle for "Shape".

Step 10: Change the "(E) Trailing Stair Length:" from 11′-0″ to **11′-11″**.

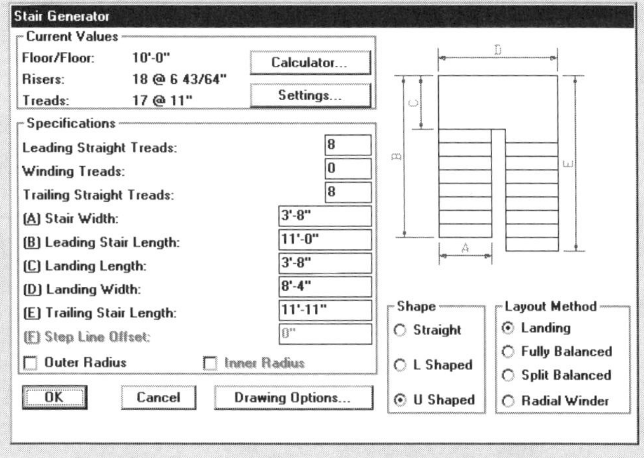

Step 11: Choose the "OK" button to draw the stair.

Step 12: Move the stair as desired and press <Enter> to end the placement process.

Step 13: Use viewports and isometric views to analyze the results of the stair design.

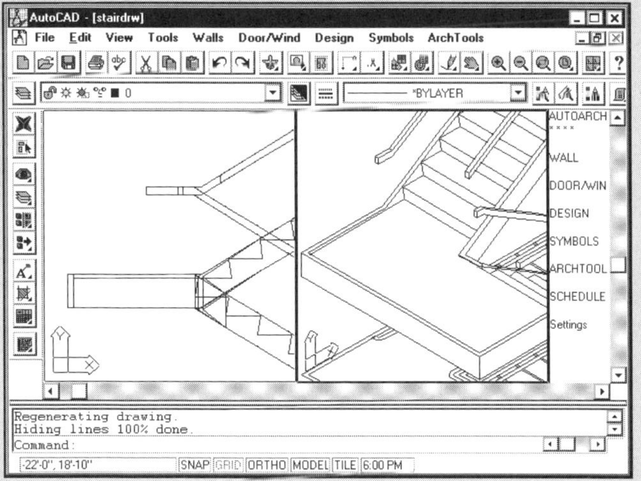

✔ Note that both 2D and 3D layers are displayed at this time.

Stair Break

You can quickly place a 2D stair break on a stair plan that you create with *Auto-Architect* stair commands.

✔ The following example shows how to place a 2D stair break using the stair drawing you just created.

Hands-on:

Step 1: Select [Design ⇨ Stairs ⇨ Add Stair Break] from the pull-down menu.

Step 2: Select a tread in the upper stair run.

Step 3: Accept the 2″ default in the "Width of stringers" prompt.

Note:

This forces the break to extend past the ends of the treads by this distance to incorporate the stringers.

Step 4: Accept the default angle in the "Break angle" prompt.

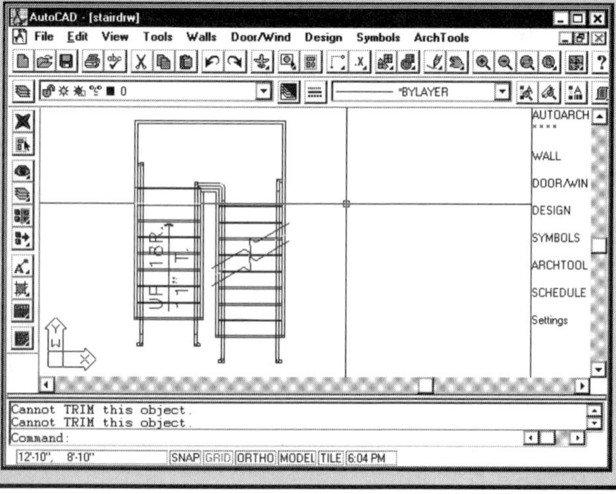

Adjust Stair Display Features

Auto-Architect may warn you that it "Cannot TRIM this object" several times as it places the break in the stair.

- ✔ The stair will not appear to be broken.
  - ✗ This is because the 3D layers are visible and *Auto-Architect* does not break the 3D objects.
- ✔ *Auto-Architect* did break the 2D stair correctly.
  - ✗ Turn off the 3D layers to display the 2D stair results.

The risers may appear as a continuous line when they should appear as a hidden line.

- ✔ You need to change the linetype for the layer.

Hands-on:

Step 1:	Use the layer command to turn off all 3D layers ("*3d*").
Step 2:	Select [ArchTools ⇨ Auto-Architect Settings…] from the pull-down menu.
Step 3:	Pick the "Layers" button.
Step 4:	Find "Stair risers" in the "Description" list and change the linetype to HIDDEN4.

Step 5: Choose the "OK" button to exit *Auto-Architect* Settings.

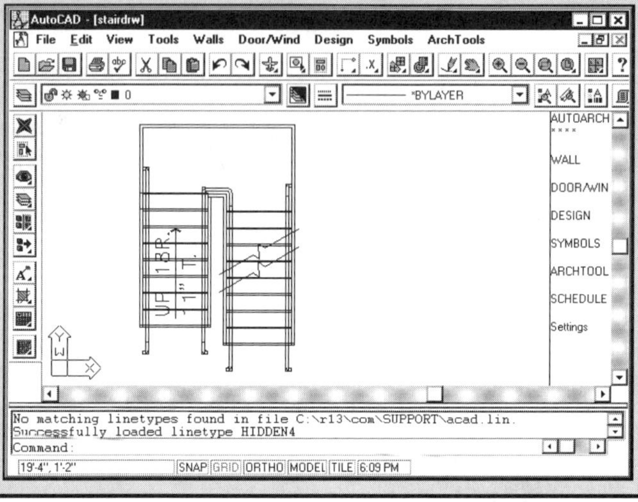

Chapter 6

Multiple Toilet Layout

Objectives

To design toilet stalls that meet the requirements of the Americans with Disabilities Act (ADA), you should be able to:

- ✔ Describe ADA guidelines that affect toilet stall design.
- ✔ Control stall dimensions with ADA renovation exceptions and toilet fixture options.
- ✔ Verify, reconfigure, and place toilet stalls.

Introduction

This chapter shows you how to design public washrooms to conform with standards set by the ADA. *Auto-Architect* includes the ADA standards in its toilet stall routines to ensure that your design conforms with the requirements of the ADA.

The introductory portions at the beginning of this chapter will familiarize you with the design parameters specific to public washrooms in the ADA. The examples in the first portion of the chapter show you how to adjust and override toilet stall parameters within the provisions of ADA standards. The second portion of the chapter leads you through the process of placing toilet stalls and optimizing your design.

The ADA

Public washrooms are one of the most critical accessibility issues in building design.

- ✔ The ADA is a federal civil rights law that prohibits discrimination against people with disabilities.
  - ✗ It ensures equal access to goods and services for people with disabilities.
- ✔ The specifications for implementing ADA law are known as the *ADA Accessibility Guidelines* (ADAAG).
  - ✗ Section 4.17 of the ADAAG specifies the layout, dimensions and clearances for accessible toilet stalls.
  - ✗ Toilet stalls for new construction or renovation must comply with these requirements; there are some exceptions for renovation or historic preservation.
- ✔ The guidelines specify a standard wheelchair-accessible stall (60″ width) as well as two alternate stalls.
  - ✗ You can use the alternate stalls for renovation work where an accessible stall is not possible or would reduce the total number of stalls required by local plumbing codes.
  - ✗ The first alternate stall is similar to the standard wheelchair-accessible stall, except that it is narrower (48″) and longer (66″).
  - ✗ The second alternate stall is narrow (36″) with handrails on both sides, providing access for people who need assistance walking but who are not in a wheelchair.

- ✗ One of these narrow stalls is also required in large toilet rooms where there are six or more stalls as specified in section A4.17.3.

✔ Stall lengths depend on the type of toilet you choose.

- ✗ You must increase the lengths by 3″ to accommodate extra space for floor-mounted toilets.
- ✗ The ADAAG provides only a federal minimal standard, which may be augmented by state building codes.
- ✗ You must confirm all building plans with local jurisdictions to ensure project compliance.

The Multi-Toilet Routine

The following example shows how to create a multi-toilet stall.

Hands-on

Step 1: Open the drawing *c:\sdskproj\workshop\dwg\int1b* and zoom to the lower rest room.

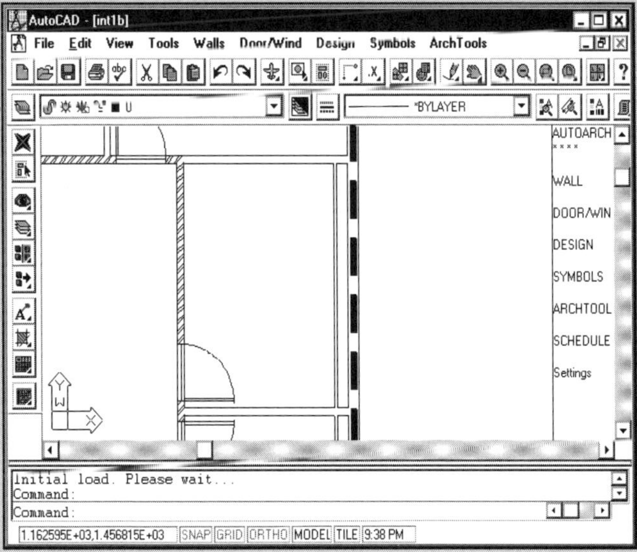

Step 2: Select [Design ⇨ Multiple Fixture Layout ⇨ Multiple Toilets...] from the pull-down menu.

Step 3: Set the Quantity of Alternate/Ambulatory stalls to 0 and press <Enter>.

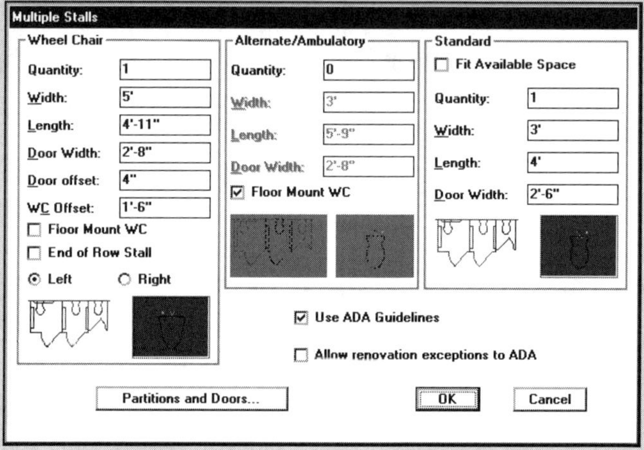

Note:

The standard accessible stall specified in ADAAG is listed as the "Wheel Chair" stall in the dialog box; the "Standard" stall in the dialog box refers to a non-accessible stall.

Step 4: Set the number of wheelchair stalls to 0 and press <Enter>. Notice that the change is not allowed.

Step 5: Turn on the toggle to "Allow renovation exceptions to ADA" and set the number of wheelchair stalls to **0** again.

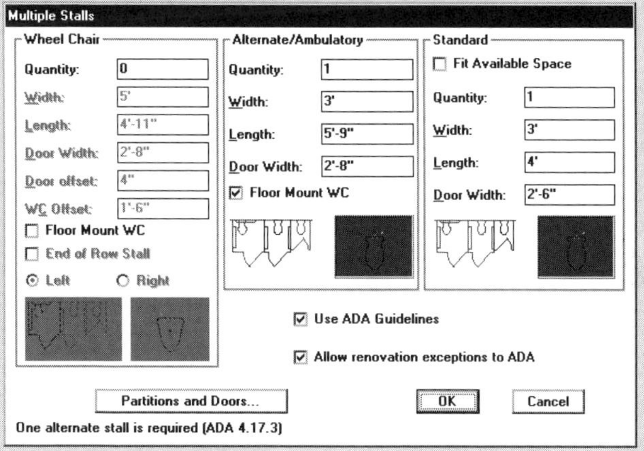

Notice the change is now allowed.

Step 6: Turn off the renovations exception toggle. Notice that the wheelchair stall is forced on.

Step 7: Set the quantity of alternate/ambulatory stalls to **0**.

Step 8: Set the quantity of standard stalls to **5** — the ambulatory stall comes back on with the reason shown at the bottom of the dialog box.

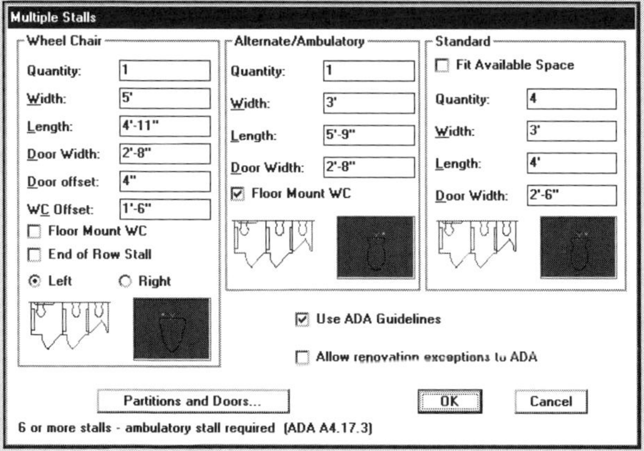

Note:

The number of standard stalls decreases by one to make the total number of standard plus alternate/ambulatory stalls match the number you enter.

Dimension Control

Auto-Architect carefully controls the dimensions of the wheelchair and ambulatory stalls.

- ✔ You can find the minimum or maximum size for an entry by entering an extreme value.
- ✔ *Auto-Architect* will correct the value with the maximum allowable value.

Hands-on:

Step 1: Try changing the width of the ambulatory stall to **2'** or **4'** — notice that only a width of 36" is allowed.

Step 2: Try changing the width of the wheelchair stall to **4'** — notice that the minimum is 5'.

Step 3: Change the length of the wheelchair stall to **3'** — notice that the minimum is 4'8" (or 4'11" for floor mount WC).

Step 4: Enable renovation exceptions to the ADA with the toggle.

Step 5: Change the width of the wheelchair stall to **4'**.

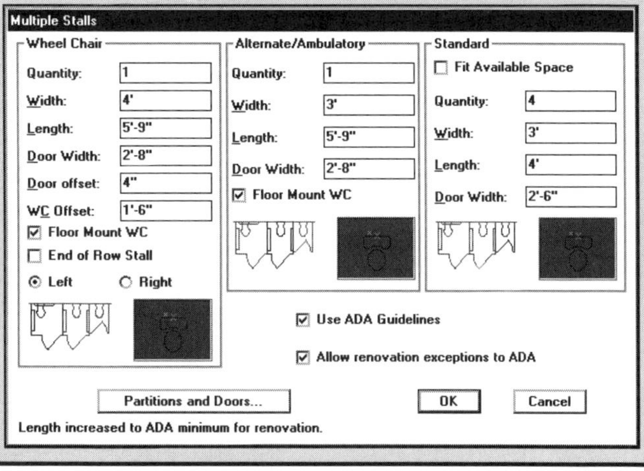

Note:

Notice that Auto-Architect *allows the width change, but the length increases to 5′6″, thus creating one of the alternate stall arrangements allowed by ADAAG 4.17.3.*

Step 6: Turn on the "Floor Mount WC" toggle and notice that the Length increases to 5′9″ to accommodate the extra space required for a floor mount fixture.

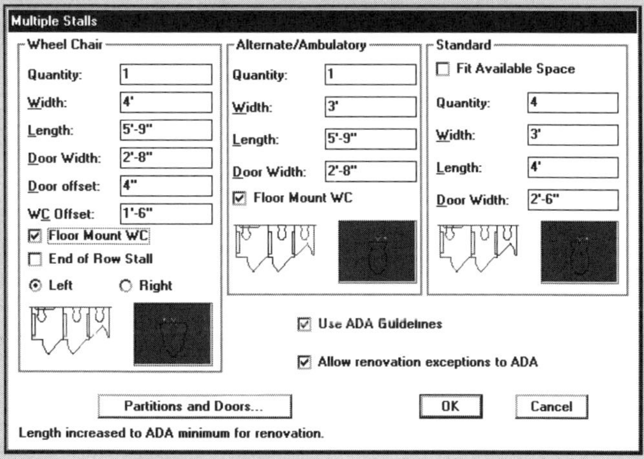

Step 7: Turn off the "Floor Mount WC" toggle and notice that the length decreases to 5′6″.

Wall and Floor Mount Fixtures

ADA guidelines require that stalls be lengthened by 3″ if you use floor mount fixtures.

✔ You can pick the "Floor Mount WC" toggle directly or let *Auto-Architect* handle this automatically.

Hands-on:

Step 1: Select the image of the toilet at the bottom of the wheelchair stall section.

Step 2: Change to the "Auto-Arch Symbol File" in the "Symbol Set" list.

Step 3: Choose the "Plumbing" category and the "Toilet" palette.

Step 4: Select "WC Flush Valve" from the list in the symbols manager.

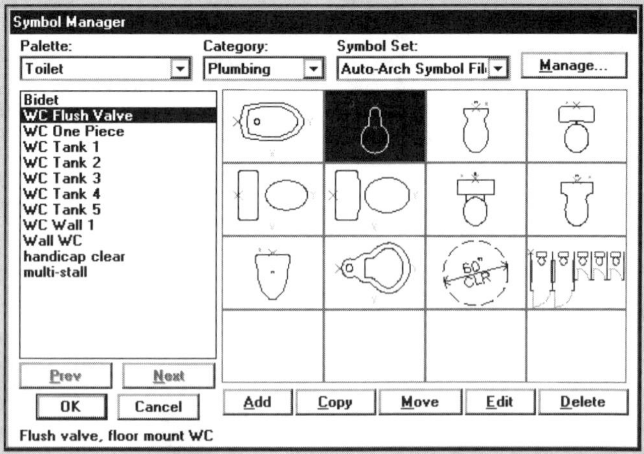

Note:

This is an example of using symbol manager as a "symbol server". Symbol manager does not insert the symbol, but it provides all insertion parameters, such as scale and layer, for the multi-stall routine.

Step 5: Double-click the symbol to display it on the Multiple Stalls dialog box.

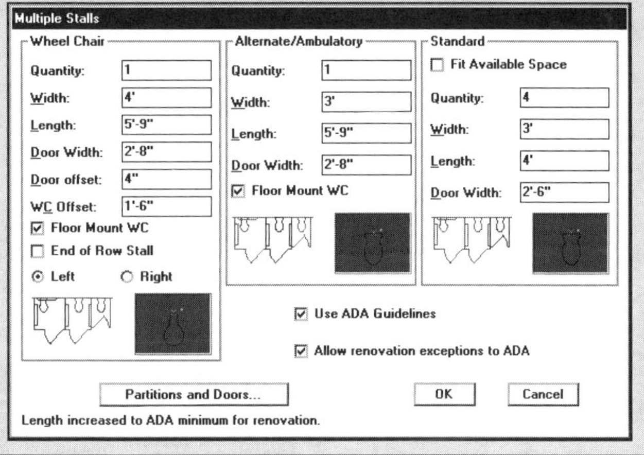

Note:

When you switch between floor mounted and wall mounted fixtures in the symbol manager, the toggle in the Multiple Stall dialog box changes, but the stall length may not. This is because you are not exceeding a minimum or maximum value.

Placing Stalls

One of the items in the Symbol Manager Toilet dialog box is the multi-stall routine.

✔ If you choose that item as your fixture, you get an invalid block alert.

✔ Choose the symbol image again to select a valid fixture.

Hands-on:

Step 1: Try the "Left" and "Right" toggle buttons in the dialog box.

Step 2: Turn on the "Fit available space" toggle for the standard stall.

Note:

The "Fit available space" toggle draws wheelchair and ambulatory stalls and divides the remaining space by the standard stall width to determine the number of standard stalls.

Step 3: Choose the "OK" button and snap to the upper-right corner of the washroom space as a start point.

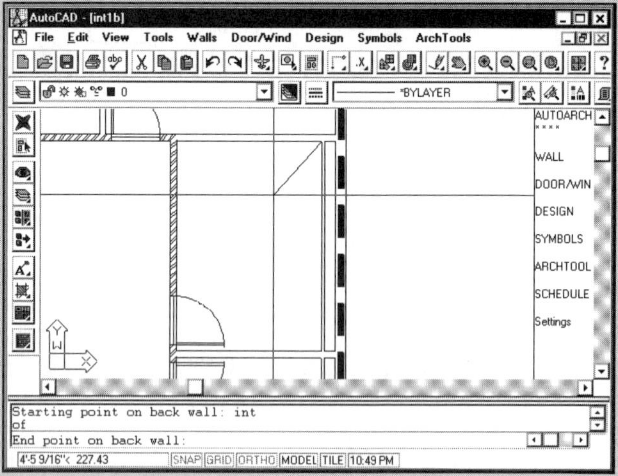

Step 4: Move the mouse down and snap to the other end of the wall.

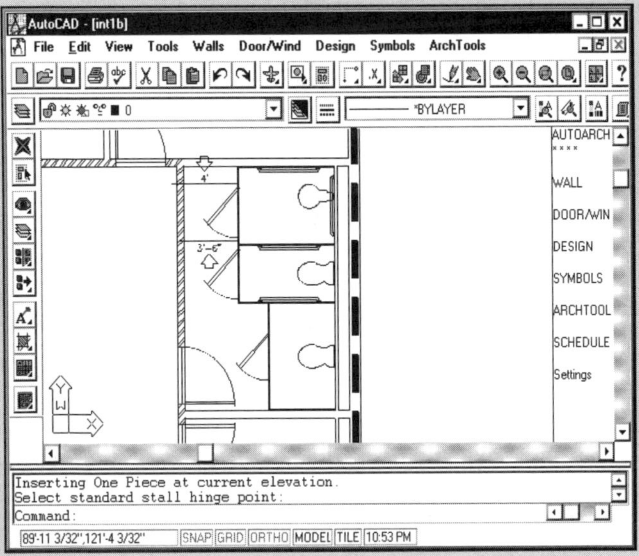

Step 5: Pick the top points when *Auto-Architect* prompts you for door hinge points.

Verify and Adjust Stall Sizes

The door clearance dimensions around the wheelchair stall show the clear area required by ADA.

- ✔ In this case, the approach is from below on the screen (latch approach) so you should use a 3′-6″ clearance.
- ✔ This means you need a clear area of 3′6″ in front of the door.
  - ✗ In this case, the toilet room is too small by a few inches.
  - ✗ You can make the wheelchair stall wider because the standard non-compliant stall is currently very large.

Hands-on:

Step 1: Undo to remove the stalls and enter SDSK to recall the Multi-toilet dialog box.

Step 2: Switch to a wall mount fixture for the wheelchair stall, set the stall length to **5′6″** and the width to **6′**.

Step 3: Set the length of the alternate/ambulatory stall to **5′6″** and recreate the design using the same points as before.

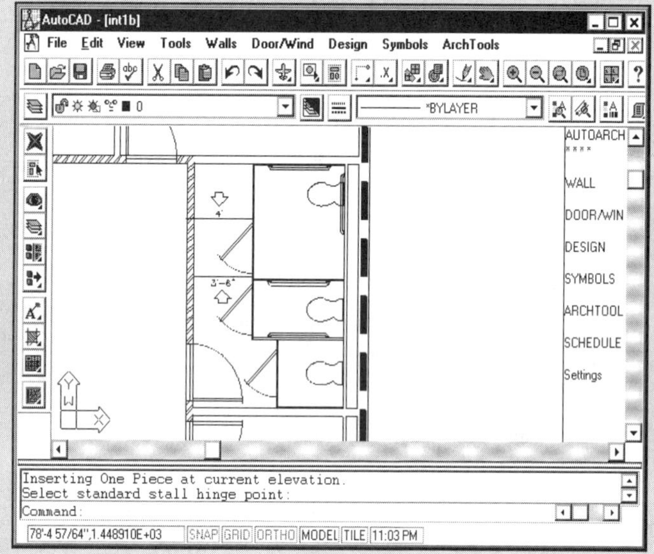

Reconfigure the Stalls

This time the stall fits properly in the rest room.

✔ There is still some room for refinements in this design.

Hands-on:

Step 1: Use the [Undo] command to remove the stalls and enter SDSK to recall the Multi-toilet dialog.

Step 2: Turn on the "End of Row Stall" toggle.

Note:

The stall length entry is disabled. You have to pick points in the drawing to set the stall length.

Step 3: Set the alternate/ambulatory Quantity to **0**.

Step 4: Set the length of the standard stall to **5'**.

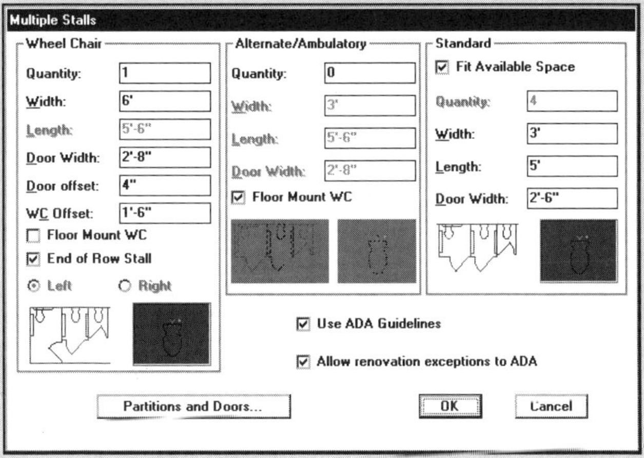

Step 5: Pick two points along the back wall and pick the length definition point for the first stall in the lower-right corner of the rest room.

Step 6: Pick the upper-right intersection when prompted for the length along the wall.

Step 7: Pick the bottom left hinge point for the standard stall doors.

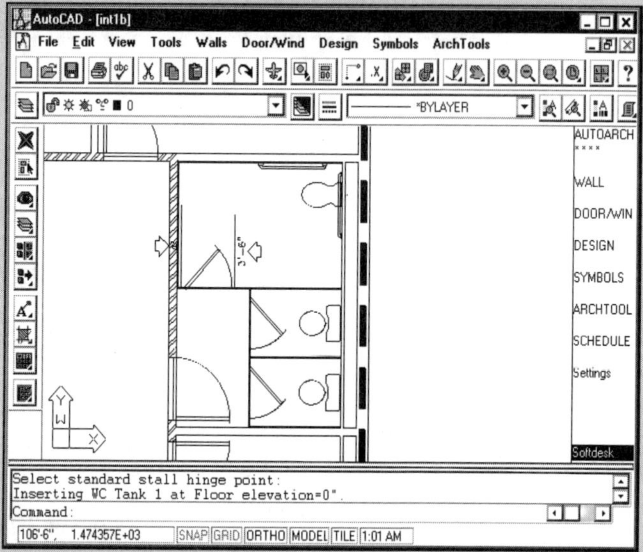

The door opens into the stall.

✔ You do not need the clearance symbol.

✔ Erase the clearance symbol.

Chapter 7

Ceilings for 3D Rendering

Objectives

To create a ceiling grid for three-dimensional modeling, you should be able to:

- ✔ Create a reflected ceiling grid with light fixtures.
- ✔ Create a ceiling surface.
- ✔ Edit light fixtures to enhance rendering.

Introduction

This chapter shows you how to generate a reflected ceiling grid and convert it into a ceiling surface for a three-dimensional model. The first section shows you how to generate the ceiling grid and balance the tiles for an attractive and cost-effective ceiling grid. From here, you can use the perimeter of the room to generate a surface above the grid, which will give the appearance of ceiling tiles. It can then place ceiling light fixtures and convert them to three-dimensional blocks to complete the design.

This chapter also shows you how to use the [Edit block] and [Replace block] commands to change three-dimensional blocks. In this case, the standard three-dimensional ceiling light fixtures do not give realistic results when you shade the model. You will replace the polyline symbol with a polyline outline and 3Dface to create a more realistic light fixture.

Ceiling Grids

You create a ceiling grid in *Auto-Architect* by picking a point inside the room where you want the grid.

- ✔ *Auto-Architect* finds the room perimeter.
    - ✗ You set the size and elevation for the ceiling.
    - ✗ *Auto-Architect* tries to balance the ceiling within the space you choose.
    - ✗ You adjust the ceiling position to define the most cost-effective, attractive ceiling layout for the space.
- ✔ You do not need to control layers for ceiling grids.
    - ✗ *Auto-Architect* ignores doors and windows; you may leave those layers on if desired.
    - ✗ The 3D wall and jamb layers above the door openings do not affect the ceiling and may be turned on or off.

- ✗ *Auto-Architect* turns on the header lines above the openings to define the room perimeter.
- ✗ The lines do not appear because their layer is defined with an invisible linetype.

Create an Initial Ceiling Grid

The following exercise shows how to start the process for creating the ceiling.

- ✔ This will result in a ceiling pattern that you must balance to meet your own design preferences.

Hands-on:

Step 1:	Open the drawing *\sdskproj\workshop\dwg \office2.dwg.*
Step 2:	Select [Design ⇨ Floor/Ceiling Grids…] from the pull-down menu.
Step 3:	Verify that the "Grid Type" toggle is set to "Ceiling" and that the "Grid Placement Options" toggle is set to "Find Boundary".
Step 4:	Set the "Grid Creation Options" toggle to "Polylines".
Step 5:	Verify that polyline width is set to **1″** and that elevation is set to **8′**.
Step 6:	Set "Thickness" to **1/16″**.
Step 7:	Press the "OK" button.
Step 8:	Pick a point inside the large open office space on the plan view.
Step 9:	Press <Enter> to select the next internal point.

Step 10:	Press <Enter> when *Auto-Architect* asks you to select the objects to avoid.
Step 11:	Enter **4'** for the first direction indicated by the direction arrow.
Step 12:	Press <Enter> to accept the default for the tile size in the second direction.

Adjust Grid Position

The grid appears balanced in the Y direction, but is offset slightly in the X direction when you look at it in the major portion of the space.

- ✔ *Auto-Architect* uses the overall area to balance the grid.
  - ✗ This area includes the corridor at the lower-right.
  - ✗ You can adjust the grid to correct the X direction imbalance without affecting the Y position.
- ✔ The following exercise moves the ceiling to compensate for the imbalance along one wall, but does not complete the ceiling design.

Hands-on:

Step 1:	Enter the **.M** midpoint filter when *Auto-Architect* prompts you to pick a new point to shift the grid.
Step 2:	Use an ENDpoint osnap to pick the end of the grid line at point A.

Step 3: Use an ENDpoint osnap to pick the end of the same grid line at point B.

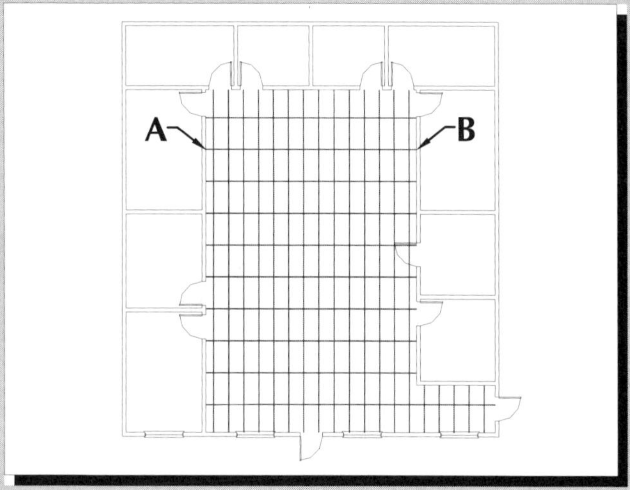

Improve the Design

The grid is now evenly balanced on this portion of the space.

- ✔ One full tile width now appears at both edges of the room, which leaves no room for error when installing the ceiling.
  - ✗ If the space is built an inch larger than specified, there will be a gap at the edge of the room.
  - ✗ A very narrow strip also appears at the corridor, which makes the ceiling difficult to install.
- ✔ The following example shows how to compensate for a common design problem that could affect the appearance and cost of the ceiling.
  - ✗ Eliminate these conditions by shifting the grid one half tile in the X direction.

Hands-on:

Step 1: Enter the **.M** midpoint filter when *Auto-Architect* prompts you to pick new point.

Step 2: Use the INTersection osnap to pick any grid intersection.

Step 3: Use the INTersection osnap to pick an intersection immediately to the right or left of your chosen intersection.

Step 4: Press <Enter> to complete the command.

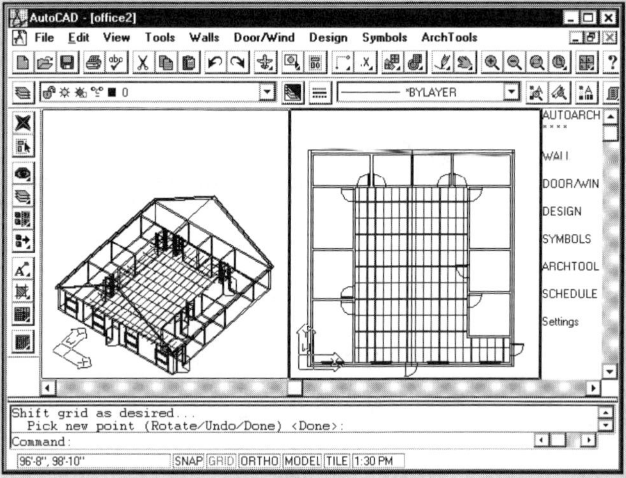

✔ The grid lines now become polylines, and the grid pattern is complete.

Adding a Grid Perimeter

As in typical commercial buildings, the ceiling grid and top of wall are at two different elevations.

- ✔ In this case, the grid is at elevation 8′ and the walls are 10′ high.
  - ✗ As a result, the grid has no perimeter line.
- ✔ You must create the perimeter line manually on the same layer as the grid.

Hands-on:

Step 1:	Select [View ⇨ Layer Controls ⇨ Set/Define Layer] from the pull-down menu and press <Enter>.
Step 2:	Choose the "Pick <" button.
Step 3:	Pick one of the grid polylines when *Auto-Architect* asks you to select objects.
Step 4:	Choose the "OK" button to continue.
Step 5:	Use the [PL] macro to draw a polyline.
Step 6:	Use the .XY point filter and then an ENDpoint osnap to pick a corner in the space.
Step 7:	Enter **8′** when *Auto-Architect* asks for the Z coordinate.
Step 8:	Use osnaps to continue drawing the polyline around the perimeter — the PERpendicular osnap works well for getting to a congested corner.

Note:

Do not use .XY filter after the first point — the [Pline] command ignores Z coordinates.

Step 9: Type "C" for close to end the [Pline] command when you come to the last corner in the space.

Step 10: Use the [SE] macro to select the new polyline and type **L** to choose that last object that you added to the drawing.

Step 11: Use the [Offset] command to copy the perimeter **1/2″** inward.

Step 12: Change the new polyline to be **1″** wide like the other grid members.

Step 13: Use the following command prompt sequence as a guide.

```
Command: OF
Macro: Offset
Offset distance or Through <Through>:  1/2
Select object to offset:Pick the polyline
Side to offset?             Pick a point within the space
Select object to offset:Press <Enter>
Command: PE
Macro: Pedit
Select polyline: L
Open/Join..../eXit <X>: W
Enter new width for all segments: 1
Open/Join..../eXit <X>:          Press <Enter>
```

Step 14: Do not erase the original polyline.

Add the Ceiling Surface

After you complete the suspended ceiling grid, you need to define a surface for the ceiling tiles.

- ✔ The ceiling grid made of polylines — there are no tiles in the grid and thus no ceiling surface.
- ✔ An easy way to create a ceiling surface is to convert the original ceiling perimeter polyline that you drew into a region surface.
  - ✗ If you move it slightly above the ceiling grid lines, it will form ceiling tiles in the three-dimensional model of the ceiling.
  - ✗ This is easier than trying to define tile surfaces for each panel in the grid.

The following example shows you how to change the perimeter polyline and create a surface with the [Region] command.

Hands-on:

Step 1: Use the [Move] command to increase the elevation of the original ceiling grid perimeter polyline by 1/4".

```
Command: M
Macro: Move
Select objects: P
1 found
Select objects:                    Press <Enter>
Base point or displacement: 0,0,1/4
Second point of displacement: Press <Enter>
```

Step 2:	Select [Tools ⇨ Construct ⇨ Region] from the pull-down menu.
Step 3:	Type **P** to choose the previous object that you selected with the [SE] macro in the last example.

```
Command: REGION
Select objects: P
1 found
Select objects:                Press <Enter>
1 loop extracted.
1 Region created.
```

Place Fluorescent Lights

You can now place fluorescent light fixtures.

✔ Before doing so, change the value of the ceiling elevation key to match the height of your ceiling grid.

Hands-on:

Step 1:	Select [ArchTools ⇨ Auto-Architect Settings...] from the pull-down menu.
Step 2:	Pick the "General" button from the Softdesk *Auto-Architect* Settings dialog box.
Step 3:	Pick the "Elevation Key Words" button from the General Settings dialog box.
Step 4:	Scroll down the "Key words" list and highlight CEILING — the current elevation for this key word appears in an edit box at the right.

Step 5: Change the elevation to **8′** and choose the "OK" button.

Step 6: Choose the "OK" button to exit all dialog boxes.

Step 7: Select [Symbols ⇨ Symbol Manager…] from the pull-down menu.

Step 8: Change the "Symbol Set" to "Auto-Arch Symbol File".

Step 9: Change the "Category" to "Electric".

Step 10: Change the "Palette" to "Fluorescent".

Step 11: Highlight the "Ceiling Light" symbol.

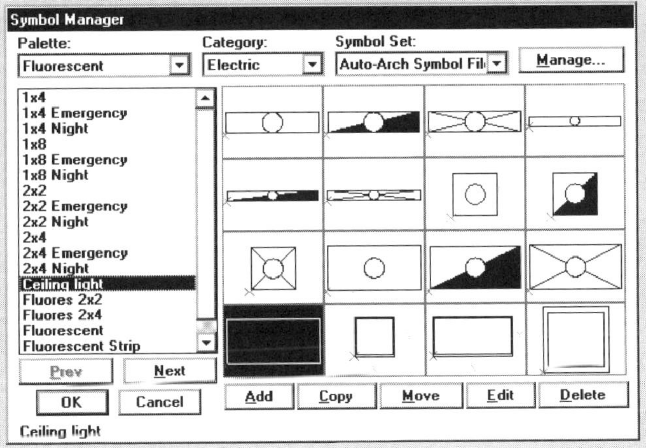

Step 12: Choose the "Edit" button and verify that "Elevation (Preset):" is set to "Ceiling".

Step 13: Choose the "OK" button.

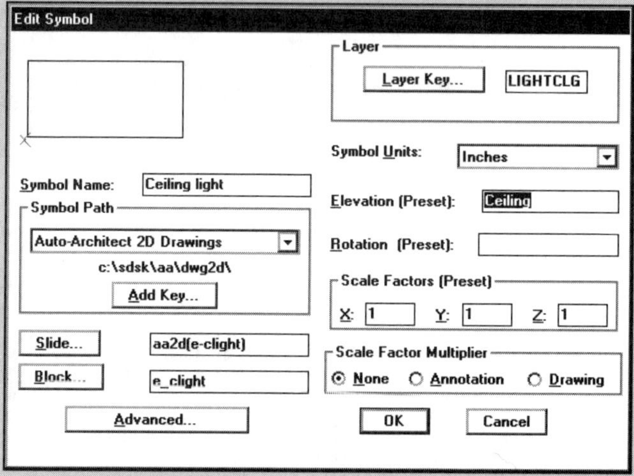

Step 14: Choose the "OK" button to insert fixtures.

Step 15: Enter **90** for the rotation angle.

Step 16: Move the fixture to location 1 as shown below — use the INTersection to help you pick the points.

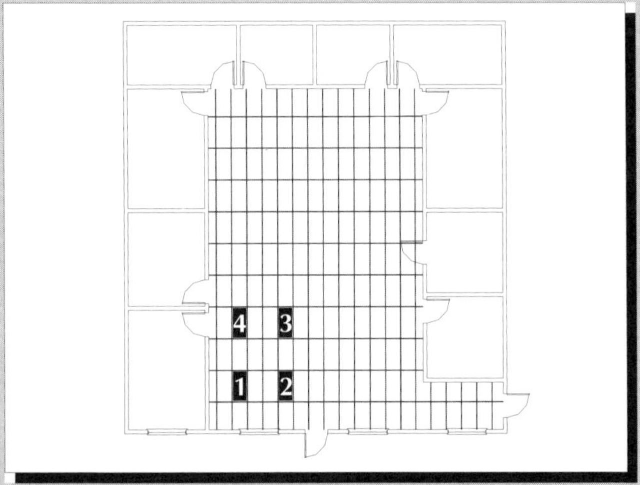

Step 17: Enter **C** for copy when *Auto-Architect* asks for a new basepoint.

Step 18: Place fixtures at locations 2, 3, and 4.

Step 19: Press <Enter> to end the command.

Convert to 3D Blocks

You now have four lights in the ceiling that you can convert from 2D symbols into 3D symbols.

Hands-on:

Step 1: Select [ArchTools ⇨ Symbol 2D<->3D] from the pull-down menu.

Step 2: Respond to the prompts as follows:

```
Convert symbols from 2D to 3D or vice versa...
Select blocks to be converted (RETURN for all)...
Select objects: W                    Select all four fixtures
First corner: Other corner: 4 found
Select objects:                      Press <Enter>
Convert to (3D/2D) <3D>:             Press <Enter>
Redefining Symbols...
Insert all future symbols in 3D <Yes>: N
```

✔ The fixtures now appear solidly filled in the plan view.

Set Up an Interior Perspective View

You are now ready to view and render the interior.

Hands-on:

Step 1: Select [View ⇨ Presentation ⇨ Eye Position] from the pull-down menu.

Step 2: Pick a point in the lower-left corner of the open office space.

Step 3: Turn ortho off and pick a point in the center of the space.

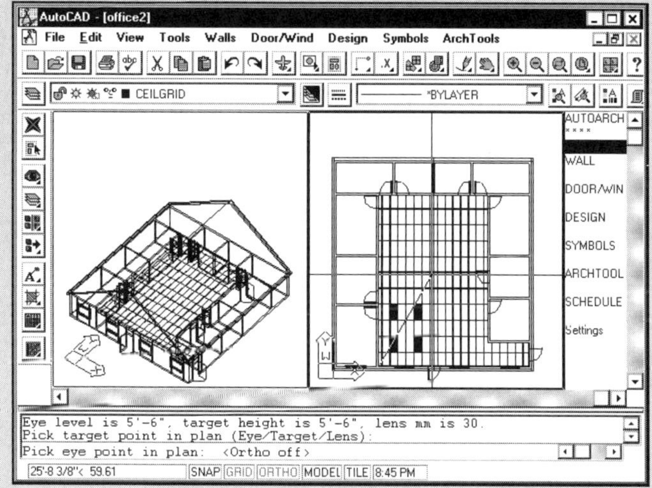

Step 4: Use a crossing windows to select the visible walls, ceiling perimeter, ceiling surface, and the light fixture closest to the eye point and then press <Enter> to continue.

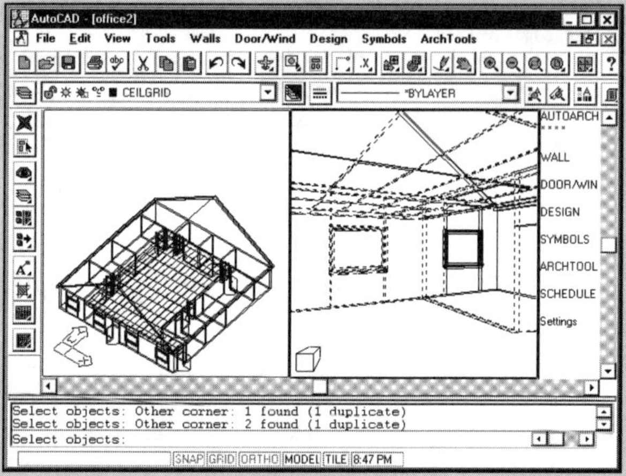

Step 5: Move the Step options dialog box to the bottom of your screen to see your model.

Step 6: Pick the "Forward" button to move one step closer — this moves the view too close.

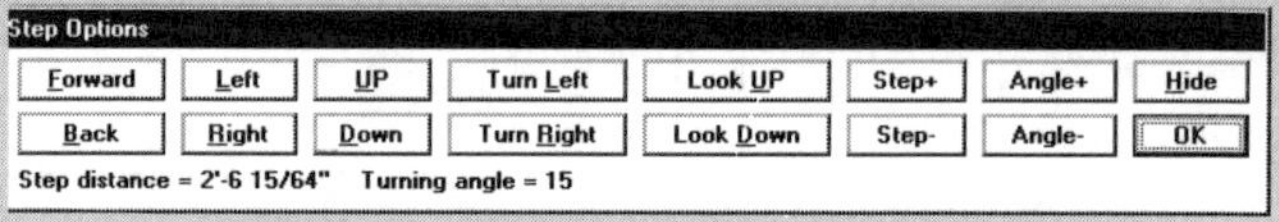

Step 7: Pick the "Back" button to move back again.

Step 8: Pick the "Step -" button to reduce the size of the step.

Step 9: Pick the "Forward" button again — this is an acceptable view.

Step 10: Pick the "Hide" button to preview the model.

Step 11: Choose the "OK" button to continue.

Step 12: Use the [Hide] command to display the model.

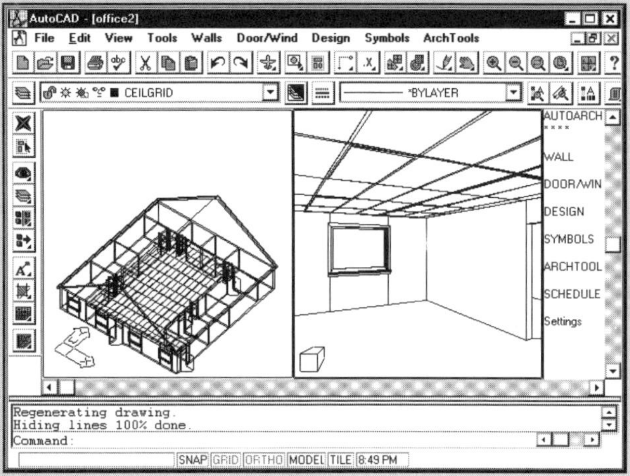

Shade the Model

The ceiling appears solid, and the light fixtures extend slightly below the grid.

- ✔ You should adjust the colors before you shade the view.
  - ✗ You can adjust the colors by restoring a layer group
  - ✗ If the color settings don't meet your needs, you can change them in the plan matrix.

Hands-on:

Step 1: Select [View ⇨ Layer Groups ⇨ Set Plan] from the pull-down menu.

Step 2: Highlight V3D-INT from the "Plan Name" list and choose the "OK" button.

Step 3: Use the [Shade] command to display the model.

Revising Light Fixtures

The edge of the lights appears with the proper color in the shaded view, but the light lenses appear to be the same shade as the ceiling tiles.

✔ Use the Softdesk *Productivity Tools* to change the light lens with the edit blocks [EB] and redefine blocks [RB] command.

Hands-on:

Step 1: Choose the left viewport to make it current before you start the next steps.

Step 2: Set layer 0 to be current.

Step 3: Copy the last light fixture to an open area at the upper-right of the viewport.

Step 4: Select [Tools ⇨ Blocks ⇨ Edit Block] from the pull-down menu.

Step 5: Select the block you just copied and place it to the left of the selected block.

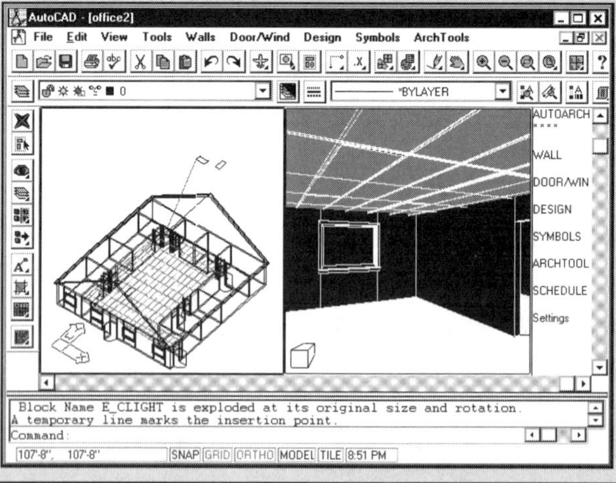

Note:

Auto-Architect *displays a message that "Block Name E_CLIGHT is exploded at its original size and rotation". A temporary line marks the insertion point.*

Step 6: Zoom in to the exploded block.

Step 7: Use the [List] command to analyze the elements in the exploded block.

polyline 3'-10" long
width of 1'-10"
thickness of 1/2"
Z value of -1/2"

Step 8: Replace this polyline with a face and extruded edge.

Step 9: Use the [RC] macro to create a rectangular polyline.

```
Macro: Rectangle
First corner:                Pick point for lower-left corner
Other corner: @3'10,1'10
```

Step 10: Make sure the width of the new polyline is 0 — use the [PE] macro to change it if necessary.

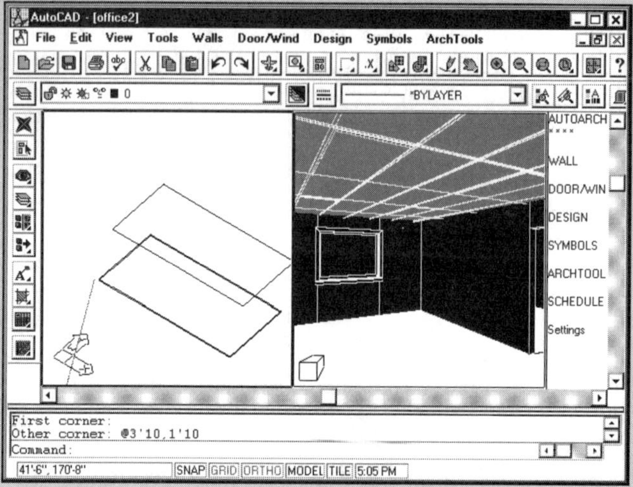

Step 11: Use the [Move] command to move the last polyline from midpoint A to endpoint B.

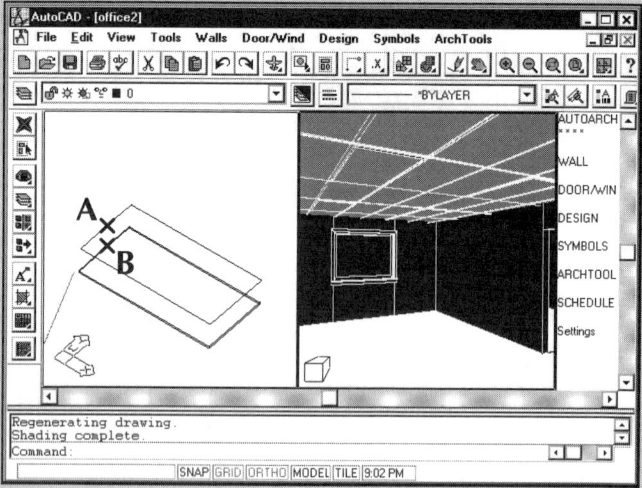

Step 12: Erase the original wide polyline.

```
Command: ER
Macro: Erase
Select objects:  C
First corner: Other corner:  2 found
Select objects:  R
Remove objects:  L
1 found, 1 removed
Remove objects:                    Press <Enter>
```

Step 13: Use the [CP] macro to change the thickness of the new polyline to 1/2".

Step 14: Draw a 3D face (using the FA macro) to fill in the polyline, osnap to the bottom of each corner.

Step 15: Select [Tools ⇨ Blocks ⇨ Redefine Block] from the pull-down menu.

```
Redefine block name <E_CLIGHT>:
                                   Press <Enter>
Insertion point <same>:            Press <Enter>
Select objects:                    Press <Enter>
Redefining E_CLIGHT...
```

Step 16: Use the [Zoom Previous] command to return to the original view.

Step 17: Erase the block in the upper-right corner.

Step 18: Switch to the right viewport.

Step 19: Use the [Shade] command to see the final model.

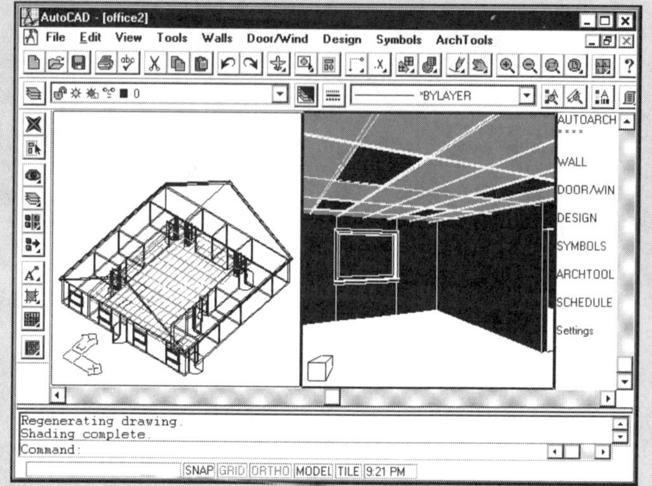

- ✔ You can use the [Wblock] command to redefine the block E_CLIGHT in the *sdsk/aa/dwg3d.*
- ✔ Do NOT do so unless you are working on your own system and no one else will be doing these same exercises.

Chapter 8

Advanced Roof Design Techniques

Objectives

To design complex roofs with roof generator, you should be able to:

- ✔ Design a complex roof layout.
- ✔ Design a roof with mixed slope values.
- ✔ Design a roof by setting and matching the ridge line.
- ✔ Design a dormer.
- ✔ Generate a flat roof.

Introduction

This chapter shows you the advanced capabilities of the roof generator in *Auto-Architect.* The first section shows you how to generate a roof on a complex building shape. From here, you use an existing building to apply the roof generator to various roof slope combinations. This chapter also shows you how to use the roof generator to create a dormer. The final section shows how to create a flat roof with drainage slope.

Throughout this chapter, you should note the flexibility with which the roof generator can solve complex roof design problems. The dormer exercise, for example, shows how to use the roof generator to create a simple roof, which you can then edit with roof commands to complete the design. This example is typical of the types of problems that you can solve with roof generator.

Roof Generator

Auto-Architect includes a simple roof routine and a more flexible roof generator.

- ✔ The roof generator routine uses slope tags that you place around the perimeter of a building to create the roof.
- ✔ The roof generator reads slope and overhang information from each tag and uses it to define a plane.
    - ✗ It then finds the intersections of the planes and sets ridge and valley locations.
- ✔ The general steps to use the roof generator include:
    - ✗ Creating a polyline
    - ✗ Placing tags on the polyline
    - ✗ Editing the tags
    - ✗ Generating the roof planes

- ✔ You can follow these steps one at a time using the Add Slope Tags and Edit Slope Tags commands, or you can start and use the [Generate Roof] command from the outset.
  - ✗ Following the steps individually gives you more flexibility for designing the roof.
  - ✗ It is also easier to undo individual steps to correct problems than to undo the entire roof generator process.

The following example shows how to use the roof generator for a complex design.

Hands-on:

Step 1: Create a new drawing called *roofdes1.dwg*.

Step 2: Start *Auto-Architect* and select the WORKSHOP project.

Step 3: Use the default sheet settings then set the snap to **1'**.

Step 4: Select [Design ⇨ Roofs ⇨ Roof Generator ⇨ Add Slope Tags] from the pull-down menu.

Step 5: Press <Enter> to draw a multi-sided polyline similar to the following illustration.

Step 6: Use the defaults in the Roof Slope Tags dialog box.

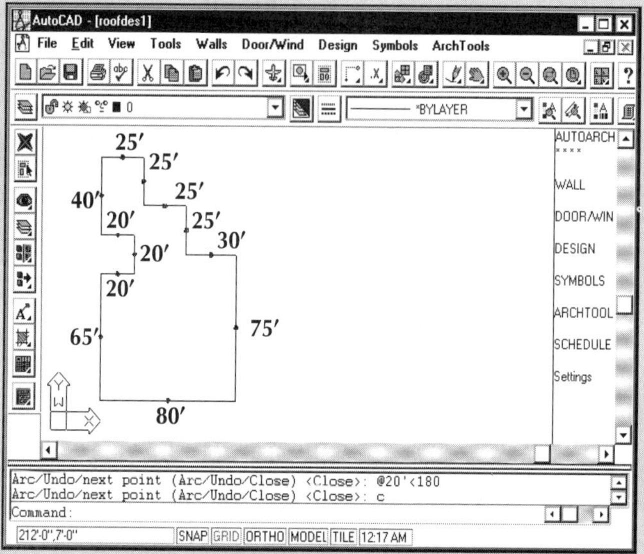

Step 7: Choose [View ⇨ View ⇨ View Presets...] from the pull-down menu and choose a "South East Isometric" view.

Step 8: Select [Design ⇨ Roofs ⇨ Roof Generator ⇨ Generate Roof] from the pull-down menu.

Step 9: Select the perimeter polyline.

Step 10: Choose the "OK" button and then accept the defaults for wall height and cutting areas.

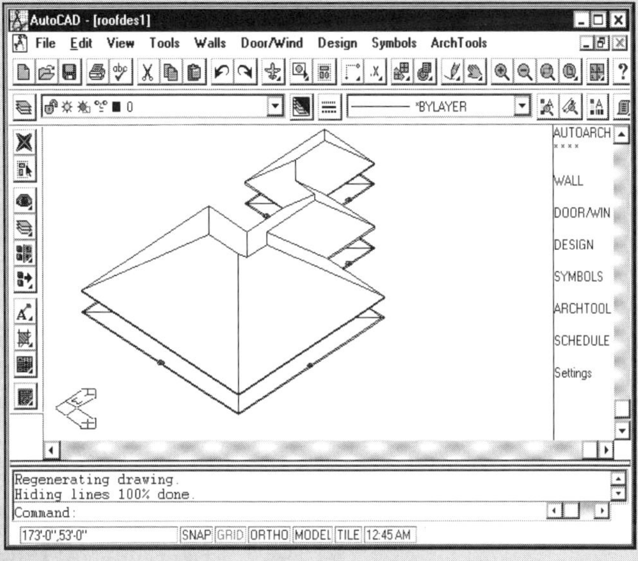

Step 11: Use the [Undo] command to return to the polyline with tags.

Step 12: Select [Design ⇨ Roofs ⇨ Roof Generator ⇨ Edit Slope Tags] from the pull-down menu.

Step 13: Pick the tag at the bottom left.

Step 14: Turn on the "Gable end (Vertical)" toggle and choose the "OK" button.

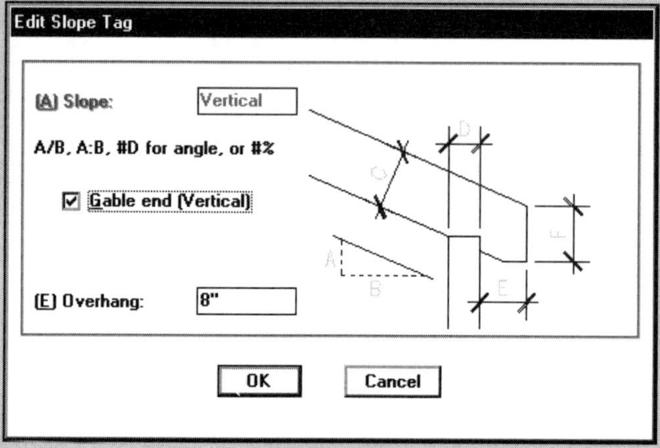

Step 15: Press <Enter> to continue.

Step 16: Select [Design ⇨ Roofs ⇨ Roof Generator ⇨ Generate Roof] from the pull-down menu and accept the defaults.

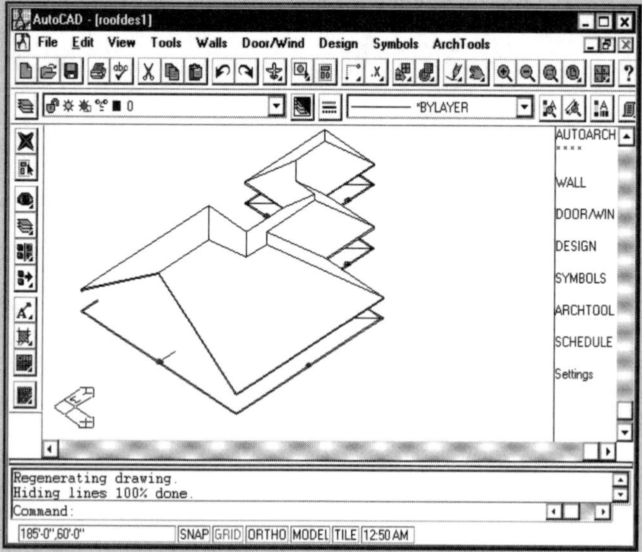

Notice that *Auto-Architect* generates a triangular wall on the gable end.

- ✔ The two-dimensional roof lines are hidden by the gable end wall.
- ✔ These triangular walls are hard to see because the edges along the bottom are invisible.
- ✔ Do not assign two adjacent edges as vertical because this creates an undefined condition.

Mixing Slope Values

The last example shows how to mix a vertical slope with other slopes.

- ✔ The following example shows how to mix several slope values.
- ✔ The first set of steps directs you to prepare an existing building for a new roof design.

Hands-on:

Step 1:	Open the drawing file called *\sdskproj\workshop \dwg\office.*
Step 2:	Use the [YE] macro to erase the existing roof objects.

Step 3: Enter the layers 3DROOF,ROOF,ROOFSOF as shown.

Step 4: Use the [Zoom Extents] command in the right viewport.

Step 5: Use the [Zoom Extents] command in the left viewport.

Step 6: Use crossing windows in the [Erase] command to remove the triangular walls.

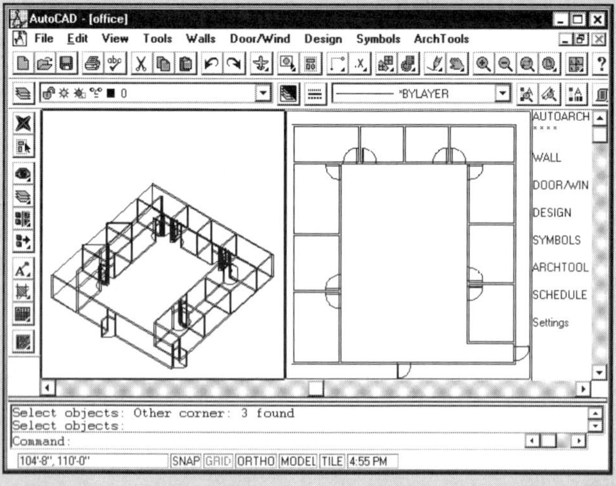

Step 7: Make sure the ROOFTAG layer is turned on.

Adjust Existing Roof Tags

You are now ready to enter a different slope in one of the tags.

Hands-on:

Step 1: Select [Design ⇨ Roofs ⇨ Roof Generator ⇨ Edit Slope Tags] from the pull-down menu.

Step 2: Pick the bottom left tag that was previously set to create a vertical end.

Step 3: Turn off the "Gable end (Vertical)" toggle and enter a **3/12** roof slope.

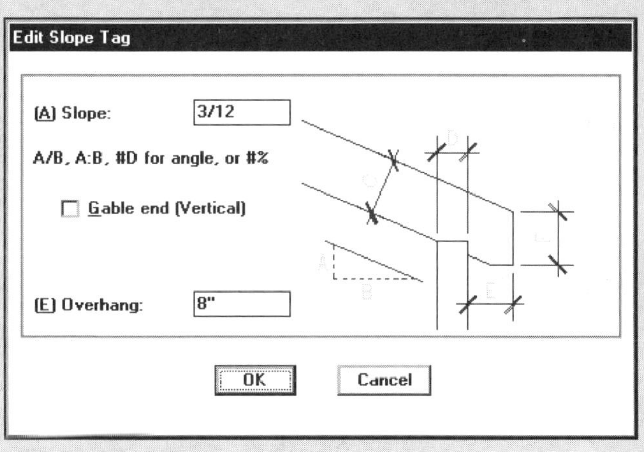

Step 4: Choose the "OK" button and change the tag at the opposite end of the building to use a **4/12** slope.

Step 5: Start the [Undo] command and type **M** for Mark.

Step 6: Select [Design ⇨ Roofs ⇨ Roof Generator ⇨ Generate Roof] from the pull-down menu.

Step 7: Choose the exterior side of any wall to select the perimeter polyline.

Step 8: Set the wall height to 10′ and no cutting areas to project.

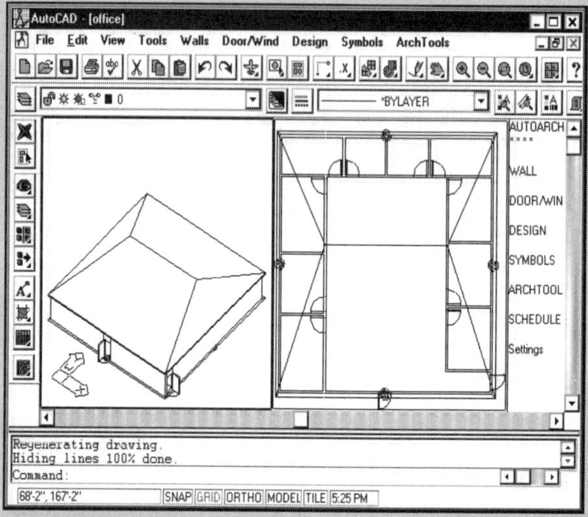

✔ The roof ridge is no longer at the center of the building.

Set and Match Ridge

Auto-Architect allows you to preset the location of the roof ridge.

✔ This eliminates trial and error process when using different slope values to locate a roof ridge.

✔ You can use the [Set Ridges] command to locate the ridge based on a slope and distance from a roof tag.

✔ You can then use the [Match Ridges] command to calculate and set slope values in other slope tags affected by the ridge that you set.

Set Ridge

The following example places the ridge based on one of the roof tags.

- ✔ *Auto-Architect* calculates the Z position by using the slope of the selected tag.
- ✔ *Auto-Architect* draws the ridge line on the ROOFTAG layer and uses it for calculations only.

Hands-on:

Step 1: Use the [Undo] command with the Back option to remove the previous roof.

Step 2: Use the [Regenall] command or the RG macro.

Step 3: Select [Design ⇨ Roofs ⇨ Roof Generator ⇨ Set Ridges] from the pull-down menu.

Step 4: Accept the dialog values and pick the tag at the bottom of the screen.

Step 5: Enter **10′** for the top of wall.

Step 6: Type **@0,30′** for the XY distance to the ridge.

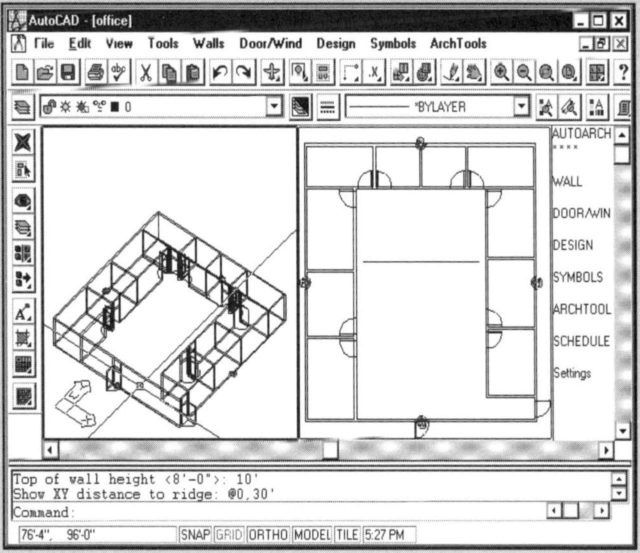

Match Ridge

When you set the ridge based on one tag, you must adjust the slope in other tags affected by the set ridge.

✔ In this example, you will set the slope in the tag at the top right side of the view with the [Match Ridge] command.

Hands-on:

Step 1:	Select [Design ⇨ Roofs ⇨ Roof Generator ⇨ Match Ridges] from the pull-down menu.
Step 2:	Accept the dialog box values.
Step 3:	Select the ridge line then the top tag and set the top of the wall to 10′.
Step 4:	Notice the new slope value reported at the command prompt.
Step 5:	Choose [Design ⇨ Roofs ⇨ Roof Generator ⇨ Edit Slope Tags] from the pull-down menu.
Step 6:	Choose the top right slope tag.
Step 7:	Notice the slope value that appears in the dialog box.
Step 8:	Choose the "Cancel" button.

Generate the Roof

When you generate the roof, the intersection of the top and bottom planes will be at the set ridge line.

✔ In the following example, generate the roof one more time to see the effect of the change.

Hands-on:

Step 1: Select [Design ⇨ Roofs ⇨ Roof Generator ⇨ Generate Roof] from the pull-down menu.

Step 2: Accept the dialog box defaults.

Step 3: Enter 10' for the wall height.

Step 4: Accept the default for cutting areas.

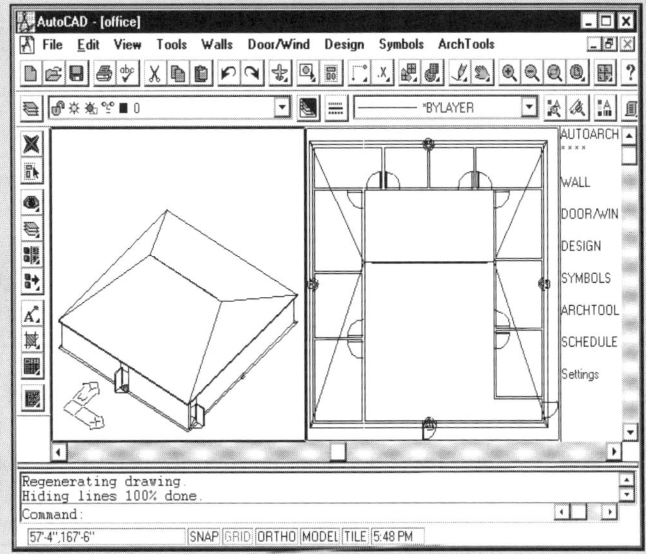

✔ The ridge is now at the location you set.

✔ Notice that the original roof ridge line is still visible along the new roof ridge.

✗ This line will disappear when you turn off the ROOFTAG layer.

Creating a Dormer

You can use several *Auto-Architect* editing tools to add a dormer to your roof design.

✔ The following example shows how to extend walls and roof surfaces to create a dormer.

Create a Dormer Space

The first step to create a dormer is to create walls which define the dormer space.

Hands-on

Step 1: Draw a rectangular space using the AB_CENTER wall style with a **6″** wall width and a **15′** wall height.

Step 2: Use an approximate size of **9′ x 9′** for the space.

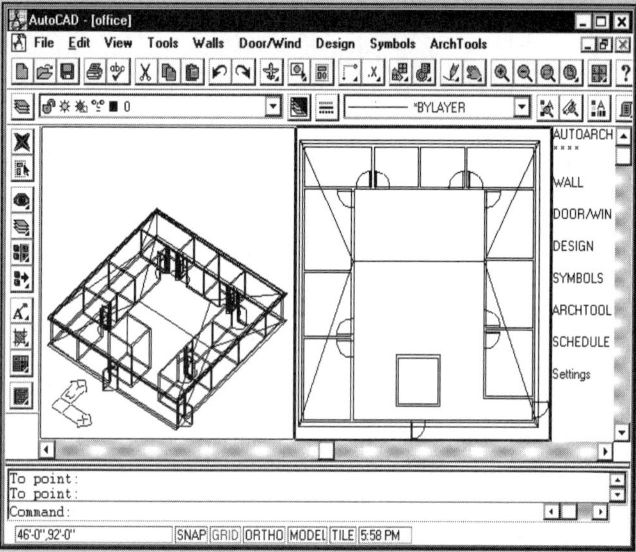

Create a Roof on the Space

Once you create a dormer space, you create a roof on that space.

- ✔ The following example shows you how to create a gable roof at the top of the dormer space with the roof generator.

Hands-on:

Step 1: Select [Design ⇨ Roofs ⇨ Roof Generator ⇨ Generate Roof] from the pull-down menu.

Step 2: Draw a polyline around the outside of the walls.

Step 3: Use the "Manual" option to place the slope tags.

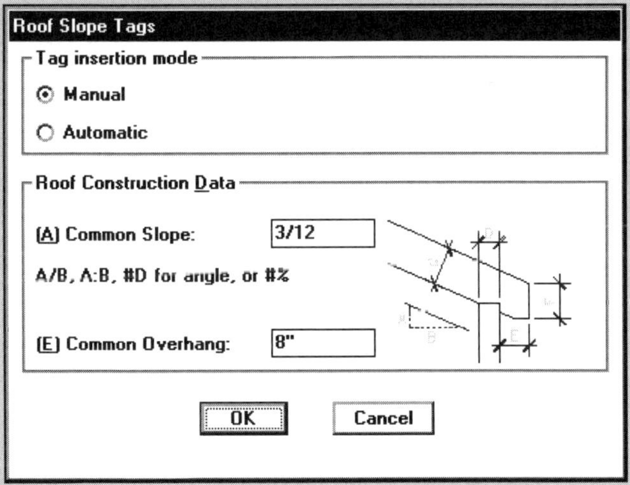

Step 4: Specify **V** for a vertical slope on the top and bottom of the space, **3/12** slope on the sides, and an **8″** overhang throughout.

Step 5: Specify 15′ for the wall height.

Step 6: Turn off the 2D roof layer "ROOF" after you create the dormer roof to avoid confusion during 3D editing.

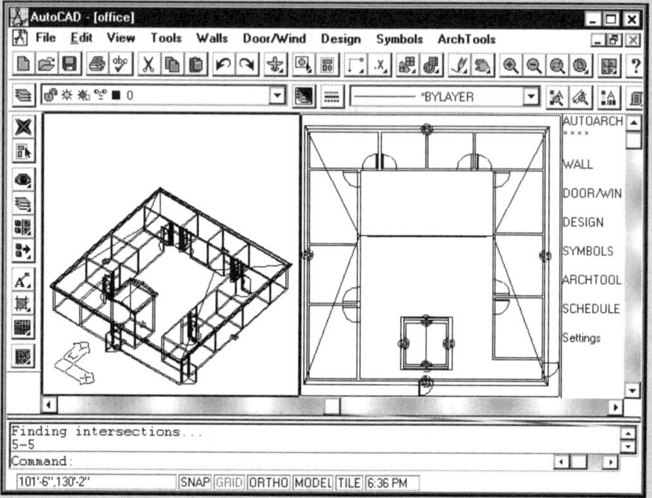

Develop the Roof Surface Intersection

The following example shows how to define the intersection between the dormer roof and the main building roof.

- ✔ The first step is to extend the roof surfaces on the dormer to the main roof surface.
- ✔ This automatically defines the location to which you have to extend the dormer walls.

Hands-on:

Step 1: Select [Design ⇨ Roofs ⇨ Roof Edit ⇨ Extend Surfaces] from the pull-down menu.

Step 2: Pick the bottom edge of the large roof surface as the stationary surface and one edge of the small gable as the surface to extend.

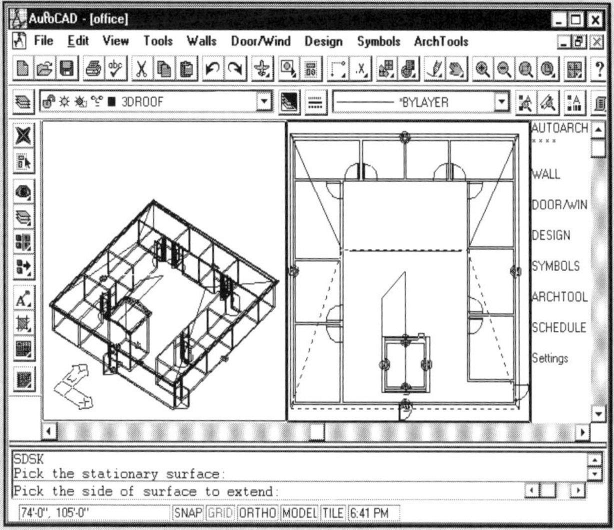

Step 3: Repeat the process for the other side of the gable.

Step 4: Erase the unnecessary soffit detail from the 3D viewport.

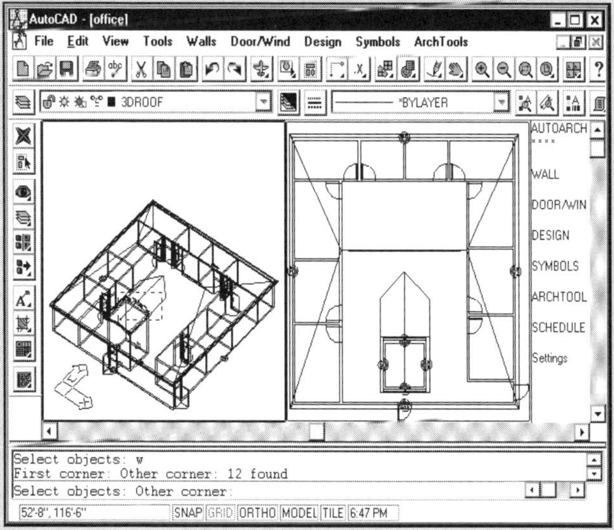

Step 5: Move back to the plan viewport, redraw the screen and stretch the walls to match the new roof position.

Step 6: Use the [ST] macro to a stretch a box as shown, and press <Enter> when prompted to remove objects.

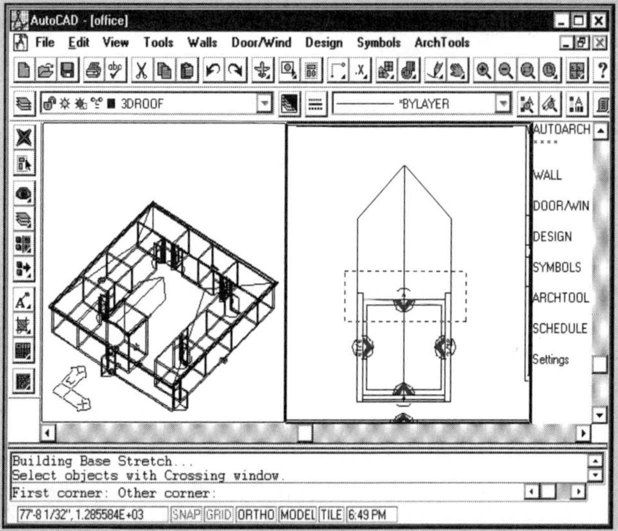

Step 7: Select the first stretch corner point on the previously generated soffit.

Step 8: Choose [Point Filters ⇨ Hold Z] from the pop-up menu for the second point.

Step 9: Pick a point at the top of the vertical line when *Auto-Architect* prompts for the XY coordinate.

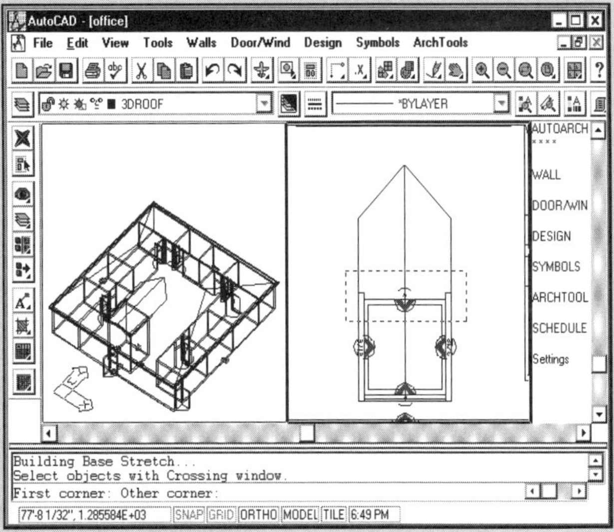

Step 10: Snap to the corner indicated in the image above using the Hold Z option again.

Use the corner that is aligned with your original basepoint.

Define Dormer Walls Above the Roof

The following example shows how to use the [Extend Walls to Roof] command to define the dormer walls above the main roof.

- ✔ The [Extend Walls to Roof] command will draw 3D wall faces from the top of the wall to the roof surface, regardless of whether the roof is above or below the top of the walls.
- ✔ This allows you to extend walls down to the roof.

Hands-on:

Step 1: Select [Walls ⇨ Wall Edit ⇨ Extend Walls to Roof] from the pull-down menu.

Step 2: Select a wall line and then type **M** for manual.

Step 3: Make a window around the dormer.

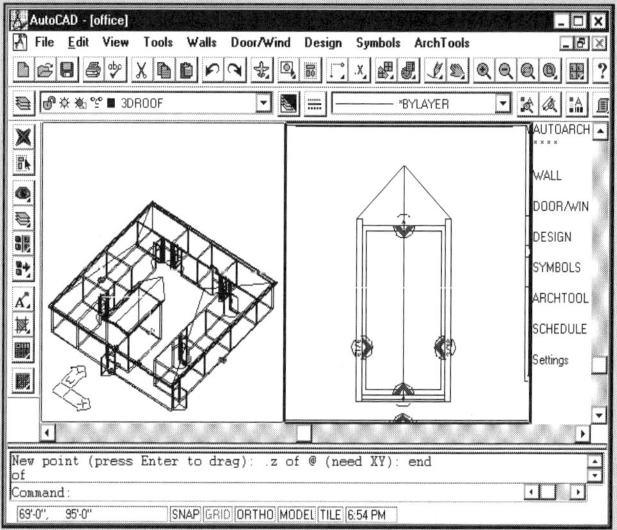

Step 4: Press <Enter> to continue.

Step 5: Select a roof face.

Step 6: Type **R** to remove the roof faces in the dormer — you want to extend only to the main roof surface.

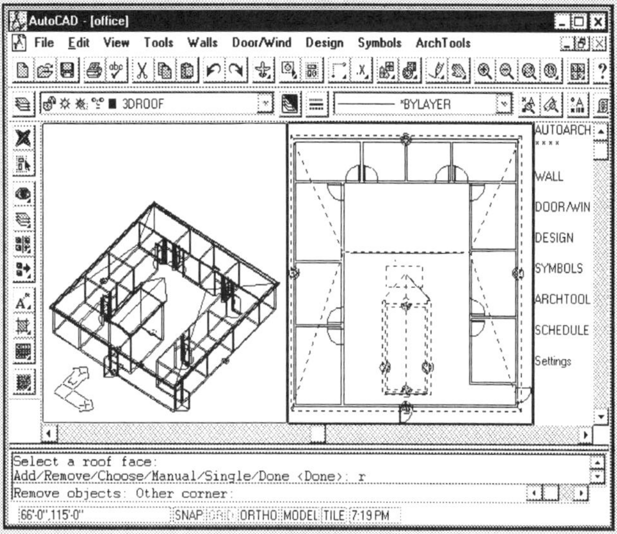

Step 7: Delete the original 15′ walls if you don't need them.

Step 8: Use crossing windows and fences to select the objects in the 3D view.

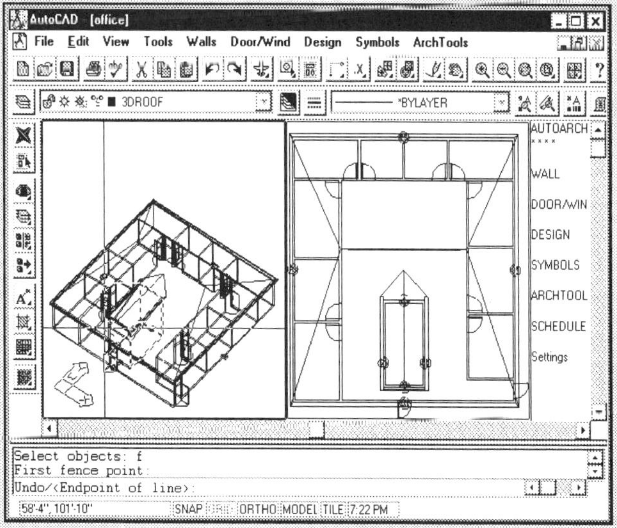

Step 9: Use the [Hide] command in each viewport to view the dormer.

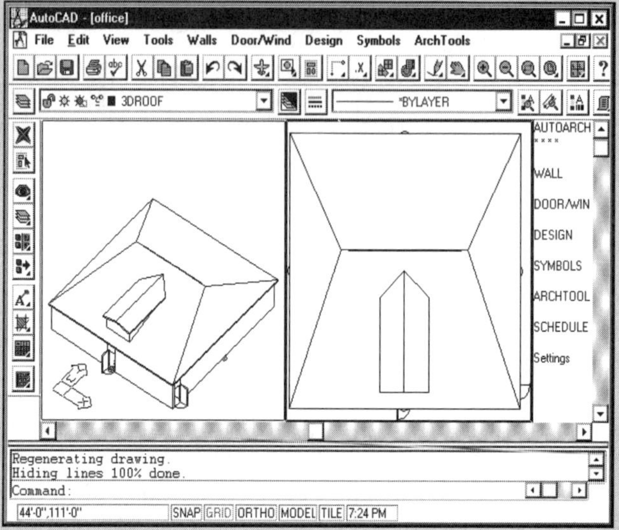

✔ You can edit the 2D roof plan manually to align it with the 3D view.

Generating Flat Roofs

You can use a negative slope with the roof generator.

✔ This allows you to define slope for drainage on a flat roof.

✔ You can also create a flat area for drains in the center of the roof.

Hands-on:

Step 1: Create a new drawing called *flatroof.dwg*.

Step 2: Start *Auto-Architect* and choose the WORKSHOP project.

Step 3: Accept the default sheet setup.

Step 4: Create a building outline as shown below using a polyline.

Step 5: Offset the polyline 22′ to the inside of the outline.

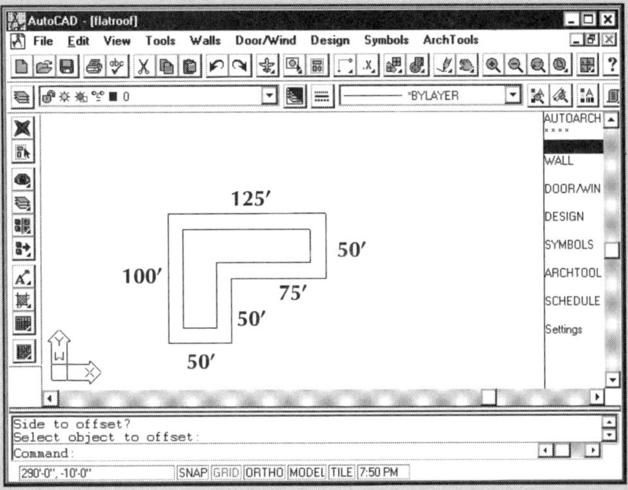

Step 6: Use the [VP] macro to create two vertical viewports.

Step 7: Set a southeast isometric view in the left viewport.

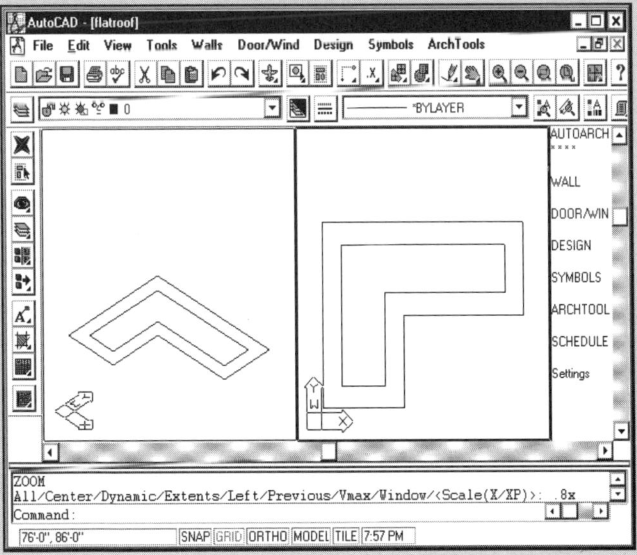

Step 8: Select [Design ⇨ Roofs ⇨ Roof Generator ⇨ Add Slope Tags] from the pull-down menu.

Step 9: Use "Automatic" insertion with a negative slope of **-0.25:12** and exit the dialog box.

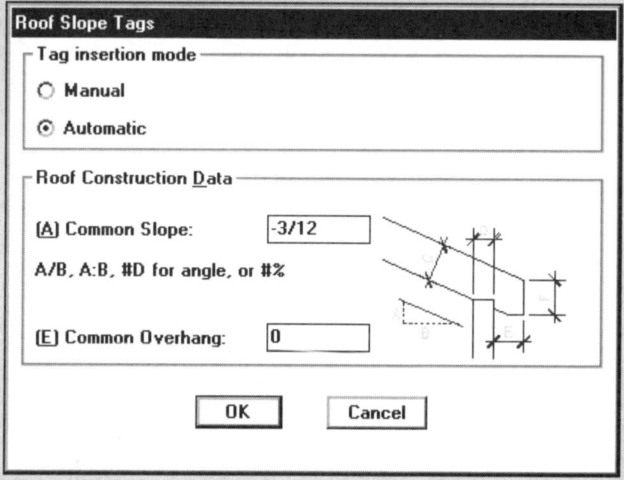

Step 10: Select [Design ⇨ Roofs ⇨ Roof Generator ⇨ Generate Roof] from the pull-down menu.

Step 11: Proceed with the steps and enter **Y** for cutting areas to project.

Step 12: Select the inner polyline.

Step 13: Set layer 3DROOF to be current and draw two faces to fill the inner area using the FA macro.

Step 14: Select [Design ⇨ Roofs ⇨ Roof Edit ⇨ Hide Faces] from the pull-down menu.

Step 15: Pick the miter as shown to hide the edges.

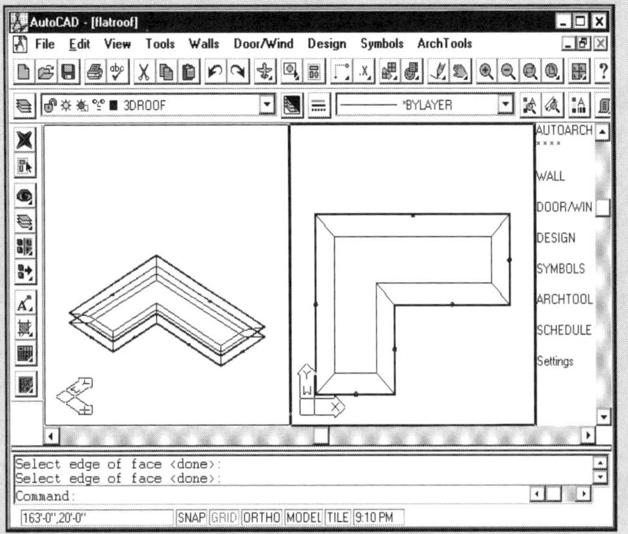

Step 16: Use the [Hide] command in the 3D viewport.

Chapter 9

Annotation and Construction Documents

Objectives

To annotate a construction document, you should be able to:

- ✔ Create a dimension style for annotating a construction document.
- ✔ Create elevations and sections from a three-dimensional model.
- ✔ Control drawing scale for sizing annotation on a drawing.

Introduction

This chapter shows you how to deal with three critical issues related to annotating a construction document. The first section shows you how to define a dimension style for architectural drawings. You will start by defining a typical AutoCAD dimension style, which you can then enhance with Softdesk dimension settings.

The next section shows you how to create elevations and sections directly from a three-dimensional model of your building. With these capabilities, you can define elevations that are associative to your design — any changes to the design automatically update the elevations and sections.

The final section in this chapter shows you how to control drawing scale as it pertains to sizing annotations on a drawing. You can use *Auto-Architect's* plan matrix system to create annotations at different scales in the same drawing that will display correctly through different viewports.

Dimension Styles

Dimensioning is one of the most important aspects of annotation.

- ✔ Architectural construction documents convey a large amount of information in a limited amount of space.
  - ✗ Dimensions are the most critical information on a drawing.
  - ✗ A dimension style must be compact and legible to allow the dimensions to be clearly visible.
- ✔ This section shows the steps to create an effective architectural dimension style.
- ✔ The following table gives a general description of each dimension style type.

Dimension Style Types

Type	Description
A	This is the default AutoCAD dimension style.
B	This dimension type shows the basic changes to create an architectural style. Annotation primary units are set to architectural. Text is above the dimension line. The dimension line is forced between the extension lines. Oblique tick marks appear instead of arrows.
C	This style is the same as dimension type B except that annotation primary units are set to architectural to display AutoCAD stacked fractions. The default size of the fraction is too large, but you can change this.
D	This style modifies dimension type B using text style DIMTEXT instead of STANDARD. It also uses a bold dimension slash (a "user arrow" block) instead of the single oblique line tick marks.
E	This style is the same as dimension type D except annotation primary units are set to architectural and the fraction size is smaller.
F	This style is similar to AutoCAD dimension type E. The difference in the fraction results from turning on the Use Special Fractions option in Softdesk Dimension Settings (with Fraction Format set to Slash) and converting the fraction.

Using Custom Dimension Styles

Types E and F are easier to read than the others.

- ✔ There are some advantages and disadvantages to each.
  - ✗ Type F is the most "architectural" looking but requires you to use a conversion command before you use AutoCAD dimension commands.
  - ✗ This conversion happens automatically when you use any Softdesk dimensioning commands.

- ✗ You can convert all dimensions at once by selecting [Tools ⇨ Dimensions ⇨ Update Dim Text] from the pull-down menu.
- ✗ Prior to the conversion, type F looks the same as type E because it is the same AutoCAD dimension style.
- ✗ Type E is not as "architectural" looking," but you do not need any conversion and it is more compact than type F.
- ✗ Style F requires that a special font in Softdesk Core be used and included with the drawing when the drawing is sent to an office that does not have Softdesk Core.

Choose a Text Style for Dimensions

The following exercise shows how to create types E and F.

- ✔ The first step is to access the drawing where you want to define the dimension style and choose a text style for the dimensions.
  - ✗ In actual practice, you should define dimensions styles in the *sdsk_i* prototype drawing.
  - ✗ For this exercise, use a temporary drawing so the results will NOT become permanent.

Hands-on:

Step 1:	Create a new drawing called *temp.dwg* — make sure you use *sdsk_i.dwg* as the prototype.
Step 2:	Start *Auto-Architect* and set the drawing scale to 1/8″.
Step 3:	Set your units precision to a minimum of 3/32 using the DDUNITS command.
Step 4:	Start the [Style] command.

Step 5: Verify that DIMTEXT is the style name and press <Enter>.

Step 6: Pick the "Type it" button in the Select Font File dialog box.

Step 7: Enter "dim,special" for the font name.

Note:

The Softdesk dim.shx *font is the same as the AutoCAD* romans.shx *font except that the hyphen is shorter and the feet and inches marks are closer to the numerals. These differences make the text more compact. Include ",special" with the style name to use the Softdesk fraction conversion. You do not need the fraction conversion if you use AutoCAD stacked fractions.*

Step 7: Leave height at **0** and specify a width of **0.75**.

Step 8: Press <Enter> to accept the remaining defaults.

```
STYLE Text style name (or ?) <DIMTEXT>:
Existing style.
Font file <dim.shx >: DIM,SPECIAL
 Height <0'-0">:
 Width factor <1.00>:  .75
Obliquing angle <0.00>:
Backwards? <N>
Upside-down? <N>
Vertical? <N>
DIMTEXT is now the current text style.
```

Choose an Architectural Dimension Tick Block

The following exercise shows how to choose a "User Arrow" for your dimension style.

✔ The block you use must be present in the current drawing before AutoCAD will accept your choice.

✗ Insert your "User Arrow" block in your prototype drawing to make it available in all new drawings that you create.

Hands-on:

Step 1: Select [Tools ⇨ Symbol Manager...] from the pull-down menu.

Step 2: Set to the Annotation Symbols symbol set.

Step 3: Choose the "Dim Pointer" palette.

Step 4: Highlight "Tick 2" and choose the "OK" button.

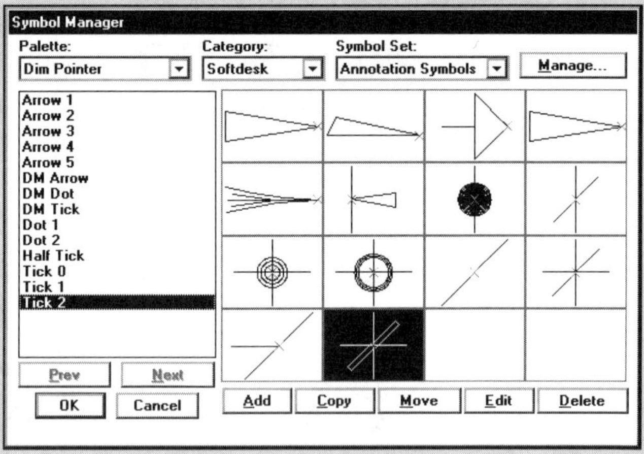

Step 5: Cancel the command at the "Insertion point:" prompt.

Step 6: Start the [Insert] command and enter "?" to list all defined blocks — notice *dimtick* block.

Define a Style with AutoCAD Settings

The following steps show how to change the dimension style to use the custom arrow and adjust dimension text.

- ✔ The dim pointers in the symbol manager are designed specifically to enhance AutoCAD dimensions.
- ✔ The result of these steps is a dimension style to match example E.

Hands-on:

Step 1: Select [Tools ⇨ Dimensions ⇨ Dim Style ⇨ Dimension Family...] from the pull-down menu.

Step 2: Verify that style "STANDARD" is the current style and then pick the "Geometry..." button in the Dimension Styles dialog box.

Step 3: Set the first arrowhead to "User Arrow..." in the Dimension Styles dialog box.

Step 4: Enter DIMTICK for the arrow name and choose the "OK" button in the User Arrow dialog box. Change the arrowhead size to **3/32"**.

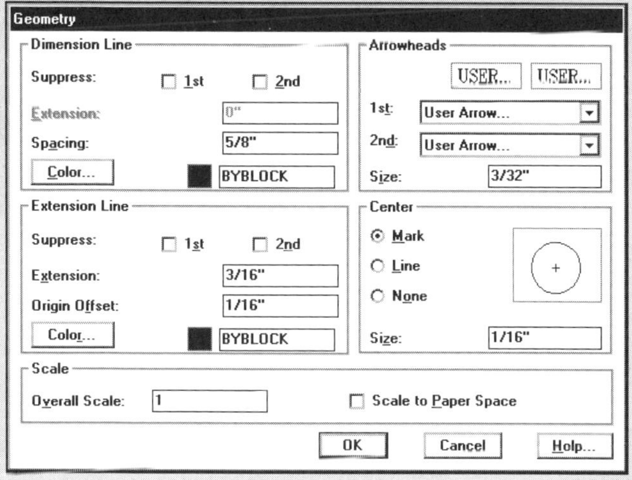

Step 5: Choose the "OK" button to continue.

Step 6: Pick the "Format..." button in the Dimension Styles dialog box.

Step 7: Set all values as shown below and choose the "OK" button.

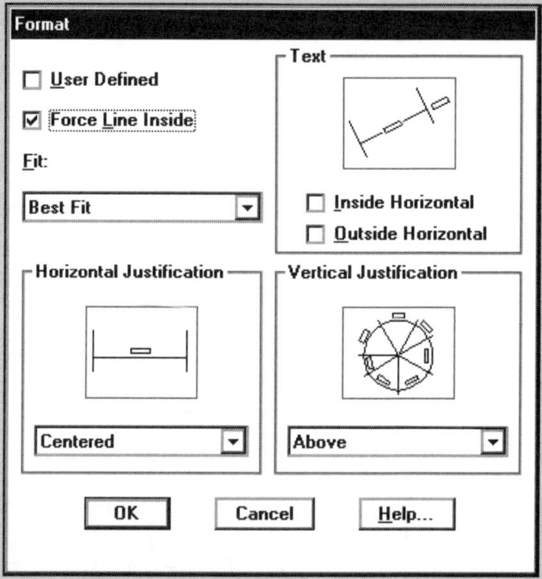

Step 8: Pick the "Annotation..." button in the Dimension Styles dialog box.

Step 9: Pick the "Units..." button in the Primary Units section of the Annotation dialog box.

Step 10: Select "Architectural (stacked)" in the Units pop-up list and choose the "OK" button.

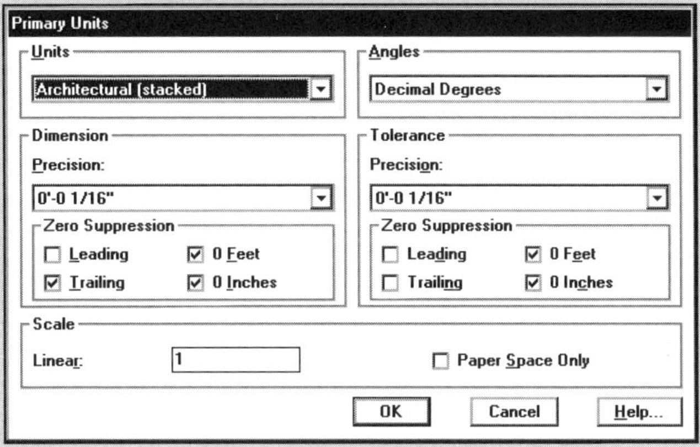

Step 11: Set "Style:" to **DIMTEXT**, "Height:" at **3/32"**, "Gap:" at **1/16"**, and "Round Off:" to **1/16"** in the Text section of the Annotation dialog box.

Step 12: Set a color to yellow.

Step 13: Temporarily set Method from none to any method except None or Basic in the Tolerance section of the dialog box.

Note:

The Tolerance Height is used by AutoCAD to size the fraction text. Although we don't want tolerances, we must enable tolerances in order to enter a tolerance Height

Note:

The size of the numerals in a fraction should be between 2/3 and 7/8 of the normal text size. The Softdesk fraction conversion shrinks them to 7/8 of whatever value you specify here.

Step 14: Enter 7/8″ for Height to obtain about 3/4 normal size.

Step 15: Set Method back to “None”.

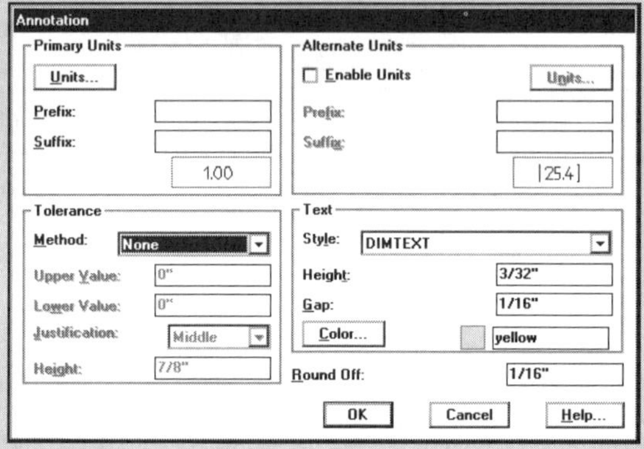

Step 16: Choose the “OK” button to continue.

Step 17: Pick the “Save” button and then choose the “OK” button to exit.

Step 18: Press <Enter> to show example dimensions.

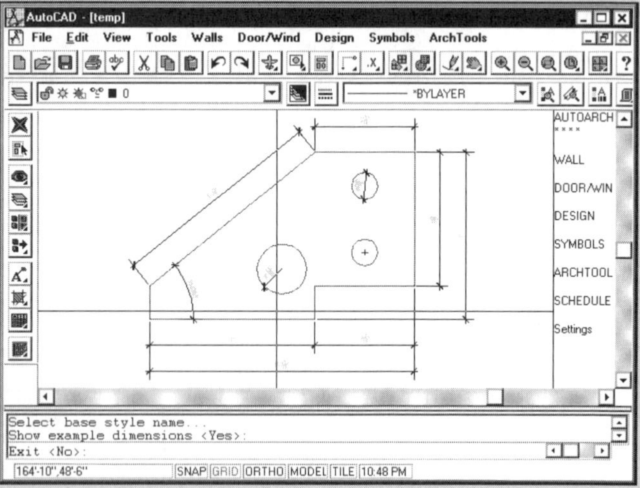

Step 19: Enter **Y** to exit from the command.

Note:

If you are not satisfied with the results, you can press <Enter> at the exit prompt to return to the Dimension Styles dialog box for further changes.

Step 20:	Choose the "OK" button to confirm the style name.
Step 21:	Press <Enter> to update the style.

Define a Style with Softdesk Settings

At this point, you have set up a style to match example E using AutoCAD stacked fractions.

- ✔ To achieve the "Architectural" looking style in example F, you need to change some Softdesk settings.

Hands-on:

Step 1:	Select [File ⇨ Project Settings…] from the pull-down menu.
Step 2:	Pick the "Dimensions…" button.
Step 3:	Turn on the "Use Special Fractions" toggle and exit the command.

Note:

The next four steps may not be necessary. The converted fractions use the special.shx *font which is a copy of either* spec_bar.shx *or* spec_sl.shx. *The system does not know which version it is, so it always assumes that it is currently the bar version, which is the default as shipped. If you know it has been changed to the slash version, you can skip the next four steps. If you are not sure, proceed with these steps.*

Step 4:	Select [Tools ⇨ Text ⇨ Set Fraction Format] from the pull-down menu.
Step 5:	Enter **S** to choose the slash text fraction format.
Step 6:	Save the changes to the *temp.dwg* file and exit AutoCAD.
Step 7:	Restart AutoCAD and open the *temp.dwg* file.

Test Dimension Style

If you change the font and style in the *sdsk_i* prototype drawing, all new drawings will be ready to dimension.

- ✔ You do not need to make any other changes to styles or fonts.
    - ✗ If you use the [Place Wall Dimensions] command, it creates the special dimension style from the current dimension style.
    - ✗ You do not need to make any changes for this method of dimensioning in new drawings.
- ✔ You can use this same procedure in existing drawings to get the same results.
    - ✗ In existing drawings, however, you will need to repeat the above procedures on both the STANDARD dimension style and on the AAWALLDIM style.

Hands-on:

Step 1:	Use the [Zoom Center] command to display a height of **20'**.
Step 2:	Select [Tools ⇨ Dimensions ⇨ Horizontal] from the pull-down menu.
Step 3:	Turn Snap off and create a few horizontal dimensions with fractions — each fraction converts automatically.

Update Dimension Text

Always start a dimensioning command from the menu or with a dimension macro, rather than typing a command.

- ✔ The menu and dimension macros set the correct layer and dimension style family.
  - ✗ Fraction conversion happens immediately as you create each dimension.
- ✔ If you type dimension commands, you must convert the fractions manually.
  - ✗ Using the dimension macros is the easiest way.

Hands-on:

Step 1:	Copy some of the dimension that you just created — the fractions appear stacked and have not converted.
Step 2:	Select [Tools ⇨ Dimensions ⇨ Update Dim Text] from the pull-down menu.
Step 3:	Press <Enter> to convert them all.
Step 4:	Select [Tools ⇨ Edit ⇨ Stretch ⇨ Stretch] from the pull-down menu and stretch one of the dimensions — the fraction is stacked.
Step 5:	Stretch the same dimension again with the [ST] macro — the fraction converts automatically.
	Use the ST macro to have dimensions update to the "Architectural" style fraction format automatically.

Elevations and Sections

This section shows how to create "live" elevations and sections — views of the current 3D model rather than an extraction taken from it.

✔ The process uses paper space viewports and externally referenced drawings for working in sections.

Hands-on:

Step 1:	Open the drawing *\sdskproj\workshop\dwg\intl.dwg*.
Step 2:	Use the [Zoom Extents] command in paper space.
Step 3:	Move the right viewport to align it across the top with the left viewport.
Step 4:	Stretch the bottom of the right viewport to align it with the bottom of the left viewport.
Step 5:	Align the titles with each other.
Step 6:	Find out what layer the existing viewports were created on and set that layer to be current.
Step 7:	Use the [Mview] command to create a viewport of similar size at the lower-right.
Step 8:	Copy one of the other titles to this viewport.

Step 9: Use the [ET] macro to change the new title to FRONT ELEVATION.

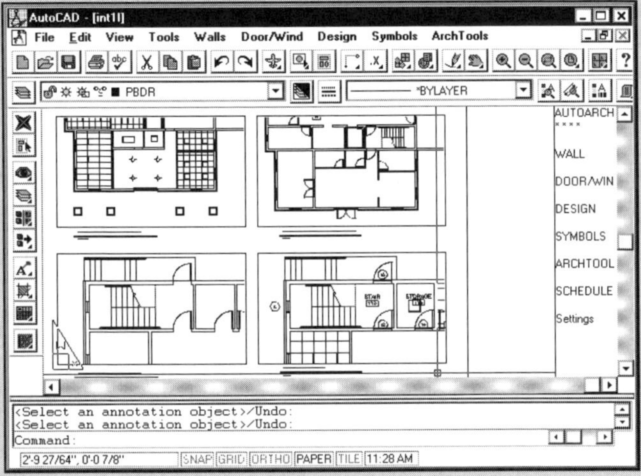

Setting Up Viewports

Hands-on:

Step 1: Open the drawing titled *model2.dwg*.

Step 2: Change to the plan view.

Step 3: Select the [Setup Drawing] command from the File pull-down menu.

Step 4: Select a predefined border by selecting the Border button and selecting "36x48".

Step 5: Turn on "Insert Border in Paper Space."

Step 6: Select the "OK" button twice for title block entry.

Step 7: Answer "Yes" to the Create Viewport prompt.

Step 8: Use option 2 for Plan, elevations, and isometric.

Step 9:	Pick two points inside the border, then accept the defaults for viewport spacing, layer, and color.
Step 10:	Pan inside each viewport to get the view of the building centered in the viewport.
Step 11:	Select [View ⇨ Viewports ⇨ Scale] from the pull-down menu.
Step 12:	Pick a point inside the viewport you want to scale.
Step 13:	Highlight **1/4" = 1'-0"** from the list of scales and pick the "OK" button.
Step 14:	Set the bottom two viewports and the top left one to 1/4".
Step 15:	Pan the top left and bottom left viewports to view the building entrance in the lower-left corner.
Step 16:	Use the Hide command on all viewports.

Attach XREFs for Generating the Elevation

Because this drawing file does not contain the complete 3D model, you must externally reference the MODEL2 drawing.

- ✔ You must make sure that the XREF layer is set for placing a new external reference.
    - ✗ There is already an external reference on layer XREF that is currently frozen in this drawing.
    - ✗ If you thaw the layer, the other external reference will appear.
    - ✗ If you attach the external reference on a frozen layer, you will not be able to see it.
    - ✗ To solve this, thaw the XREF layer and freeze all layers that belong to the external reference that is attached to the drawing.
    - ✗ Do this before you attach the new external reference.

- ✔ The main reason for using a special XREF layer is so you can lock the external references.
  - ✗ This prevents you from inadvertently erasing or moving external references.

Hands-on:

Step 1: Start the [Layer] command and enter the following sequence:

```
Command: LA
Macro: Layer
?/Make/..../Thaw/LOck/Unlock:  T
Layer name(s) to Thaw:  XREF
?/Make/..../Thaw/LOck/Unlock:  S
New current layer <0>:  XREF
?/Make/..../Thaw/LOck/Unlock:  LO
Layer name(s) to Lock:  XREF
?/Make/..../Thaw/LOck/Unlock:  ?
Layer name(s) to list <*>:  *|*
Layer name       State   Color       Linetype
---------------- ------ ----------- ------------
COLGRID|DIMLINE  On      1 (red)     CONTINUOUS
Xdep: COLGRID
COLGRID|GRIDBUB  On      2 (yellow)  CONTINUOUS
Xdep: COLGRID
COLGRID|GRIDLINE On      2 (yellow)  COLGRID|CENTER
Xdep: COLGRID
Current layer: XREF
?/Make/..../Thaw/LOck/Unlock:  F
Layer name(s) to Freeze:  COLGRID|*
?/Make/.../Thaw/LOck/Unlock:          press <Enter>
Regenerating drawing.
```

Step 2: Use the [MS] macro to switch to model space.

Step 3: Pick inside the lower-right viewport to make it current.

Step 4:	Use the [XREF] command to attach *model2.dwg* into your drawing.
Step 5:	Enter 0,0 for the insertion point and press <Enter> to accept the defaults in the remaining prompts.

Adjust Viewport Layers

The model drawing now appears in all four viewports.

✔ Use the [Vplayer] command to control in which viewport you want the model to appear.

Hands-on:

Step 1:	Start the [Vplayer] command and follow the example:

```
Command: LVP
Macro: Viewport Layer Controls
?/Freeze/Thaw/Reset/Newfrz/Vpvisdflt: F
Layer(s) to Freeze: model2|*
All/Select/<Current>: S
Switching to Paper space.
Select objects:            pick first window corner
Other corner: 2 found      select left two viewports
Select objects:            press <Enter>
Switching to Model space.
?/Freeze/Thaw/Reset/Newfrz/Vpvisdflt: F
Layer(s) to Freeze: ~MODEL2|*
All/Select/<Current>: S
Switching to Paper space.
Select objects:            pick first window corner
Other corner: 2 found      select two right viewports
Select objects:            press <Enter>
Switching to Model space.
?/Freeze/Thaw/Reset/Newfrz/Vpvisdflt: T
```

```
Layer(s) to Thaw: 0,XREF          these were frozen also
                                  and must be re-thawed
All/Select/<Current>: S
Switching to Paper space.
Select objects: P 2 found         same two viewports on right
Select objects:                   press <Enter>
Switching to Model space.
?/Freeze/Thaw/Reset/Newfrz/Vpvisdflt: press <Enter>
Regenerating drawing.
```

- ✔ The two viewports on the left should now look just as they did before attaching the model drawing.
- ✔ The two viewports on the right show only the model.

Completed Viewport Layout

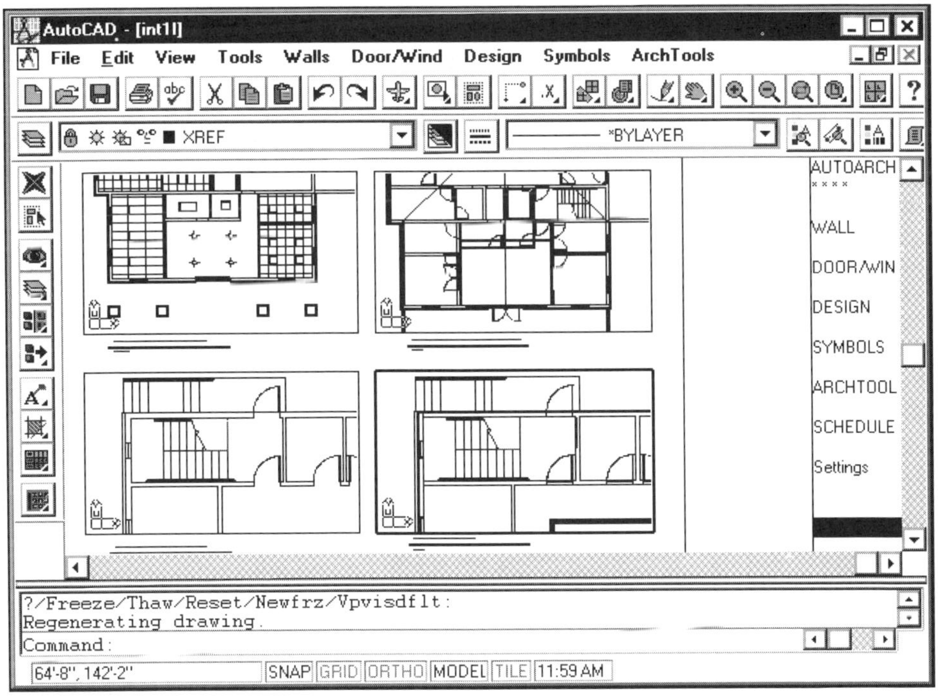

Set Up Views

We can now set up our views, starting with the front elevation (lower-right viewport).

Hands-on:

Step 1:	Select [View ⇨ View ⇨ View Presets...] from the pull-down menu.
Step 2:	Highlight "Front" and choose the "OK" button.
Step 3:	Select [View ⇨ Viewports ⇨ Scale] from the pull-down menu.
Step 4:	Pick a point inside the viewport where you want to set the scale.
Step 5:	Highlight "1/8″ = 1′-0″" from the list of scales and choose the "OK" button.
Step 6:	Use the [Pan] command with ortho toggled off to raise the image into view.
Step 7:	Position the right end of the building just inside the viewport.
Step 8:	Use the [PS] macro to switch to paper space.
Step 9:	Stretch the right edge of the lower-left viewport and the left edge of the lower-right viewport to show the entire elevation.
Step 10:	Use the [MS] macro to switch back to model space.

Step 11: Use the [Hide] command to display the elevation.

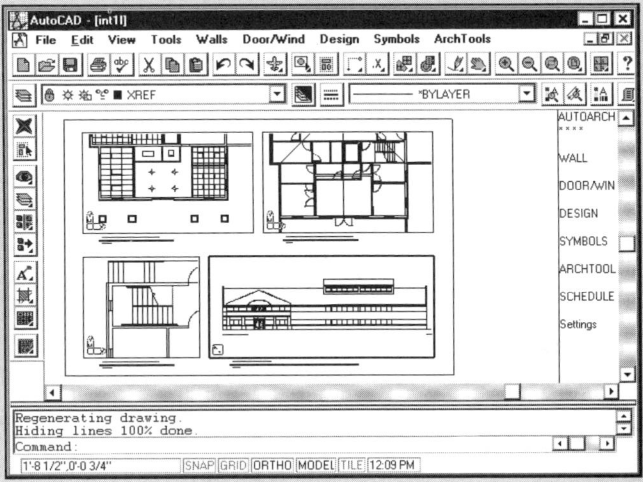

Set Elevation Display for Plotting

The elevation in the last example is of much better quality than an extracted 2D elevation.

- ✔ Notice that the columns in front of the reception area are present.
  - ✗ The [Extract 2D Elevation] command ignores them because they are a block the program does not recognize as an element of the building.
- ✔ Notice also that a portion of the door is showing at the second floor balcony.
  - ✗ This is not possible with the [Extract 2D Elevation] command.
- ✔ The [Hide] command is limited to viewing your elevations on-screen.
  - ✗ To make the view hide when you plot the drawing, you must set the viewports to hide during the [Plot] command.

- ✗ You could plot to a DXB file, and import the elevation in 2D just as it appears within this viewport (including hidden lines).

Hands-on:

Step 1:	Use the [MV] macro to start the [Mview] command.
Step 2:	Enter **H** to use the Hideplot option.
Step 3:	Enter **ON** to turn the Hideplot option on.
Step 4:	Select the top left, bottom left and right viewports on the right and press <Enter>.

The viewports that you select will now plot as a hidden view.

- ✔ Do not specify a "hidden" plot when plotting the drawing — the drawing will hide automatically.
  - ✗ Unlike other methods of producing an elevation, this one needs no further attention.
  - ✗ Any future changes to the model appear automatically whenever you reopen the drawing or reload the external reference.

Create a Sectional View

- ✔ You can now set up a "live" sectional elevation of the reception area in the top left viewport.
  - ✗ In this process, you will create a tag on the current layer.
  - ✗ You do not want to plot this tag, so you should make the NOPLOT layer current.

Hands-on:

Step 1: Pick inside the upper-right viewport to make it current.

Step 2: Use the [LS] macro to set the layer NOPLOT to be current.

Step 3: Enter the name NOPLOT and choose the "OK" button to create the layer if it does not exist.

Step 4: Select [View ⇨ Section ⇨ Define Section] from the pull-down menu.

Step 5: Enter **2′** for the section width.

Step 6: Pick a point in front of the wall and to the left of the reception area to locate the first point of the section cut line.

Step 7: Pick the second point of section line to the right of the reception area with ortho toggled on. The section cut line should pass through the entrance door symbol.

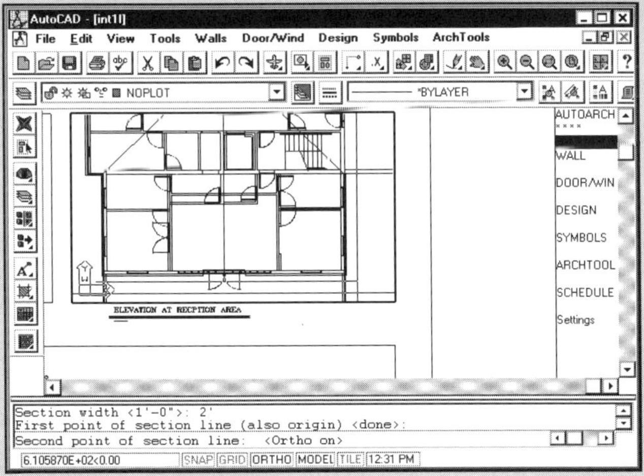

Step 8: Pick a point anywhere below the section line to choose the viewing side — the drawing flashes the section view then returns to the plan view.

Step 9: Press <Enter> to complete the command — a small tag appears at the origin of the section line.

Step 10: Select [View ⇨ Section ⇨ Go to Section] from the pull-down menu.

Step 11: Select the new tag as the section view tag block — the elevation view appears.

Step 12: Use the [Hide] command to see the finished results — the columns and balcony do not appear in front of the elevation, but the balcony appears in section.

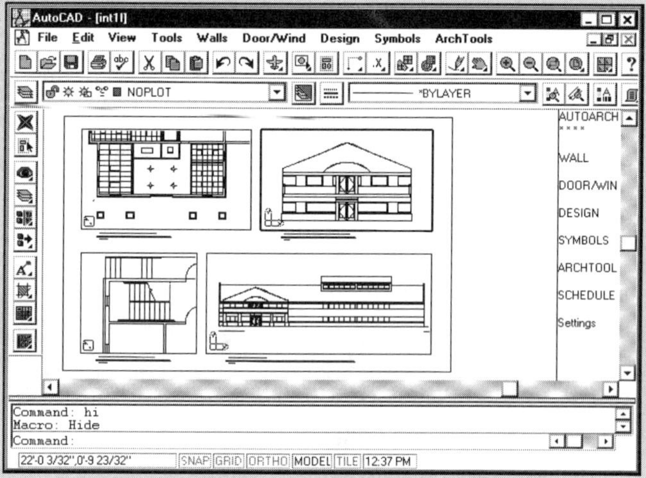

Step 13: Switch to paper space and use the [LI] macro and pick the viewport boundary to verify that this viewport will plot with hidden lines removed.

Step 14: Switch back to model space.

Notice how the 3DDOOR SWNG LINES appear continuous.

Step 15: Set the PSLTSCALE = 1 and Ltscale = 1 and regenerate the drawing so that the dashed and hidden linetypes look consistent from one viewport to another, regardless of viewing scale.

Elevation and Section Notes

You can switch between the normal UCS and the section view UCS.

- ✔ There are two ways to return to the previous UCS.
- ✔ One way is to select [View ⇨ Section ⇨ Go to Plan] from the pull-down menu.
  - ✗ This method also restores the plan view, which you do not want in this case.
- ✔ Another way is to use the UCS command to return to the previous UCS.
  - ✗ You can return to the section UCS at any time by selecting [View ⇨ Section ⇨ Go to Section] from the pull-down menu.
- ✔ You can create as many section views as you need.
  - ✗ Each section has a unique tag.

You must set the [Visretain] system variable to keep the current layer settings for external references when you open the drawing file.

- ✔ Set [Visretain] to 1.
- ✔ If [Visretain] is set to 0, the visibility of XREF layers in the current drawing is determined by the settings in the source drawing.
  - ✗ You may want to change this setting in the *sdsk_i* prototype drawing.
- ✔ Verify that [Visretain] has been set to 1 in the current drawing.

Working with Multiple Scales

You can use standard AutoCAD viewports in paper space to scale different parts of the building.

- ✔ For example, you can set one viewport to show the entire floor plan at 1/8″ scale and another to show a core plan at 1/4″ scale.
- ✔ Change the scale of each viewport with the [Zoom] command.
  - ✗ You can create annotation at the correct scale for each viewport.
  - ✗ The following examples show how to set up a multi-scale drawing and create annotation at the correct scale for each viewport.

Hands-on:

Step 1:	Open the drawing *\sdskproj\workshop\dwg \intp.dwg.*
Step 2:	Use the [Preferences] command to display the side-screen menu if it does not appear on the screen.

Side Screen Menu Controls

Some handy controls appear in a status area on the bottom of the side-screen menu.

- ✔ The drawing scale feature is not available anywhere else:
  - ✗ -------- ← (refresh display)
  - ✗ E>0″ ← Elevation
  - ✗ T>0″ ← Thickness
  - ✗ S>1/8″ ← Drawing Scale
  - ✗ L>. ← Level
  - ✗ P>FLR ← Plan Type

- ✔ Depending on the size and resolution of your display, you may not see all (or any) of the above options.
  - ✗ If only some of these options display, pick the refresh bar to display them in the upper top area of the side-screen.
  - ✗ You can also use the [=] macro to display these options.

Create a Building Core Plan Matrix

Notice that the side-screen status area shows the drawing scale is 1/8″=1′-0″ and the plan type is set to FLR.

- ✔ Dimensions (except for the grid dimensions) are drawn on layer FLR_DIMLINE with a 1/8″ plotting size.
  - ✗ You need to annotate the reception area at 1/4″ scale.
- ✔ It is a common practice to include a "core" plan, enlarged to 1/4″ scale along with a floor plan at 1/8″ scale.
  - ✗ Although you will not actually show a building "core", you will create a new core plan type and use it for a similar purpose.

Hands-on:

Step 1: Zoom into the reception area in the lower-left part of the building.

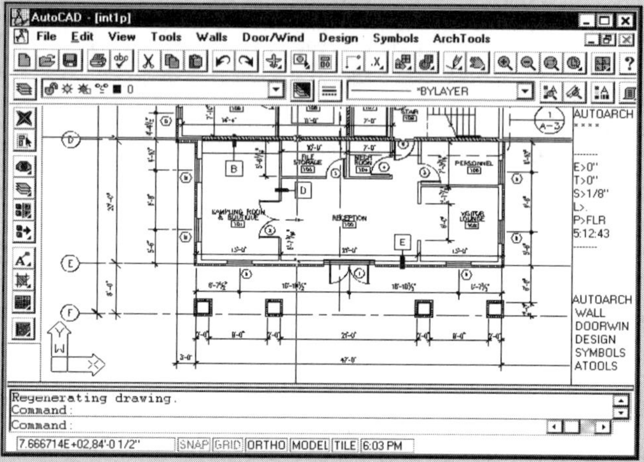

Step 2: Select "P>" from the side-screen menu.

Step 3: Highlight "?" and choose the "OK" button.

Step 4: Pick the "-->" button to make the FLR plan visible.

Step 5: Select the "Column" radio button.

Step 6: Pick any box in the FLR column to make it current.

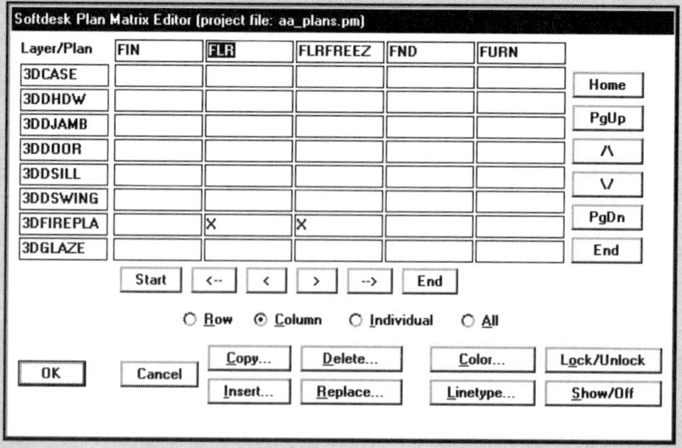

Step 7:	Pick the "Copy" button to copy the FLR Plan to XXXXXXXX..
Step 8:	Change XXXXXXXX to CORE.

Edit the Building Core Plan Matrix

The FLR (Floor) plan displays several layers you do not want to plot, but which display while working in this plan.

- ✔ Some 3D layers are on to prevent 3D components of some objects from separating with their 2D counterparts during editing.
  - ✗ You will need to take an extra step to plot the floor plan later on
- ✔ Because you edit most major objects in the floor plan, you can turn these layers off in the core plan.

Hands-on:

Step 1:	Pick the "Individual" radio button.
Step 2:	Go through the list of layer names with the "PgDn" button in the CORE column and turn each 3D layer off.
Step 3:	Pick inside the cell and then pick the "Show/Off" button.
Step 4:	Turn off the SPACE layer.
Step 5:	Choose the "OK" button — CORE should appear on the list.
Step 6:	Choose "Cancel" in the dialog box and enter **No** to the "Restore layers now?" message if CORE does not appear on the list.
Step 7:	Choose "P>" from the side-screen menu to repeat the command — CORE will appear when you repeat the command.

Step 8: Highlight CORE and choose the “OK” button.

Step 9: Press <Enter> to restore the layers now.

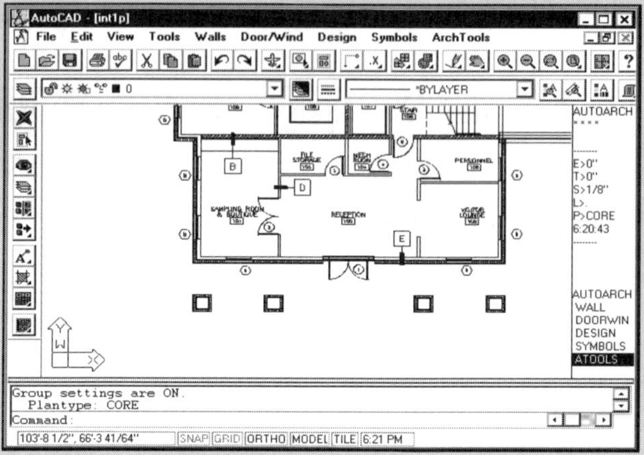

Notice that the floor plan dimensions, detail, and section annotation no longer display.

- ✔ The various tags still appear just as in the floor plan.
- ✔ This is because they are linked to real objects.
  - ✗ They are treated as objects (rather than annotation) that may appear in more than one plan type.
  - ✗ If you do not want them in this plan type, go back to the plan matrix editor and turn them off.
- ✔ The grid and its dimensions do not display because they are on the frozen XREF layer.
  - ✗ You can add this layer to the plan matrix as well.
  - ✗ You should also add the DEFPOINTS layer (which is used to create the paper space viewports) to the plan matrix.

Hands-on:

Step 1:	Return to the plan matrix editor and turn off door tags, window tags, and construction tags for the CORE Plan Type.
Step 2:	Pick the "Row" radio button.
Step 3:	Pick the "Insert" button to insert a new row.
Step 4:	Enter XREF for the layer name.
Step 5:	Pick the "Show/Off" button.
Step 6:	Choose the "OK" button to turn on all cells in the new row.
Step 7:	Turn layer XREF off in the FLRFREEZ plan type.
Step 8:	Repeat the previous steps to create the DEFPOINTS layer.
Step 9:	Choose the "OK" button to exit the plan matrix editor.
Step 10:	Choose the "OK" button to restore the updated core plan display.

Adjust Scale for Placing Annotation

If you place annotation now, it will be for the core plan and it will be at 1/8″ scale.

- ✔ To create annotation at 1/4″ scale as desired, you must temporarily reset the drawing scale.

Hands-on:

Step 1:	Select **S>** from the side-screen status area (use the "=" macro if it is not displayed.
Step 2:	Highlight **1/4″=1′-0″** and choose the "OK" button.

Step 3: Place some dimensions using either the [Place Wall Dimensions] command or the dimension macros.

Step 4: Place some text using the [TL] macro — use the default height of 1′-0″.

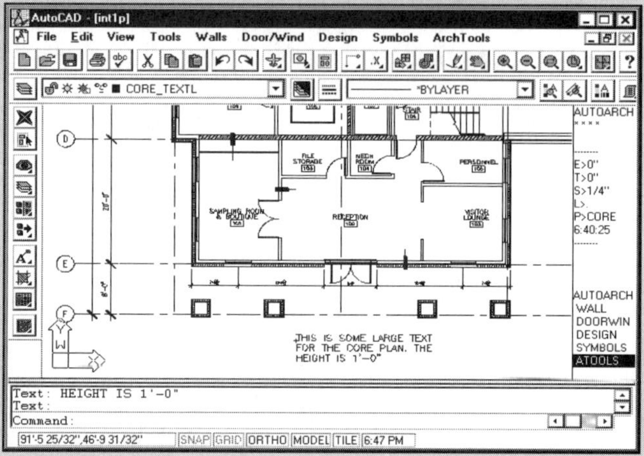

Step 5: Select **P>** on the side-screen status area and restore the FLR plan type.

Step 6: Select **S>** at the side-screen status area and restore the scale to 1/8″=1′-0″.

Step 7: Place some text using the [TL] macro using the default height of 2′-0″.

Notice the fractions in the dimensions — they now appear as AutoCAD stacked fractions instead of Softdesk architectural fractions.

- ✔ You can convert the fractions back again using [Tools ⇨ Dimensions ⇨ Update Dim Text] from the pull-down menu.
- ✔ Suppose you want to edit the floor plan.
  - ✗ The FLR display turns on layers not meant to be plotted.
  - ✗ To obtain the correct display for plotting, you need to freeze the unwanted layers.

Hands-on:

Step 1:	Select [View ⇨ Layer Groups ⇨ View Group] from the pull-down menu.
Step 2:	Enter **F** to choose the freeze option.
Step 3:	Press <Enter> at the "Trade name:" prompt.
Step 4:	Highlight FLRFREEZ and choose the "OK" button in the Plan Name dialog box.
Step 5:	Choose the "OK" button at the Level Name dialog box.
Step 6:	Press <Enter> at the "Modifier:" prompt.

The FLRFREEZ plan type is never set as the current plan type; FLR is still current.

- ✔ Return to the plan matrix editor and take a look at FLRFREEZ.
  - ✗ The layers in FLRFREEZ that seem to be on (having an "X") are actually subtracted from the current display when using the "Freeze" option of view group.
  - ✗ Compare CORE with FLRFREEZ and turn off every layer in CORE that has an "X" in FLRFREEZ.
- ✔ You can use the same FLRFREEZ technique when working with paper space viewports.
  - ✗ Do this before switching to paper space.
  - ✗ You can now go to paper space and control the display in each viewport.

Hands-on:

Step 1:	Use the [TI] macro to return to paper space.
Step 2:	Use the [Layer] command to thaw layers FLR_* — core plan annotation and floor plan annotation display in both viewports.

Note:

The [Vplayer] command can control only those layers which are thawed and turned on with the normal [Layer] command. The [Vplayer] command can then freeze any of these layers in one or more viewports, or it can thaw any layers which have been previously frozen by the [Vplayer] command. The [Vplayer] command cannot thaw layers which have been frozen (globally) by the [Layer] command.

Step 3: Start the [Vplayer] command and complete the following steps:

```
Command: LVP
Macro: Viewport Layer Controls
?/Freeze/.... /Vpvisdflt: F
Layer(s) to Freeze: CORE_*
All/Select/<Current>: S
Select objects: 1 found          Select Floor Plan viewport
Select objects:                  Press <Enter>
?/Freeze/.... /Vpvisdflt: F
Layer(s) to Freeze:
FLR_*,COLGRID|*,CONSTTAG,DOORTAG,WINDTAG
All/Select/<Current>: S
Select objects: 1 found          Select Reception Area
                                 viewport
Select objects:                  Press <Enter>
?/Freeze/.... /Vpvisdflt:        Press <Enter>
Regenerating drawing.
```

You now have a floor plan and a core plan (the Reception Area) at two different scales, complete with annotation.

- ✗ Each viewport will remember which layers should be frozen.

✗ Unfortunately, when you freeze CORE_* in the floor plan viewport, AutoCAD does not remember the wild card specification — it remembers only the layers which matched it at the time.

✗ When you introduce new annotation layers for the Core Plan, they will appear in both viewports until you use [Vplayer] to freeze CORE_* for the floor plan viewport.

Fixing Dimension Fractions

Dimensions with special fractions reconvert to standard AutoCAD fractions when you restore layers after a change of plan type.

- ✔ This happens because the layer restore program regenerates objects by erasing them and restoring them with the [OOPS] command.
- ✔ You can fix this with a little bit of simple programming.
  - ✗ As an added benefit, the process will run a little faster.
- ✔ Create or edit the file called *sdsk/acad.lsp.*
  - ✗ This file exists only if someone has already done some customization.
  - ✗ This file should have a startup function and this function must define a replacement for the Softdesk function that does the object regeneration.
  - ✗ Unless *acad.lsp* already exists, the entire contents of the file is as follows:

```
(defun s::startup ()
; the next line replaces a Softdesk function
(defun zz_regen_visible ()(command "_.regen")) )
```

✔ You can edit this file with any ASCII text editor, such as Edit (DOS) or Notepad (Windows).

✗ If there is already an *acad.lsp* file and it already has a startup function, just add the one line to it.

✗ You must toggle on the automatic initialization in Softdesk preferences for this to work.

Chapter 10

Managing Details

Objectives

After completing this chapter, you should be able to:

- ✔ Compose details.
- ✔ Annotate details.
- ✔ Add details to libraries.
- ✔ Create detail sheets.
- ✔ Annotate externally referenced details.

Introduction

Two of the most important aspects of construction documentation are details and specifications. The AIA Masterformat standard defines a clear approach for preparing construction specifications. Aside from the Con-Doc standard, there are few industry-wide standards for composing and managing details.

Firms have various methods for composing and managing their details.

This chapter shows examples of composing and managing details. The Softdesk *Details* module provides a complete set of tools to create details, generate annotation, and compose detail sheets. While you create details, you can also add them to your project libraries so that the detail becomes part of your firm's standard detail library.

As you compose the example detail in this chapter, you will see how to access a standard library of materials. Using this library to compose your details allows you to automate the annotation process. The *Details* module knows what materials the detail is composed of and automatically includes the material description in the keynote. You can also use this information to generate keynote charts.

This chapter prepares you to create and annotate a detail and add it to your detail library. Make sure you are comfortable with these skills before you continue with the following chapter on advanced *Detail* module skills.

Library of Standard Details

A standard detail library is an important part of managing your details.

- ✔ You need to organize your details so they are easy to find and retrieve.
  - ✗ How you organize your details will depend on the standards in your design firm and the type of work you perform.
- ✔ The Softdesk *Details* module contains utilities that help you organize detail libraries.
  - ✗ You can group your details to best suit your application.

  - ✗ Detail libraries are stored in their own directories on a local hard disk drive or a network drive.
  - ✗ For example, your firm may want all metal frame window details in a library such as *\dets\mtlwind*, while wood frame window details reside in *\dets \wdwind*.

- ✔ While some firms choose to include all details from all projects in their library, other firms find this cumbersome.

  - ✗ You should have an approval procedure for adding new details to the library.
  - ✗ Some details are unique to a specific project design condition and will not be used again.
  - ✗ Sometimes, it is more time consuming to red-line an existing detail and make changes than to compose a new detail.
  - ✗ The decision to add a detail to the library should come from experienced staff who can identify whether the detail will be useful in the future.

Managing Details

An important aspect of managing details is to determine the method for creating and inserting details into construction documents.

- ✔ The most common methods include:

  - ✗ Placing multiple details on detail sheets.
  - ✗ Inserting individual details into a project manual.
  - ✗ Placing details on the plan sheets they are associated with.
  - ✗ A combination of these methods.

- ✔ Annotation methods also vary between conventional annotation and keynoting (which may incorporate the Con-Doc keynote system).

  - ✗ You can use the Softdesk *Details* module with any of these methods.

✔ The following exercises demonstrate how to compose and annotate details to use conventional and Con-Doc keynoting with the same detail.

Composing a Detail

The following examples direct you to draw a CMU retaining wall with a reinforced concrete footing.

✔ The first step directs you to open an existing detail sheet and begin to define a material for the new detail.

Hands-on:

Step 1:	Open the drawing *\sdskproj\workshop\dwg \detsheet.dwg*.
Step 2:	Switch to the *Details* module if it is not already current.
Step 3:	Select [Manager ⇨ Setup New Detail] from the pull-down menu.
Step 4:	Highlight 3/4"=1'-0" in the "Scales" list box on the Drawing Scale and Units dialog box.

Note:

This is a temporary scale set for consistent creation of annotation and hatch patterns.

Step 5:	Select [Compose ⇨ Material Compose] from the pull-down menu.

Step 6: Review the selections in the "Default Material — Division" pop-up list and notice the materials are categorized using the CSI format.

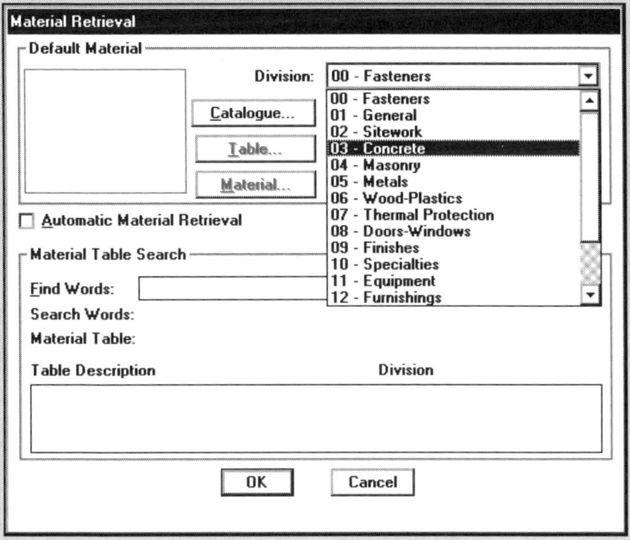

Step 7: Highlight 03 — Concrete in the "Division" pop-up list.

Note:

The "Catalog," "Table," and "Material" buttons reflect either the last material selected from this division or the first item located in the database. A slide of the current material displays in the image area.

Step 8: Enter an asterisk (*) in the "Find Words" edit box and press <Enter>.

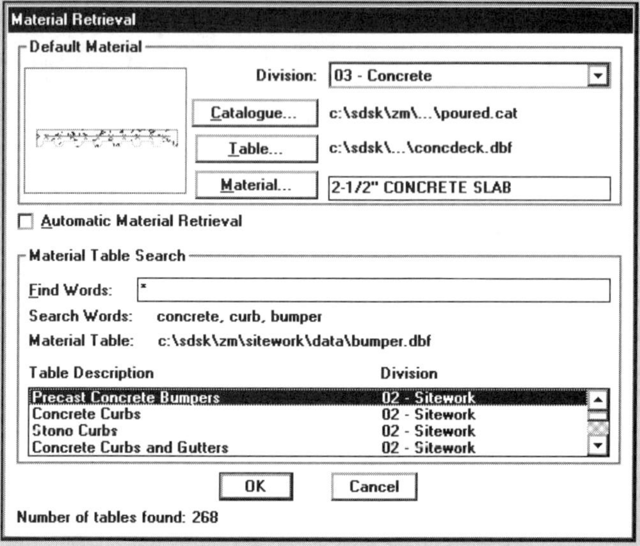

Choose a Material

You can now examine all of the material tables in the "Table Description" list box.

✔ The following example shows you how to find a material category, select a material, and example the properties of that material.

Hands-on:

Step 1: Enter MASONRY in the "Find Words" edit box and press <Enter>.

Step 2: Click twice on 2 Core CMUs to display the 2 Core CMUs dialog box.

Step 3: Scroll down the "Description" list and pick various items — notice the change in the "Size" section of the dialog box.

Step 4: Highlight the 8″ x 8″ x 16″ CMU.

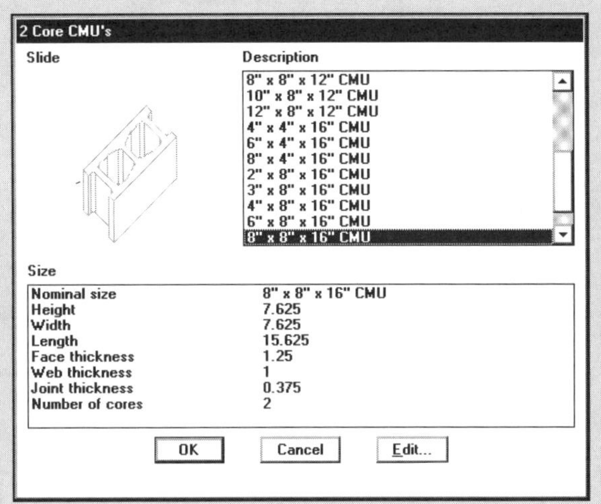

Note:

The bottom of the dialog box includes an "Edit..." button to access the Edit Table dialog box. You can edit, add, or delete materials from this dialog box.

Step 5: Choose the "Edit..." button to view the contents of this dialog box.

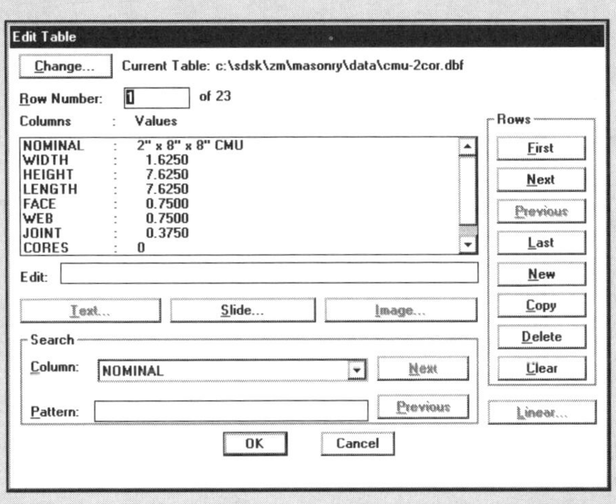

Step 6: Pick the "Cancel" button to exit this dialog box without making any changes and return to the 2 Core CMUs dialog box.

Step 7: Pick the "OK" button to return to the Material Retrieval dialog box.

Note:

Another method for selecting tables and materials from the Material Retrieval dialog box is to use the "Table..." and "Material..." buttons.

Step 8: Pick the "Table..." button to access the Material Tables dialog box and look at the selections in the "Description" list box.

Step 9: Highlight 2 Core CMUs.

Step 10: Pick the "OK" button to access the Material Tables dialog box for 2 core CMUs.

Step 11: Choose the 8″ x 8″ x 16″ CMU.

Step 12: Pick the "OK" button to return to the Material Retrieval dialog box.

Note:

You can also use the "Material..." button to access the material-specific dialog box or enter the material description into the edit box for retrieval.

Step 13: Verify that 8″ x 8″ x 16″ CMU is the highlighted material and pick the "OK" button.

Define Block Specifications

The following example shows you how to complete the steps to specify the material and begin to define the detail.

- ✔ The "View" section of the Block Specifications dialog box provides the means to view the CMU in section, top, or elevation views.
  - ✗ The "End Conditions" section of the dialog box provides display options for each end of the CMU.

Hands-on:

Step 1: Toggle the "Section" radio button on.

Step 2: Verify that the "Regular" radio buttons are toggled on for the left and right end conditions, then toggle the "Hatch block" check box on.

Step 3: Verify that the "Left" and "Right" pop-up lists both display "Rodded" in the "Mortar Joints" section.

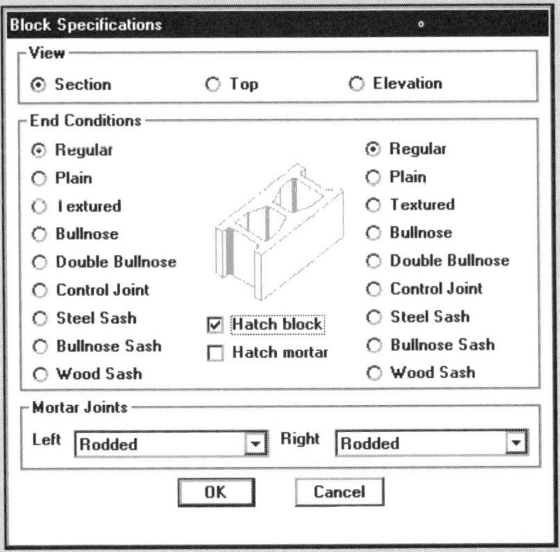

Step 4: Pick the "OK" button to continue and pick a point in an open area of the drawing sheet to define the insertion point for the material.

Step 5: Choose the "Select" option to access the Mortar dialog box.

Step 6: Highlight MORTAR in the "Description" list box.

Step 7: Pick the "OK" button to resume drawing the masonry wall section.

Note:

If this is the first time using this command, additional dialog boxes will appear. Choose "Mortar" in each of these.

Step 8: Press <Enter> for the new base point prompt to accept the current location for the wall.

Step 9: Press <Enter> to accept the default to draw courses.

Step 10: Enter **9** for the number of courses.

Step 11: Zoom in to examine the masonry unit wall section.

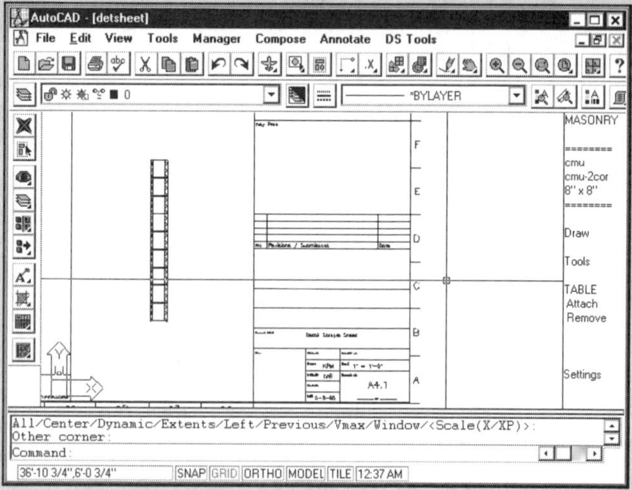

Add a Footing

The following example shows you how to add a footing to the retaining wall detail.

✔ This example shows the complete sequence to define materials and settings to create part of a detail.

Hands-on:

Step 1: Select [Compose ⇨ Materials Compose] from the pull-down menu.

Step 2: Highlight 03 — Concrete in the "Division" pop-up list.

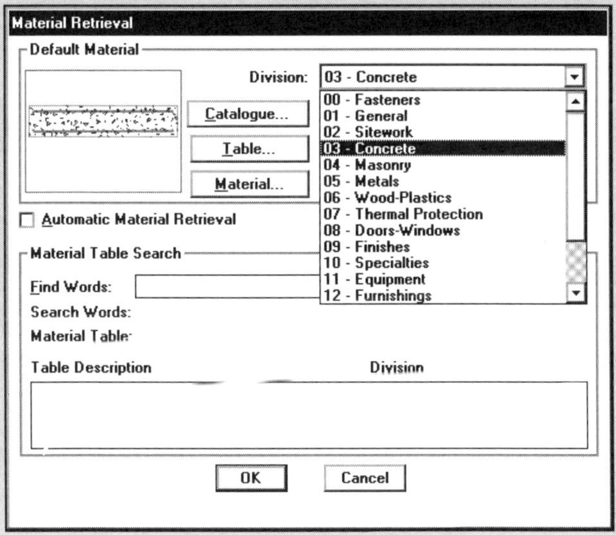

Step 3: Select the "Catalog..." button, select Cast-in-Place and choose "OK".

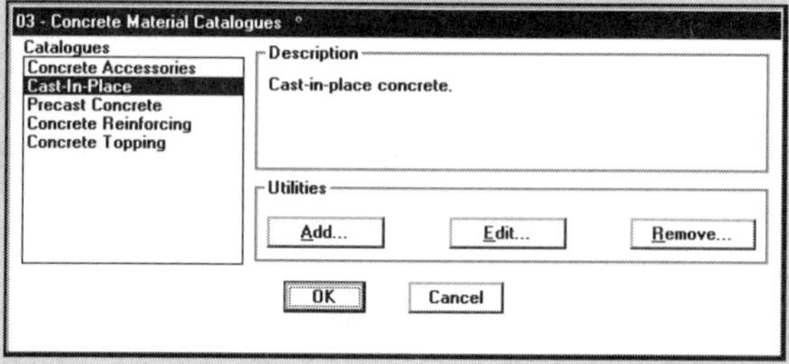

Step 4: Choose Strip Footings and choose "OK".

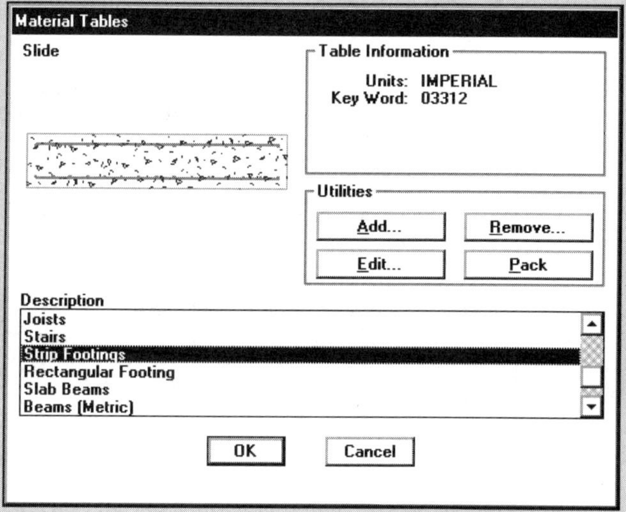

Step 5: Choose 18″ x 12″ Concrete Footing and choose "OK".

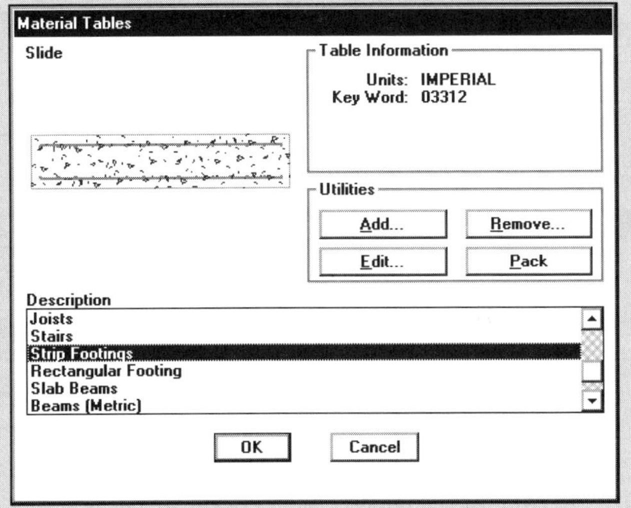

Step 6: Pick the "OK" button to return to the drawing and place the footing.

Step 7: Accept the defaults for section view, hatching, and reinforcing.

Step 8: Choose "Rebar" for the reinforcing type and make sure the edge distances are set to **2″**.

Step 9: Choose the "Catalogue" option at the lateral bar size prompt.

Step 10: Choose Concrete Reinforcing in the "Catalogues" list box and choose "OK".

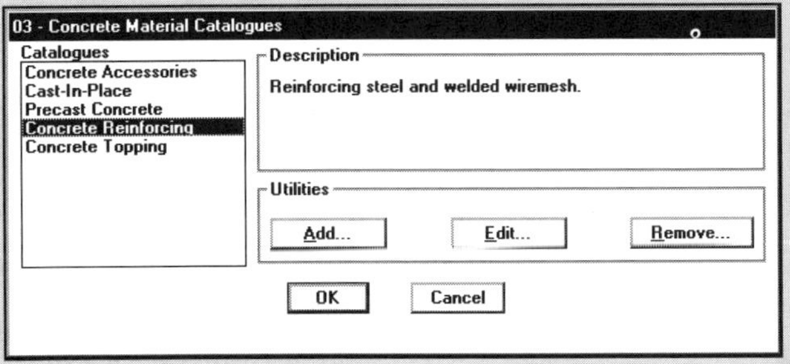

Step 11: Choose ACI Reinforcing Bar in the "Description" list box and choose "OK".

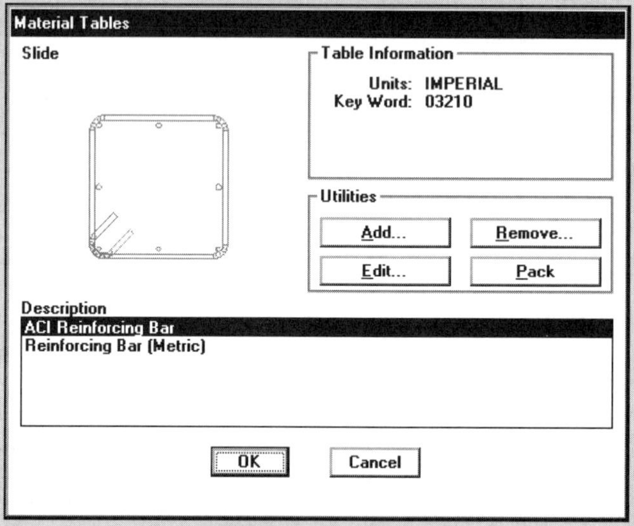

Step 12: Choose #4 REBAR in the "Designation" list box and choose "OK".

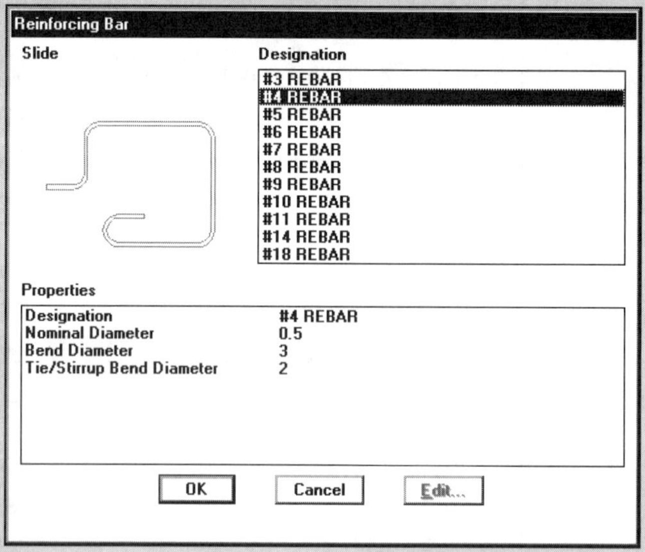

Step 13: Repeat these same steps when prompted for the longitudinal reinforcing bar size.

Step 14: Divide the longitudinal bar spacing by **3** bars and enter **Yes** for placement of the lateral bars on outside.

Step 15: Enter **S** for "Skip" at the "Edge 2 clear distance:" prompt.

Step 16: Pick the bottom endpoint of the lowest left-hand mortar joint to position the footing as shown in the following figure.

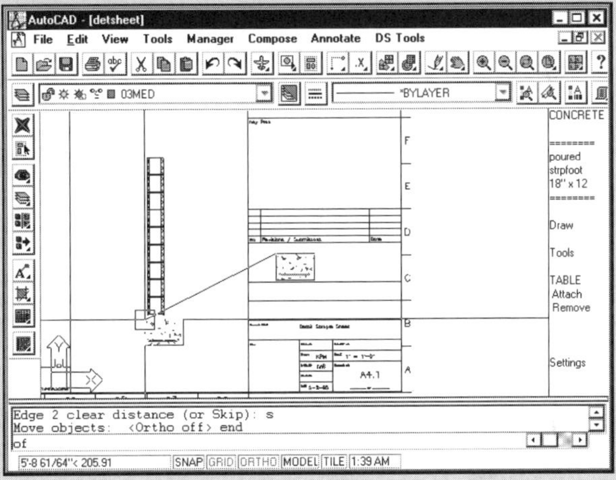

Step 17: Press <Enter> to complete the command.

Step 18: Use the AutoCAD [Pline] command to draw an L-shaped polyline with a thickness of 1/2″ to represent additional rebar as shown in the following figure.

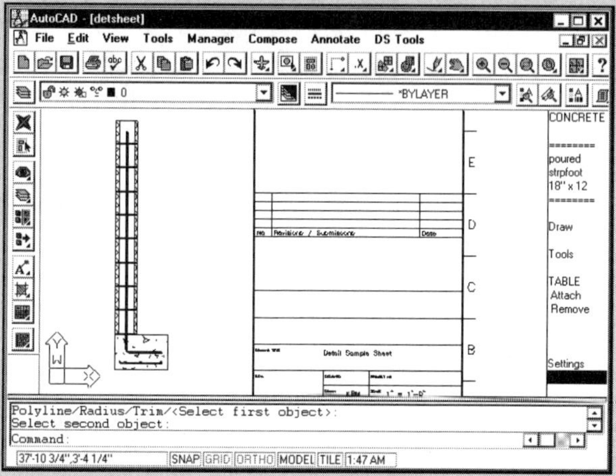

Step 19: Use the AutoCAD [Fillet] command to apply a bend to the rebar with 1-1/2″ radius fillet.

Prepare a Detail for Annotation

To utilize the automatic annotation features in the *Details* module for the rebar polyline, you must attach it to the material table.

✔ The following example shows how to attach the rebar that you drew with the [Pline] to the material list.

Hands-on:

Step 1: Use the [CL] macro to set the layer of the polyline to 03MED.

Step 2: Pick the [Attach] command from the side-screen menu.

Step 3: Pick the polyline and press <Enter>.

Note:

The polyline now matches the material settings as shown on the screen menu. The width of the wall footing was purposefully drawn too narrow.

Step 4: Use the [ST] macro to increase the width of the footing from 18″ to 36″.

Step 5: Select [DS Tools ⇨ Hatch Materials] from the pull-down menu.

Step 6: Pick the concrete hatch inside the footing and press <Enter>.

Step 7: Draw two lines on the HEAVY layer as partial boundaries for an earth hatch pattern to designate back fill — use the following illustrations as a guide.

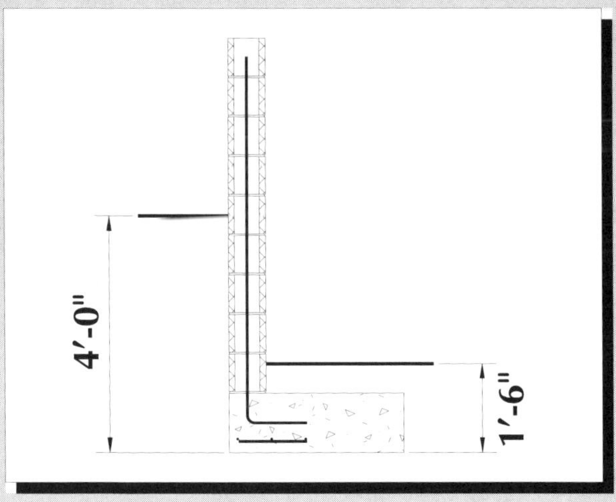

Note:

The dimensions are for the purpose of locating these lines only.

Step 8: Select [Compose ⇨ Materials Compose] from the pull-down menu.

Step 9: Enter BACKFILL in the "Find Words" edit box and press <Enter>.

Step 10: Double click the Backfill item in the 'Table Description" list and select COMPACTED SOIL from the Back fill dialog box.

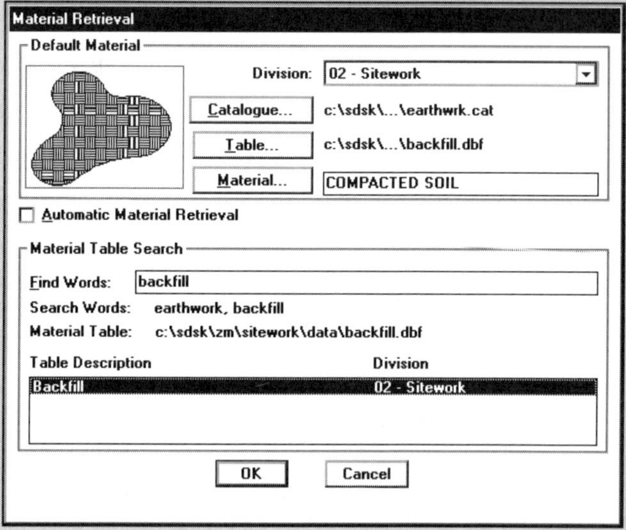

Step 11: Exit the dialog boxes and type **D** to draw an outline for the hatch pattern.

Step 12: Erase the boundary polyline once the hatch pattern is complete.

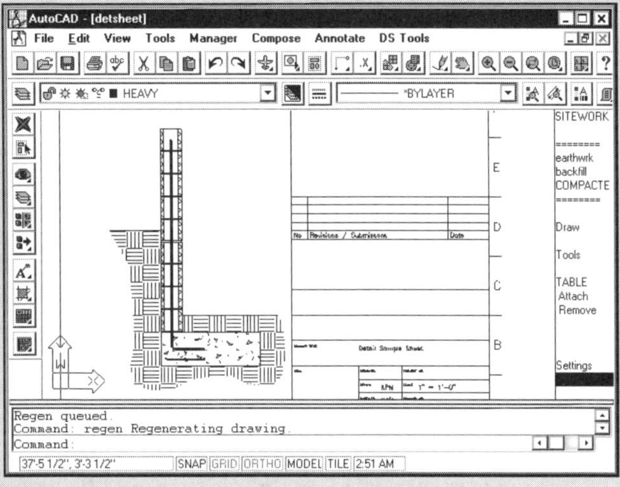

Detail Annotation

The following example shows you how to keynote the materials in your detail.

- ✔ The first step is to choose to include the material key and a note when you place the leader.
- ✔ After that, you choose the material and pick a location for the note.
  - ✗ The *Details* module reads the material information associated to the object you select and places the key.
  - ✗ You can then type any additional notes below the key.
- ✔ If you take the time to carefully assign materials to objects while you create your details, adding keynotes will be quick and easy.

Hands-on:

Step 1: Select [Annotate ⇨ Keynote Leader Settings...] from the pull-down menu.

Step 2: Toggle the "Key and Notes" radio button on in the Project Keynote Leader Settings dialog box.

Step 3: Toggle the "Database table file for material" radio button on in the "Key Word Source" section.

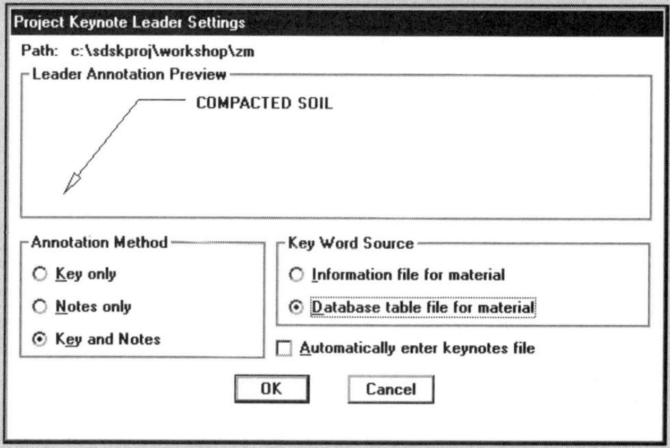

Step 4: Pick the "OK" button to return to the drawing.

Step 5: Select [Annotate ⇨ Keynote Leaders] from the pull-down menu.

Step 6: Pick a point on the vertical rebar in the wall.

Step 7: Press <Enter> to accept the default object point.

Step 8: Drag the leader line to the right to insert the note text.

Note:

The command retrieves the keynote from the database and allows you to type additional notes.

Step 9: Enter **@ 32″ O.C.** and press <Enter> when done.

Step 10: Add additional keynotes as desired.

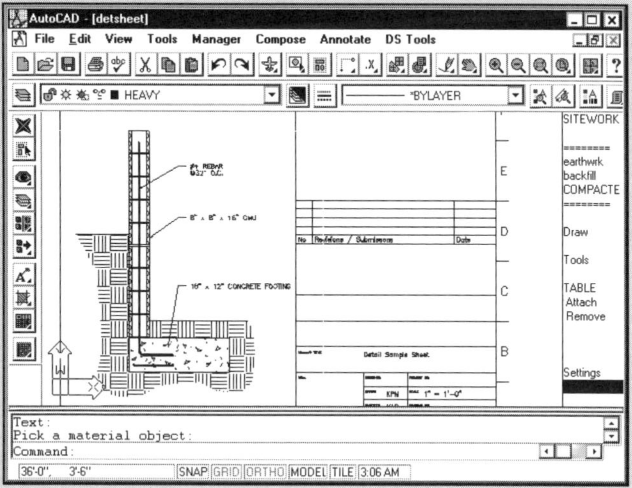

Adding a Detail to the Library

When you finish the detail, you can add it to your details library.

✔ The first step in adding a detail to the library is to create a slide of the detail.

- ✗ The slide becomes a visual reference of the detail in the library dialog box.
- ✗ You should make sure that only the detail will appear on the slide — freeze any layers or move the detail to isolate it from other details on the drawing.
- ✗ The [Create Detail] command automatically creates a slide of current screen view for subsequent use.

Hands-on:

Step 1: Zoom in on the detail so that it is framed on your screen without any other entities — use the [LF] macro to turn off any layers that may interfere with your detail's display.

Step 2: Select [Manager ⇨ Create Detail] from the pull-down menu.

Step 3: Pick a point in the center of the retaining wall detail as the basepoint.

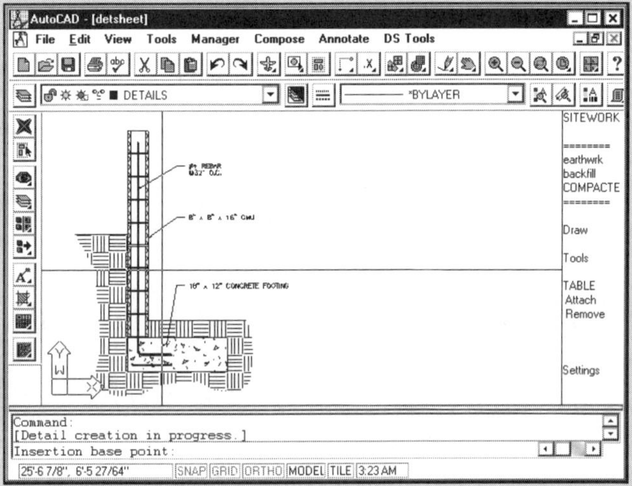

Step 4: Enter **Yes** to automatically select objects for detail and press <Enter> once all the objects appear highlighted.

Step 5: Enter **Yes** to save the detail to the library.

Step 6: Highlight WORKSHOP in the "Library Name" list box on the Select Detail Library Path dialog box.

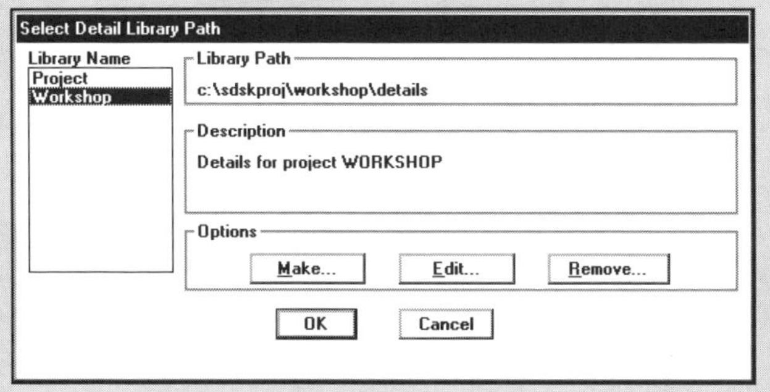

Step 7: Pick the "Edit..." button to access the Edit Detail Library Path dialog box.

Define Detail in the Library

You can choose from a variety of settings to govern the library name, path, and description of the detail.

- ✔ Use the "Make" button to create new detail libraries.
- ✔ Use the "Remove" button to delete detail libraries.

Hands-on:

Step 1: Pick the "Cancel" button to return to the Select Detail Library Path dialog box.

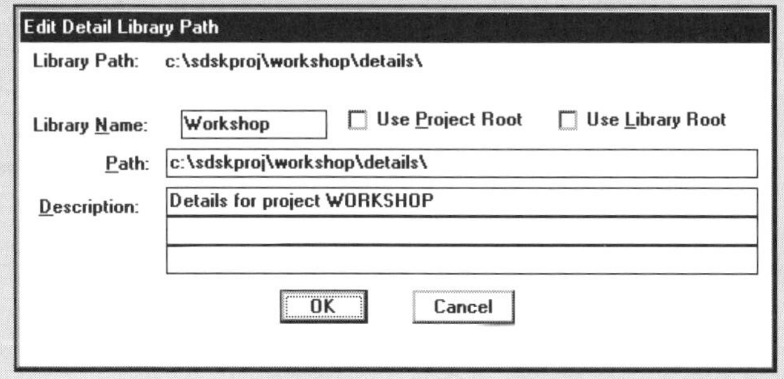

Step 2: Make sure the WORKSHOP library is highlighted in the "Library Name" list box and pick the "OK" button to add the detail to this library.

Step 3: Enter GARDNWAL for the "Drawing" and "Slide" on the Save Detail dialog box.

Step 4: Enter the title and description as shown below.

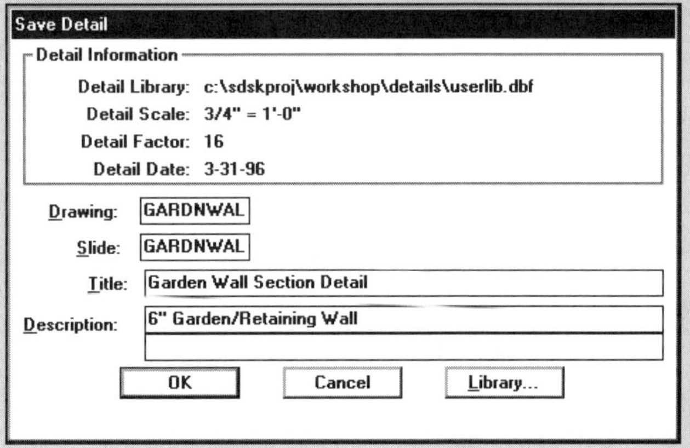

Note:

You can use the "Library" button to attach the detail to another library.

Step 5: Pick the "OK" button to add the detail to the Workshop library.

Step 6: Enter **No** to end the command without inserting the detail.

Insert the Detail

After you add the detail to the library, you can prepare the drawing to place the detail.

Step 1: Restore any layers that you may have removed from the display before you added the detail to the library.

Step 2: Zoom in on the area next to the title block to place the detail.

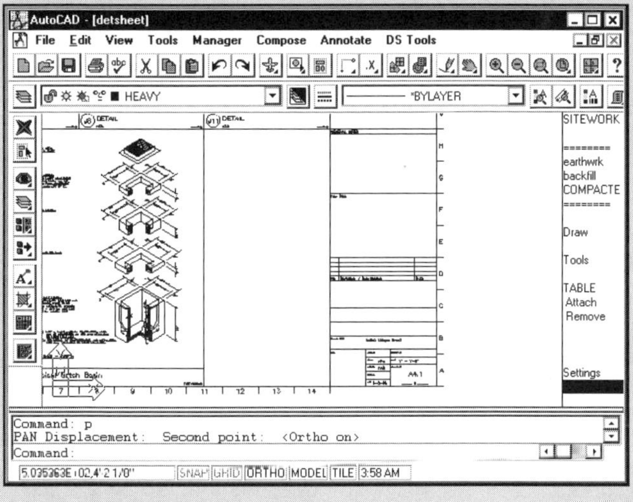

Step 3: Select [Manager ⇨ Title Settings...] from the pull-down menu.

Step 4: Toggle the "Use Border Grid for Detail Identification" check box on.

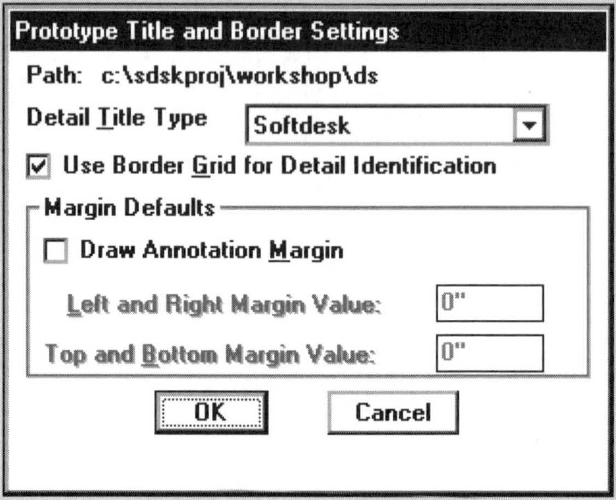

Step 5: Pick the "OK" button to return to the drawing.

Step 6: Select [Manager ⇨ Insert Detail...] from the pull-down menu.

Step 7: Choose the GARDNWAL detail and review how the detail information and illustration appears in the dialog box — choose "OK" to continue.

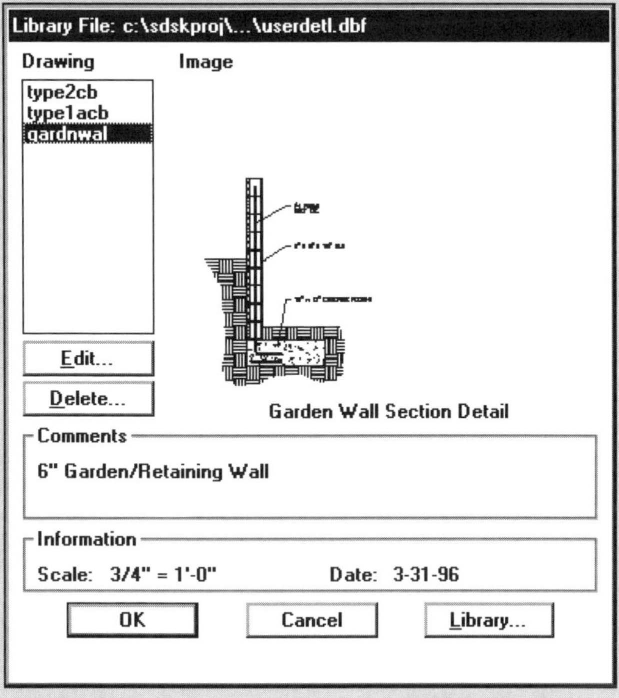

Step 8: Choose to insert the detail as an XREF and pick a point in the center of the area where you want to insert the detail.

Step 9: Enter **Yes** to add a detail title.

Step 10: Enter GARDNWAL.DWG for the "Detail Reference".

Step 11: Pick the lower left-hand corner and the upper right-hand corner of the detail area.

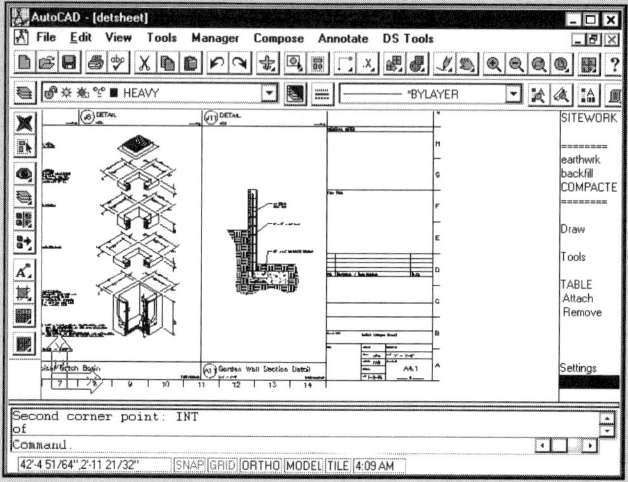

Annotating Externally Referenced Details

The following example shows how to replace the conventional annotation with keynotes on the garden wall detail.

✔ You can choose to place only keynote information with your leaders.

✔ Once you place keynotes, you can generate a keynote chart.

Hands-on:

Step 1: Use the [LZ] macro to freeze the annotation layers for the garden wall detail — GARDNWAL|ANNOBJ and GARDNWAL|ANNTEXT.

Step 2: Zoom in on the garden wall detail and annotate the detail with keynote leaders again.

Step 3: Specify a material that can be used as an example in the dialog box before changing the keynote leader settings.

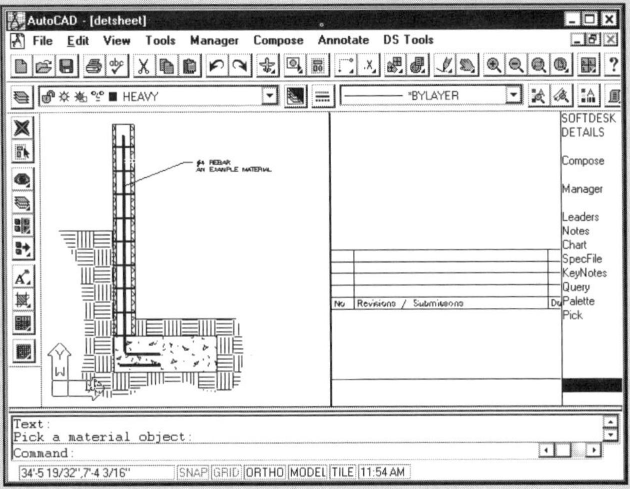

Step 4: Select [DS Tools ⇨ Pick Material Object] from the pull-down menu.

Step 5: Pick one of the components of the Garden Wall detail, then cancel the draw material.

Step 6: Select [Annotate ⇨ Keynote Leader Settings...] from the pull-down menu.

Step 7: Turn on the "Key Only" radio button in the "Annotation Method" section on the Project Keynote Leader Settings dialog box.

Step 8: Turn on the "Information file for material" radio button in the "Key Word Source" section.

Step 9: Pick the "OK" button to return to the drawing.

Step 10: Select [Annotate ⇨ Keynote Leaders] from the pull-down menu.

Step 11: Annotate the detail as necessary.

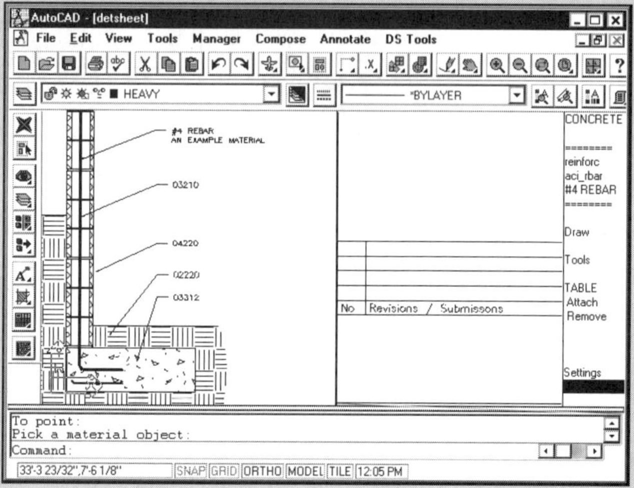

Create a Keynote Chart

The following example shows how to create a keynote chart from a detail.

✔ In this case, you will choose only one detail.

✔ On a complete detail sheet, you can choose all details to generate a single keynote chart.

Hands-on:

Step 1: Select [Annotate ⇨ Chart Keynotes] from the pull-down menu.

Step 2: Pick the garden wall detail when prompted to select objects.

Step 3: Locate the chart in the Materials Keying Legend area of the title block sheet.

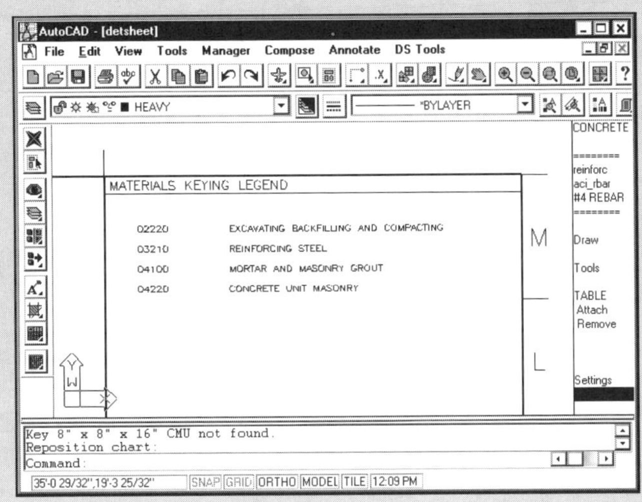

Chapter 11

The Fine Points of Details

Objectives

To manage material and detail libraries, you should be able to:

- ✔ Find and use materials in the *Details* module materials library.
- ✔ Add new material catalogues and tables to the materials library.
- ✔ Create component assemblies in the *Details* module.
- ✔ Annotate details using material keynote descriptions and ConDoc methods.
- ✔ Add details from other CAD systems and scanned drawings

Introduction

This chapter shows you how to control the advanced features of the *Details* module. The first section deals with how to use and customize the most powerful feature of the *Details* module — the materials library. The materials library allows you to associate a part of your detail with material specification information. Through this association, you can automate the detail annotation process. An important part of the materials library is how the material information is organized. You should be familiar with the Masterformat method for organizing construction specifications to help you take full advantage of the materials library.

Once you have control of the materials library, you can use it to help you automate the process of annotating details. This chapter shows you how to set what information you want to show on the detail from the materials library. This gives you the ability to generate traditional annotations as well as ConDoc keynote charts.

This chapter also shows you how to use details created outside of the *Details* module. You can import details created with regular AutoCAD or other CAD programs and associate the existing geometry with the materials library. You can also integrate your existing paper-based details library through *CAD Overlay ESP.*

Inside the Details Module

Use the Softdesk *Details* module to create construction details quickly and efficiently.

- ✔ The Details module has the ability to incorporate custom material database information and custom geometry generation programs.

  - ✗ You can customize the *Details* module to use the specific construction materials and methods you commonly work with.
- ✔ The *Details* module helps you generate construction specifications.
  - ✗ You can attach intelligent information to your details to maximize the benefits of these features.
- ✔ The *Details* module uses standard dBASE IV files to store non-graphical information.
  - ✗ You should have a dBASE compatible editor to help you take full advantage of the *Details* module.
  - ✗ This guide shows examples using Microsoft Excel, although you can use any dBASE compatible editor.

Materials

The key to success with the *Details* module is being able to use the materials library.

- ✔ You should take time to familiarize yourself with the structure of the library, including how to customize the database, and how to organize information with the Masterformat.
- ✔ You may want to keep a copy of the Masterformat specification handy while you begin to use the materials library.

Access the Material Settings

The *Details* module stores material settings with the current project.

- ✔ You can find material settings in the directory *\<projectname> \zm\material.dfm*.
- ✔ The Material Project Settings dialog box allows you to determine how to generate certain materials when you draw them.

  - ✗ Material boxes that appear "grayed-out" do not require additional settings.
- ✔ The following example shows how to access the material project settings.
  - ✗ You should experiment with the other material settings.
  - ✗ These settings allow you to configure the *Details* module to meet your requirements and standards.

Hands-on:

Step 1: Create a new drawing called *material.dwg*

Step 2: Initialize the Softdesk *Details* module and choose the WORKSHOP project.

Step 3: Set the drawing scale to 1′-0″=1′-0″ with a sheet size of 24x36.

Step 4: Do not insert a sheet border.

Step 5: Select [File ⇨ Project Settings...] from the pull-down menu.

Step 6: Pick the "Edit..." button below Details in the "Application Settings" section of the dialog box.

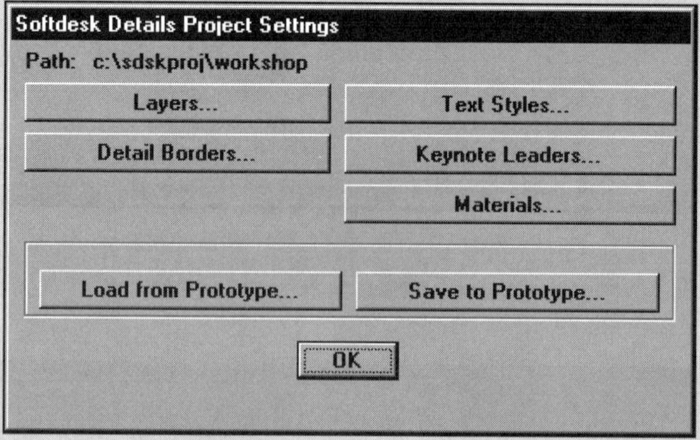

Step 7: Pick the "Materials..." button.

Step 8: Pick the "Fasteners..." button.

Step 9: Change the "Nut Type:" to Chamfered Hex in the "Bolt Settings" section of the dialog box.

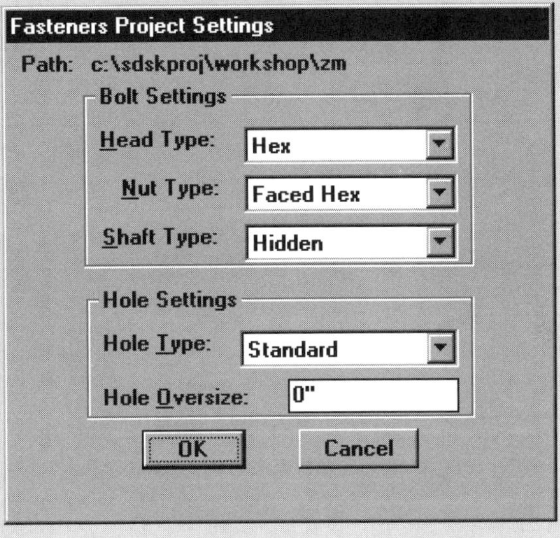

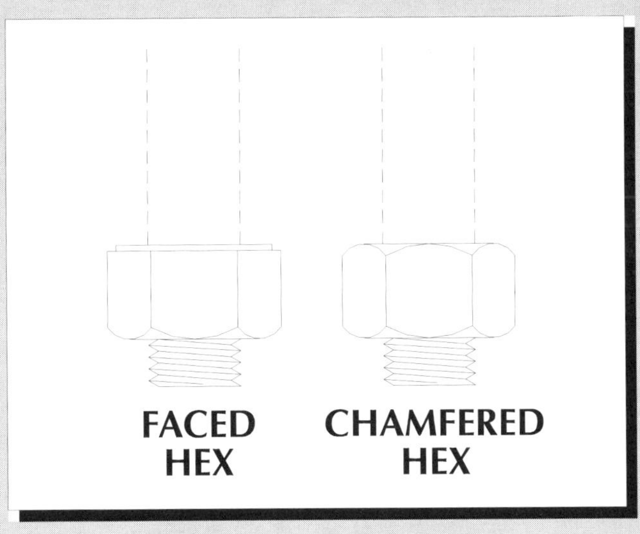

Step 10: Choose the "OK" button four times to return to the command prompt.

Material Overview

The Softdesk *Details* module stores all material information according to the Masterformat standard set by the Construction Specifications Institute (CSI) and Construction Specifications Canada (CSC).

- ✔ There are sixteen divisions in the Masterformat:

  1. General Requirements
  2. Sitework
  3. Concrete
  4. Masonry
  5. Metals
  6. Wood and Plastics
  7. Thermal and Moisture Protection
  8. Doors and Windows
  9. Finishes
  10. Specialties
  11. Equipment
  12. Furnishings
  13. Special Construction
  14. Conveying Systems
  15. Mechanical
  16. Electrical

- ✔ Each division is divided into catalogs.

How Softdesk Uses the Divisions

Division 1 of the Masterformat is reserved for regulatory requirements and references.

- ✔ The *Details* module uses this division to display sample tables and LISP routines.

- ✔ You can use these to design custom material catalogues and tables for any application.

Note:

> *The division 1 samples in the exercises draw basic circles and rectangles. They are here to help you learn how to customize the software. Do not use them to create geometry for construction details. For more information on customizing the* Details *module, see Appendix A of the* Details Reference Manual.

The *Details* module also includes an additional Division 0 for fasteners.

- ✔ Though this is not a defined division in the Masterformat, it gives you convenient access to fastener information within the *Details* module.

Choosing a Material

You can find a material in the *Details* module by choosing the Masterformat division where the material resides, and then selecting the catalogue containing the material.

- ✔ The following exercise shows you how find a metal cap for a wooden column in division 6.

Hands-on:

Step 1:	Select [Compose ⇨ Material Compose] from the pull-down menu to access the Material Retrieval dialog box.
Step 2:	Select 06 - Wood-Plastics from the "Division:" scroll list.
Step 3:	Pick the "Catalogue..." button.
Step 4:	Highlight "Metal Connectors" and pick the "OK" button to access the Metal Connectors catalogue.
Step 5:	Highlight the "Column Caps (CC)" material table from the list and pick the "OK" button.

Step 6: Select a material and pick the "OK" button to retrieve it — the column cap is now the current (default) material.

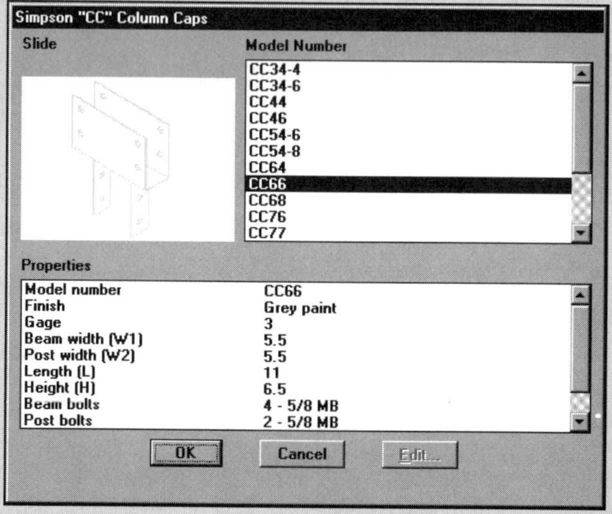

Step 7: Spend some time reviewing the Masterformat divisions in the Material Retrieval dialog box.

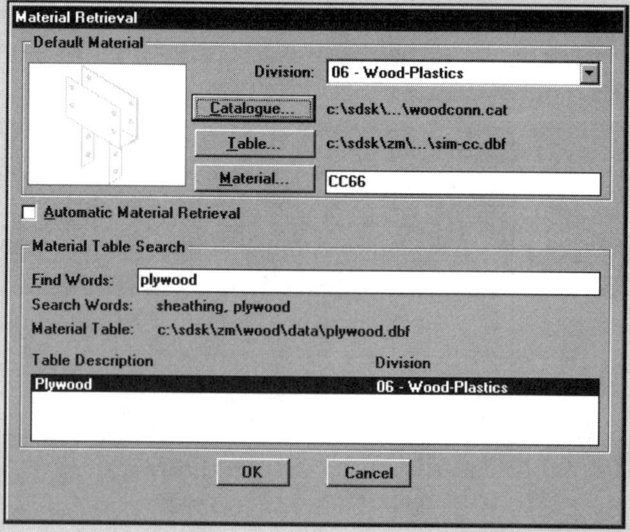

Perform a Material Search

If you are not an expert at the structure of Masterformat divisions, you can search the library with a keyword to find the material you want.

- ✔ The *Details* module reports every instance of the keyword in the material list.

Hands-on:

Step 1: Enter **Plywood** into the "Find Words:" edit box in the "Material Table Search" section of the dialog box.

Step 2: Press the <Enter> key to start the search.

Step 3: Double-click on "Plywood" in the list box to access the material table.

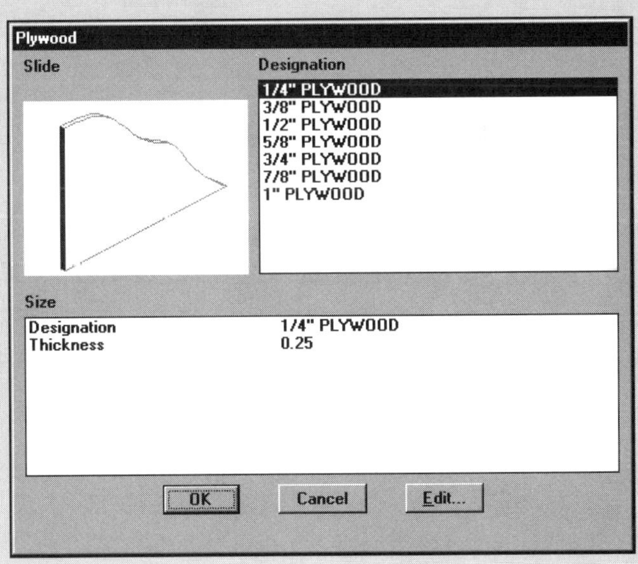

Modifying Existing Material Tables

You can add additional information to the materials database.

- ✔ The material description in the database becomes the annotation when you use the material in a detail.
  - ✗ You can add additional descriptions of common materials to speed up the annotation process.
- ✔ The Edit Table dialog box displays the contents of the table file one row at a time.
  - ✗ The rows display individually and each column occupies a separate line within the list box.
  - ✗ You can scroll through the columns of a particular row by highlighting them in the list box.
  - ✗ You can scroll through the available rows with the buttons found in the "Rows" section of the dialog box.

The following exercise shows how to expand the material database by adding a new plywood size to the database.

Hands-on:

Step 1:	Pick the "Edit" button in the Plywood dialog box.
Step 2:	Pick the "New" button from the "Rows" section of the dialog box.
Step 3:	Highlight "DESCRIPT:" in the list of columns.
Step 4:	Enter **1 1/8" PLYWOOD** in the "Edit:" edit box.
Step 5:	Highlight "THICKNESS:" in the list of columns.

Step 6: Enter **1.125** in the "Edit:" edit box.

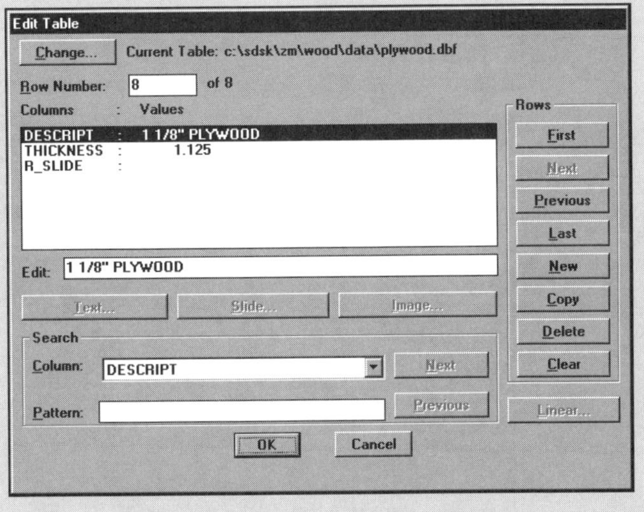

Step 7: Pick the "OK" button to add the new value to the material table.

Step 8: Pick the "OK" button again to select 1 1/8″ PLYWOOD as the current material.

Step 9: Exit the dialog box and end the command without drawing any plywood.

Adding a Detail Description

You can add detail descriptions to existing materials.

- ✔ A good example is the nominal cut lumber database.
  - ✗ The description in this database shows only the size (i.e., 2x4, 2x6 etc.).
  - ✗ You can modify the database to include a 2x6 PRESSURE TREATED SILL PLATE in addition to the generic 2x6 material.
- ✔ The Edit Table dialog box has similar search capabilities to the "Find Words" function of the Material Compose dialog box.

✗ You can enter search criteria based on any of the columns within the table.

Hands-on:

Step 1: Select [Compose ⇨ Material Compose] from the pull-down menu to access the Material Retrieval dialog box.

Step 2: Type **LUMBER** in the "Find Words" edit box.

Step 3: Double-click on the Nominal Cut Lumber table description in the list box.

Step 4: Choose the 2x6 designation.

Step 5: Pick the "Edit..." button to access the Edit Table dialog box.

Step 6: Verify that "Column" is set to DESCRIPTION in the "Search" section of the dialog box.

Step 7: Enter **2x6** in the "Pattern:" edit box.

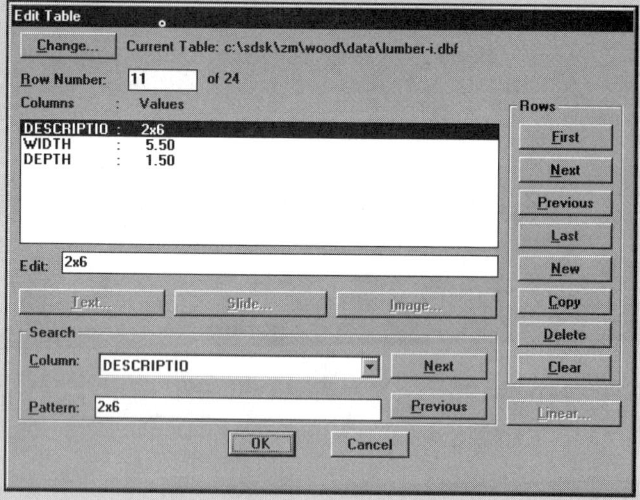

Step 8: Pick the "Copy" button in the "Rows" section of the dialog box — this creates a new row in the table.

Step 9: Highlight the 2x6 description in the list of columns as shown in the above figure.

Step 10: Type **2x6 P.T. SILL PLATE** in the "Edit:" edit box beneath the list of columns and press <Enter>.

Step 11: Notice that the dialog box reports the *"string is too long"* in the lower-left corner.

Step 12: Pick the "Cancel" button to exit the Edit Table dialog box.

Step 13: Pick "Cancel" to exit all dialog boxes and return to the command prompt.

Adjust Database File

The lumber database file includes enough room for six characters in the description column.

- ✔ The database file and path appear at the top of the Edit Table dialog box.
- ✔ You can modify this file to allow a longer description.
  - ✗ You need a dBASE IV compatible editor to modify this setting.
- ✔ You cannot edit a database file that is currently being accessed by the *Details* module.
  - ✗ You must exit to the command prompt before you modify the database.

The following example shows how to increase the width of the DESCRIPTIO column from 6 characters to 24 characters.

- ✔ This example uses Microsoft Excel to change the database.
- ✔ You can use any dBASE compatible editor.

Hands-on:

Step 1:	Make sure you have exited the [Material Compose] command.
Step 2:	Minimize the AutoCAD window and start Microsoft Excel.
Step 3:	Open the file *\sdsk\zm\wood\data\lumber-i.dbf.*
Step 4:	Highlight any of the rows within the DESCRIPTIO column.
Step 5:	Select [Format ⇨ Column ⇨ Width…] from the pull-down menu.
Step 6:	Enter **24** in the "Column Width" edit box.
Step 7:	Choose the "OK" button to continue.
Step 8:	Save the file and exit Microsoft Excel.
Step 9:	Maximize the AutoCAD window.

Add a New Description

The following example repeats the steps for adding a new material description to the database.

✔ The *Details* module will now accept your description.

Hands-on:

Step 1:	Select [Compose ⇨ Material Compose] from the pull-down menu to access the Material Retrieval dialog box.
Step 2:	Access the Nominal Cut Lumber dialog box.
Step 3:	Highlight your new 2x6 material (located at the end of the list).
Step 4:	Pick the "Edit…" button to access the table editor.
Step 5:	Highlight the 2x6 description within the list of columns.

Step 6: Type **2x6 P.T. SILL PLATE** in the "Edit:" edit box beneath the list of columns and press <Enter>.

Step 7: Select your new material from the list.

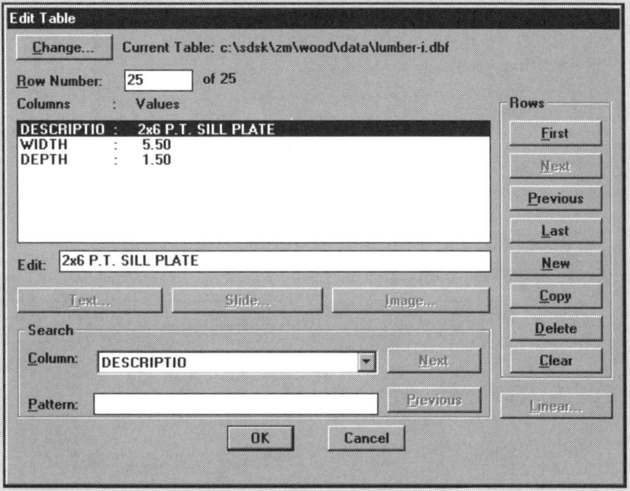

Step 8: Pick the "OK" button twice to return to the Material Retrieval dialog box.

Step 9: Pick the "Cancel" button to exit to the command line.

Material Palettes

The information in the Material Retrieval dialog box is normally organized into Masterformat divisions.

- ✔ You can choose to organize the information into material palettes.
  - ✗ Material palettes allow you to organize your materials in any fashion you desire.
  - ✗ You can organize groups of materials that you commonly use together.
  - ✗ For example, you can include anchor bolts, sill plates, plywood, and floor joists into a floor assembly palette.

- ✔ Each palette can hold up to 16 materials.
  - ✗ You can have as many palettes as you want.
- ✔ You must define a palette before you add materials.
- ✔ *Auto-Architect* stores material palettes in the *\zm* subdirectory under the project directory.
  - ✗ You can change this to read a shared directory containing material palettes from other projects.

The following example shows how to create a material palette.

Hands-on:

Step 1: Select [DS Tools ⇨ Material Palette] from the pull-down menu and press <Enter> to access the dialog box.

Step 2: Select the "New..." button to create a new material palette file.

Step 3: Enter **WDFLOOR** for the filename and choose the "OK" button.

Step 4: Pick the "Add..." button to access the Material Retrieval dialog box.

Step 5: Retrieve the sill plate you added in the previous exercise and pick the "OK" button.

Step 6: Highlight position 2 in the Material Palette dialog box.

Step 7: Pick the "Add..." button.

Step 8: Retrieve the 1-1/8″ plywood and pick the "OK" button.

Step 9: Add the following items to the palette:

1/2″ ANCHOR BOLT

2x12 (for use as floor joist)

2x6 (for use as wall studs)

Step 10: Pick the "Save" button when you finish adding the materials.

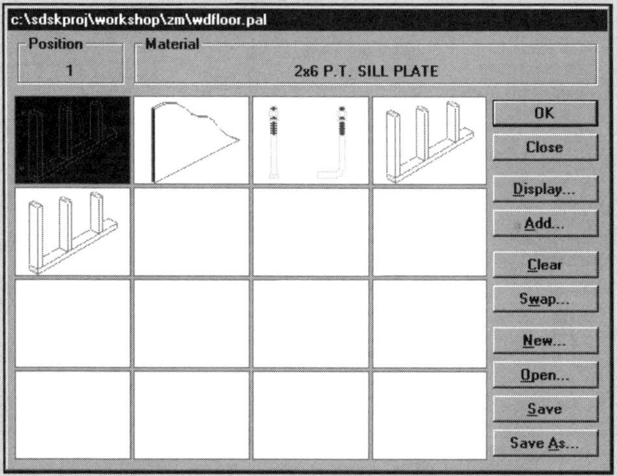

Step 11: Pick the "Close" button to exit the palette without drawing a material.

Adding New Catalogues and Tables

The *Details* module includes numerous catalogues and material tables.

- ✔ You may need to add additional materials to compose your custom details.
- ✔ The *Details* module has an open interface for you to add your own catalogues and material tables.
    - ✗ You can add your own custom drawing routines, although it is easier to copy existing detail routines and modify the database.

Copying an Existing Table

The following example shows how to add built-up roofing material for flat roofs.

- ✔ The *Details* module does not have this material.

- ✔ This material is usually shown as a single line or a series of parallel lines in a detail.
  - ✗ You can define the material by copying a material from a table with similar qualities.
  - ✗ Vapor Barriers are shown on a detail in a similar fashion to built-up roofing.
  - ✗ You will find vapor barriers in the same division where built-up roofing is defined.
  - ✗ This allows you to use the same AutoLISP routine without having to modify its layer properties.
- ✔ There are several ways to copy and edit the material.
  - ✗ The following example combines duplicating and editing the file at the same time.

Hands-on:

Step 1:	Minimize your AutoCAD window and start Microsoft Excel.
Step 2:	Open the file *\sdsk\zm\thermal\data\vapor-i.dbf.*
Step 3:	Modify the first field below DESCRIPTIO to read 2-PLY BUILT-UP ROOF.
Step 4:	Modify the next field to read 3-PLY BUILT-UP ROOF.

Step 5: Remove any of the remaining fields as shown in the following figure.

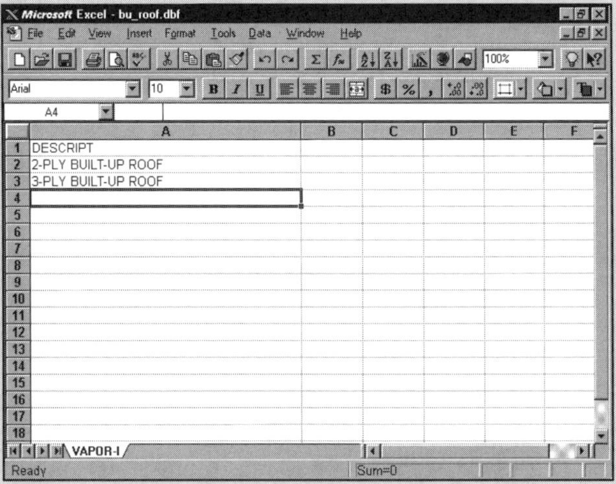

Step 6: Select [File ⇨ Save As...] from the pull-down menu.

Step 7: Save the file as **bu_roof.dbf** in the same directory as the current file.

Step 8: Exit Excel and return to AutoCAD.

Step 9: Select [Compose ⇨ Material Compose] from the pull-down menu to access the Material Retrieval dialog box.

Step 10: Select the 07 - Thermal Protection division.

Step 11: Pick the "Catalogue..." button.

Step 12: Pick the "Add..." button.

Step 13: Enter **buroof** for the file name.

Note:

You should use a different name for the catalogue and the material table you create. If you use the same name, the Details *module assumes you want to use the table as the catalogue definition and returns an error message.*

Step 14: Enter **Built-up Roofing** for the title.

Step 15: Enter **Built-up Roofing Assembly** for the description.

Step 16: Pick the "OK" button to continue.

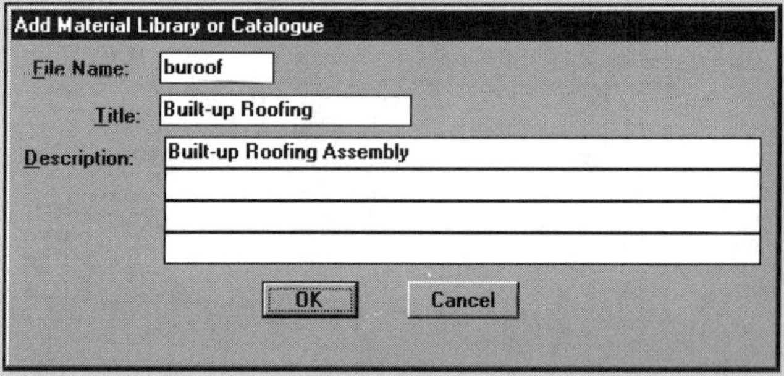

Step 17: Pick the "Create Catalogue" button on the New Material Catalogue dialog box.

Step 18: Enter **bu_roof** in the "Information File" edit box.

Step 19: Enter **Built-up Roofing** in the "Description" edit box.

Step 20: Enter **roofing** in the "Search Words" edit box.

Step 21: Enter **thermal(vapor)** as the slide name.

Step 22: Enter **vapor.lsp** as the Draw program.

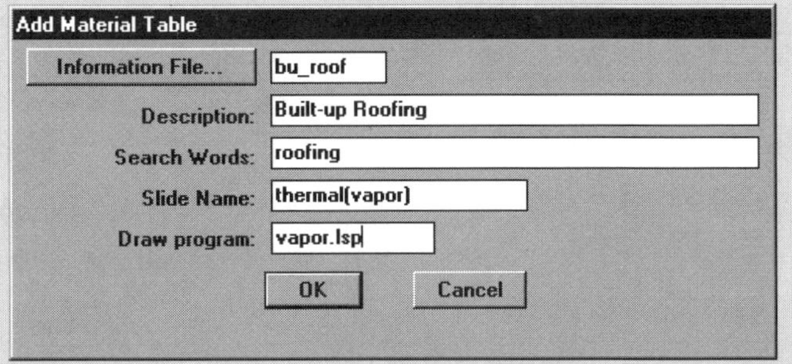

Note:

The slide and draw program are existing files. The slide or slide library must be in the \data *directory with the material table. The slide is optional, but if you do not specify a file* Auto-Architect *will not display an image. The draw program should reside in the materials root directory (i.e.,* \sdsk\zm\thermal*). The program can be a LISP routine or an ADS application.*

Step 23: Pick the "Information File..." button to edit the *.ifm* file.

Step 24: Enter the information as shown in the following figure.

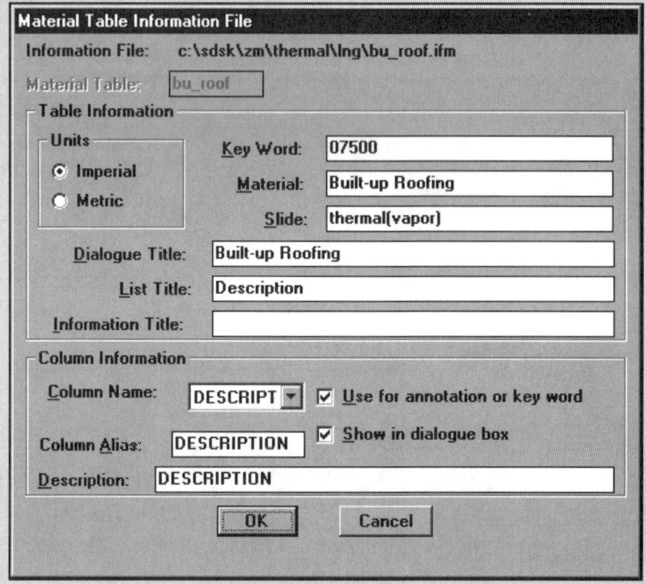

Step 25: Choose the "OK" button three times to return to the Thermal Protection Material Catalogues.

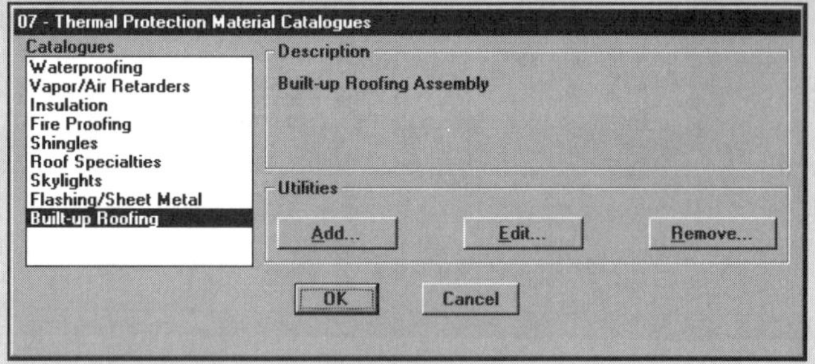

Step 26: Highlight "Built-up Roofing" in the list of catalogues and then choose the "OK" button.

Step 27: Choose the "OK" button again to access the Built-up Roofing material table.

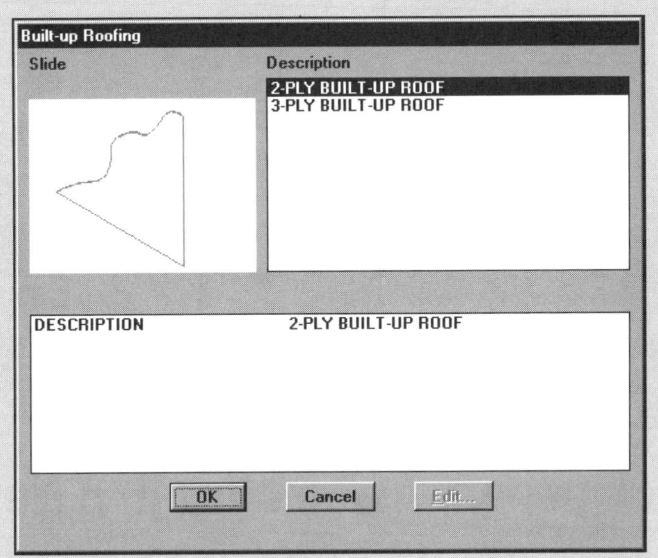

Step 28: Highlight 3-PLY BUILT-UP ROOF and choose the "OK" button to accept the new material.

Step 29: Pick "Cancel" to exit without drawing the new material.

Practice Example

Complete the following example to help reinforce your ability to add and locate material tables.

- ✔ You will create new materials definitions for suspended acoustical ceiling tiles (keyword 09510).

Hands-on:

Step 1:	Locate in Division 9 — Finishes within the Acoustic Treatment catalogue.
Step 2:	Copy the *\sdsk\zm\finish\data\r-flr-1.dbf* material table.
Step 3:	Modify the table to include ½″, 5/8″ and ¾″ Ceiling Tiles.
Step 4:	Use the r_floor.lsp routine as the draw program (found in Div. 9 in the Resilient Flooring catalogue).
Step 5:	Use finish (r-floor) as the slide.

Component Assemblies in a New Library

Material palettes are a great way to organize individual components that you use together when you generate details.

- ✔ This section takes this concept a step further by showing how to create and store common assemblies of different materials for easy access.
- ✔ The following example shows how to create components for typical steel column/beam connection details.

Hands-on:

Step 1: Compose the following detail at ¾″=1′-0″ – use the example in the previous chapter to guide you through the process.

Step 2: Use the notes in the following illustrations for your reference — do not add annotation to the detail at this time.

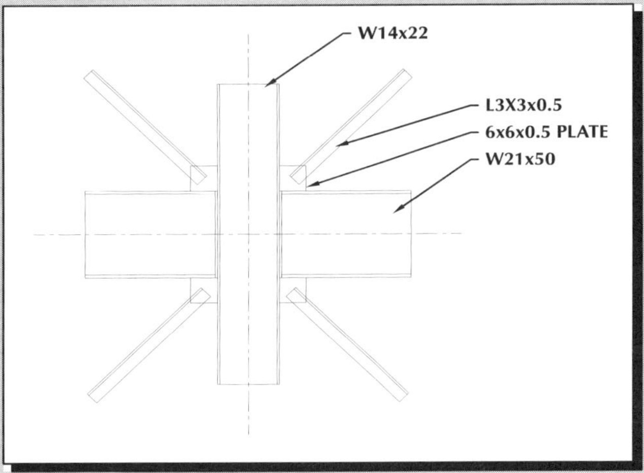

Step 3: Select [Compose ⇨ Steel Connection Angles] from the pull down menu.

Step 4: Type **E** to draw the elevation view of the Connection Angle.

Step 5: Pick the "Select…" button within the "Material" section of the dialog box.

Step 6: Retrieve an L4x3.5x0.5 from the AISC Angle Shapes table.

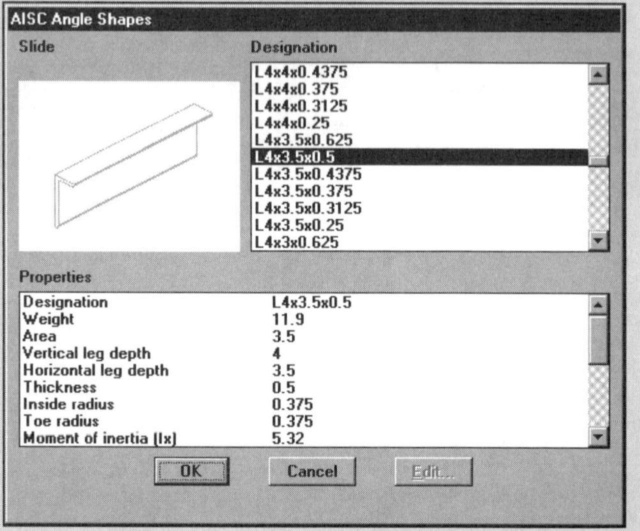

Step 7: Pick the "OK" button twice to accept the material and return to defining the connection angle.

Step 8: Enter the connection angle parameters as shown in the following images.

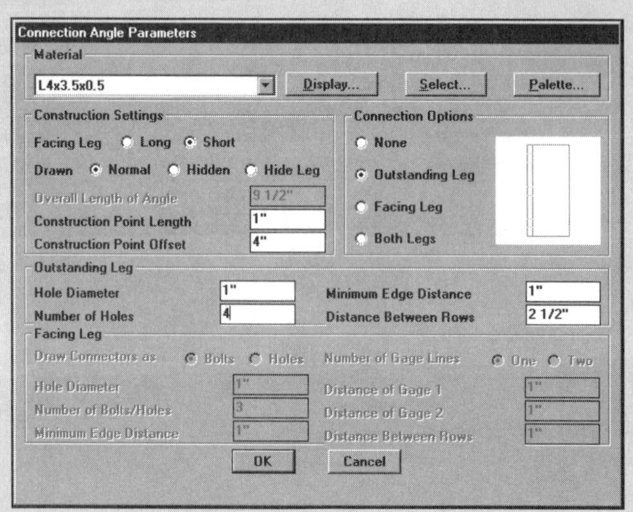

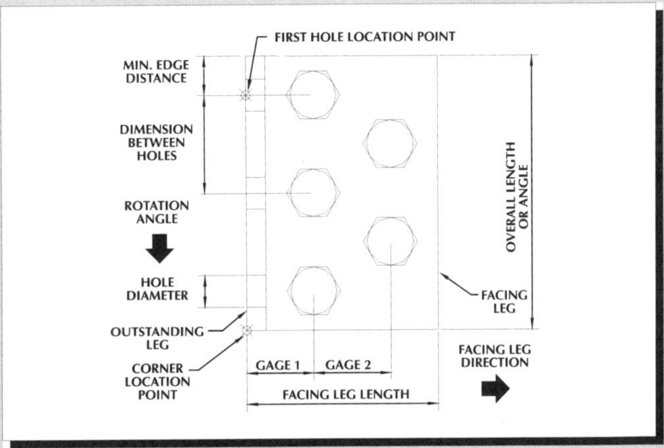

Step 9: Insert an angle to connect the right beam to the column.

Step 10: Add four ¾″ A307 BOLTS to each angle as shown in the following figure.

Step 11: Mirror the angle and bolt to the left side of the detail.

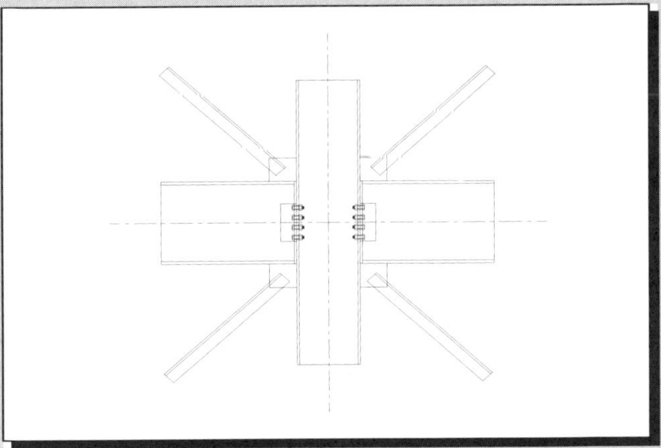

Step 12: Select [Manager ⇨ Create Detail] from the pull-down menu to add the first component to the library.

Step 13: Pick the intersection of the centerlines for the insertion base point.

Step 14: Select only the objects that make up the vertical column.

Step 15: Press <Enter> to accept your selection.

Step 16: Choose <Yes> when *Auto-Architect* prompts you to save the detail to the library.

Step 17: Pick the "Make..." button when the Select Detail Library Path dialog box appears.

Step 18: Edit the detail library path as shown below.

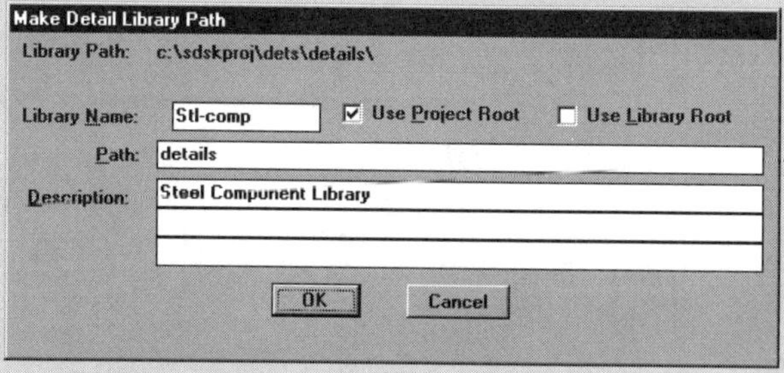

Step 19: Pick the "OK" button to continue.

Step 20: Highlight the new library path and pick the "OK" button.

Step 21: Enter the detail information as shown below to save the first component.

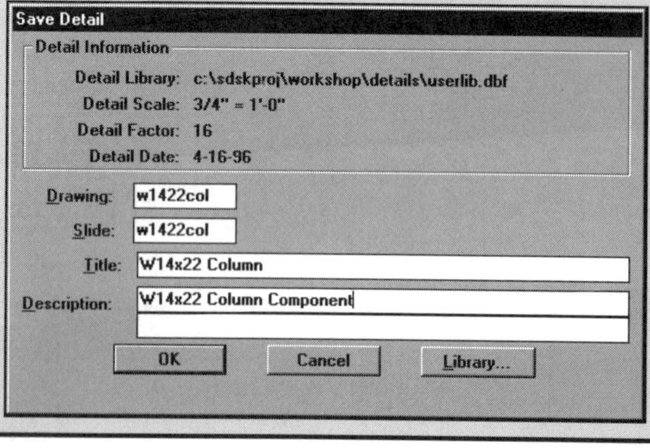

Note:

The Details *module automatically generates this slide. The slide consists of all the elements on the screen. You must redefine the slides later to create slides that show only the detail.*

Step 22: Pick the "OK" button to save the detail to the library.

Step 23: Choose "Yes" to insert the detail.

Step 24: Select the XREF insertion option.

Step 25: Insert the detail into a clear area so that you can create slide.

Step 26: Enter "No" when prompted to add a detail title.

Step 27: Zoom in on the component.

Step 28: Type **[Mslide]** at the command prompt to redefine the existing slide.

Step 29: Save the slide as *\sdskproj\workshop\details \w1422col.sld.*

Step 30: Pick the "Yes" button when the *Details* module prompts you to replace the existing file.

Step 31: Select [Manager ⇨ Insert Detail…] from the pull-down menu to access the library and view the new component.

Step 32: Pick the "Cancel" button when you are done.

Step 33: Detach the XREF from the drawing and return to the remaining geometry.

Step 34: Select [Manage ⇨ Setup New Detail…] from the pull-down menu.

Step 35: Set the drawing scale to 3/4″=1′-0″.

Step 36: Choose the "OK" button to continue.

Step 37: Repeat the process to create a detail for each component in the assembly — use the same insertion point.

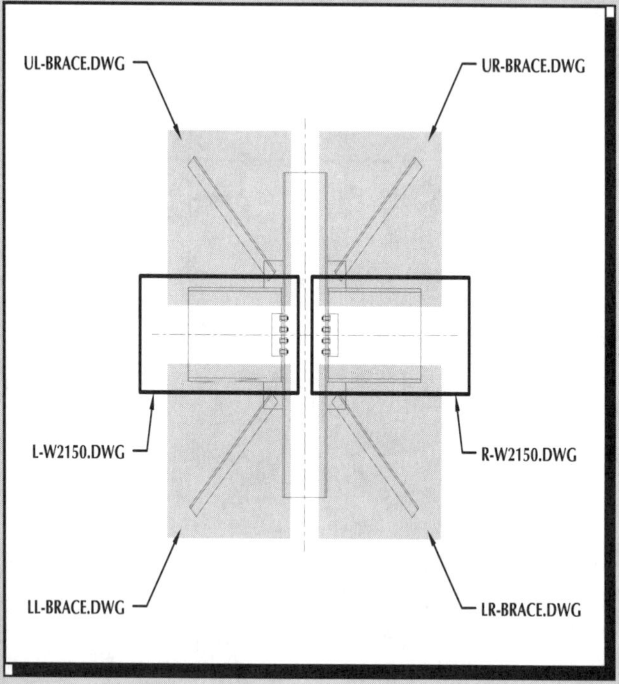

- Upper right brace (ur-brace.dwg)
- Lower right brace (lr-brace.dwg)
- Upper left brace (ul-brace.dwg)
- Lower left brace (ll-brace.dwg)
- W21x50 right (r-w2150.dwg)
- W21x50 left (l-w2150.dwg)

You can now combine the components to create several steel column/beam connection details for your project.

- ✔ You will have an opportunity to insert and annotate these components in the next section.

Annotating Details

Detail annotation styles vary between different projects and different design firms.

- ✔ You can use the *Details* module for industry standard annotation methods as well as custom techniques.
- ✔ The following section shows the key annotation features of the Softdesk *Details* module, including:
  - ✗ Keynote leader settings
  - ✗ Annotating using material table descriptions
  - ✗ Welding symbols
  - ✗ Keynotes database annotation
  - ✗ ConDoc system annotation

Keynote Leader Settings

You choose the method for annotating details in the Keynote Leader Settings dialog box.

Hands-on:

Step 1:	Select [Annotate ⇨ Keynote Leader Settings...] from the pull-down menu.

Step 2: Verify the settings are set as shown below.

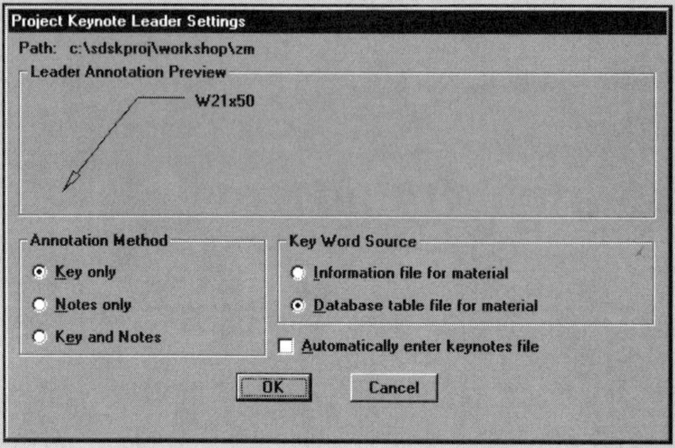

Step 3: Pick the "OK" button to continue.

The annotation method and keyword source options are described below.

✔ The "Key Word Source" establishes which file becomes the source of the keyword to use for keynoting.

Annotation Methods

Method	Description
Key Only	This option places the material key or description at the end of the leader.
Note Only	This option adds one note to the end of the leader and then prompts you for additional text.
Key and Notes	This option adds a keyword and the corresponding note to the end of the leader and then prompts for additional text.

Keyword Sources

Keyword Source	Description
Information file for material	Use this field to retrieve the material keyword annotation from the material tables information file. Every material table file has an associated .ifm file that contains the information for the material. These files contain a specific keyword for that material and associate the material with every row in the table. The [Keynote Leaders] command uses this keyword to find the associated keynote in the *keynotes.dbf* file.
Database table file for material	Use this field to set the source for the keyword to a column in the material table. By default the keyword column is the first column in the table unless the material information file specifies an alternate column. This column is generally the material description or part number. It is usually used as the material description in the Material Table Viewer dialog box.

Annotate Using Material Table Descriptions

The following example shows the effect of the settings in the Project Keynote Leader Settings dialog box.

Hands-on:

Step 1:	Select [Manager ⇨ Insert Detail…] from the pull-down menu to access the detail library.
Step 2:	Access the Stl-comp library and insert W1422COL.
Step 3:	Choose the “OK” button and choose XREF as the insertion option.
Step 4:	Insert the column in a clear area within your drawing.
Step 5:	Use a rotation angle of 0.

Step 6: Type **No** when prompted to add a title.

Step 7: Zoom into the column to add more components.

Step 8: Insert the following components as external references using the insertion point of the column as their basepoint:

r-w2150

r-angle

Step 9: Select [Manager ⇨ Setup New Detail...] from the pull-down menu.

Step 10: Setup the detail at 1'-0"=1'-0".

Step 11: Select [Annotate ⇨ Keynote Leaders] from the pull-down menu and annotate the detail as shown.

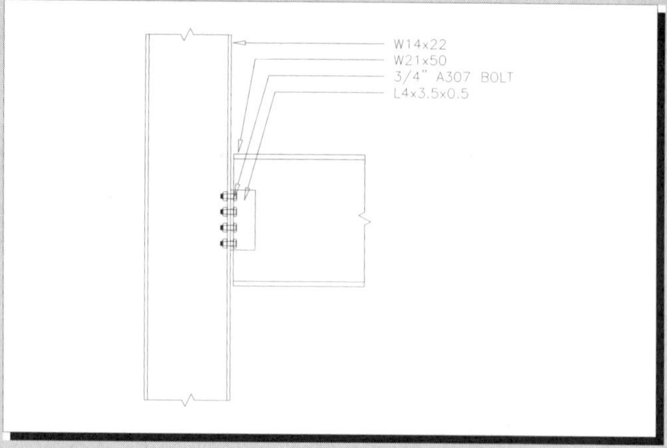

Step 12: Edit the Keynote Leader Settings to read **Key and notes** in the "Annotation Method" section.

Step 13: Annotate a material.

Step 14: Enter any additional information you want and press <Enter> twice to exit to the command line.

Using Welding Symbols

The [Welding Symbols] command creates standard symbols for welding, brazing, and nondestructive examination.

- ✔ The *Details* module uses welding symbols defined by the American National Standards Institute (ANSI) and the American Welding Society (AWS) for imperial and metric units.
  - ✗ All welding symbols are blocks.
  - ✗ Welding symbol files are stored in the *\sdsk\zw\dwg* directory.
- ✔ You should study the [Welding Symbols] command in detail, specifically how to save and restore welding symbols per project.
  - ✗ This tool provides an efficient, easy-to-use method of annotating and editing welding symbols.

Hands-on:

Step 1:	Select [Annotate ⇨ Welding Symbols] from the pull-down menu.
Step 2:	Type **New** at the command prompt to access the Welding Symbols dialog box.

Step 3: Edit the Welding Symbols dialog box as shown in the following figure.

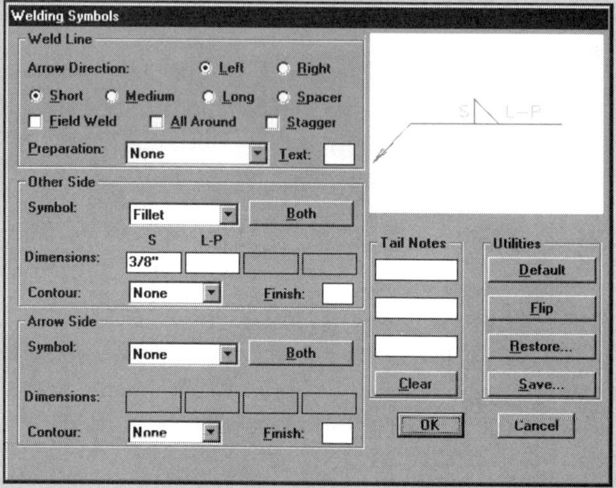

Step 4: Pick the "OK" button and insert the symbol and leader as shown in the following figure.

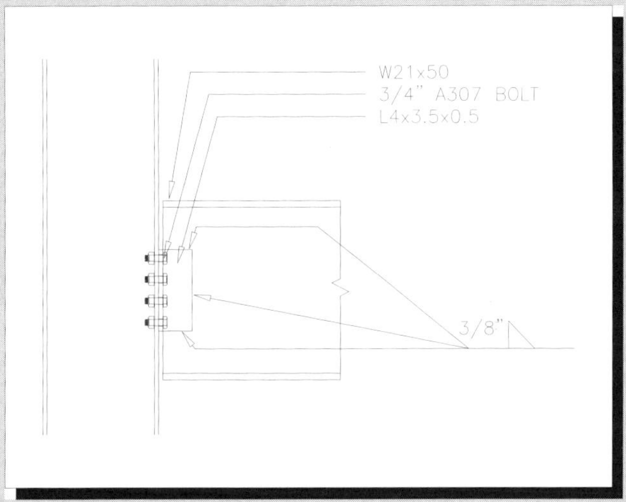

Step 5: Repeat the [Welding Symbols] command and choose the "Edit" option.

Step 6: Pick the welding symbol you just inserted.

Step 7: Pick the "Both" button within the "Other Side" section of the dialog box to duplicate the fillet symbol to the other side.

Step 8: Choose the "OK" button to continue.

Save Your Detail

The following steps direct you to save the detail in the details library.

Hands-on:

Step 1: Use the [Zoom] command to display the full detail within your screen area.

Step 2: Select [Manage ⇨ Save Detail...] from the pull-down menu.

Step 3: Enter the settings as shown below.

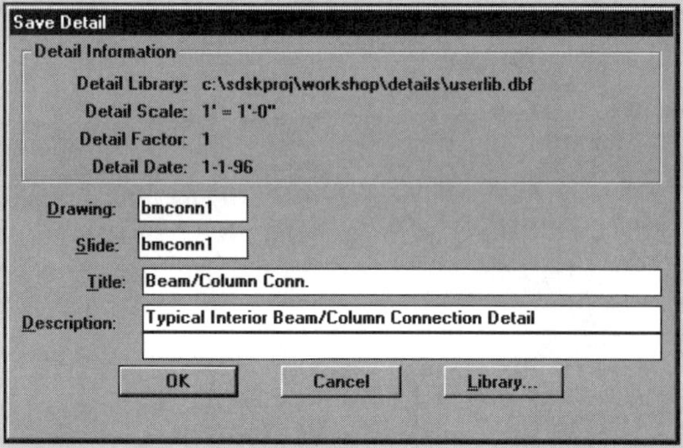

Step 4: Choose the "OK" button to create the slide and save the detail in the library.

Keynotes Database Annotation

The keynotes database is an efficient and powerful tool for generating details and specifications.

- ✔ The flexibility of the keynotes database lets you to use most of the common annotation methods.
  - ✗ You can replace the keynotes file that comes with the *Details* module with any form of keynoting that associates a keyword with a paragraph of text.
  - ✗ If you delete a keynote file, the *Details* module creates an empty keynote file the next time you use the command.
- ✔ The following example shows how to implement some of these methods.

Keynoting with CSI Key Words

The *Details* module includes a standard keynote table file called *keynotes.dbf*.

- ✔ This file contains keywords and keynotes based on the CSI and CSC Masterformat.
- ✔ This file is an outline for creating a complete project keynote file.
- ✔ The following section shows how to modify this file and annotate a detail using the default keynote table.

Hands-on:

Step 1:	Select [Manage ⇨ Insert Detail...] from the pull-down menu.
Step 2:	Select the Project detail library and highlight ROOFASSY as the detail to insert.
Step 3:	Choose the "OK" button to continue.
Step 4:	Choose the "Block" option for insertion.
Step 5:	Accept the default of 0 for the rotation.
Step 6:	Type **No** at the prompt to insert a detail title
Step 7:	Select [Manage ⇨ Setup Existing Detail] from the pull-down menu to edit the detail.

Step 8: Zoom out to display the exploded detail.

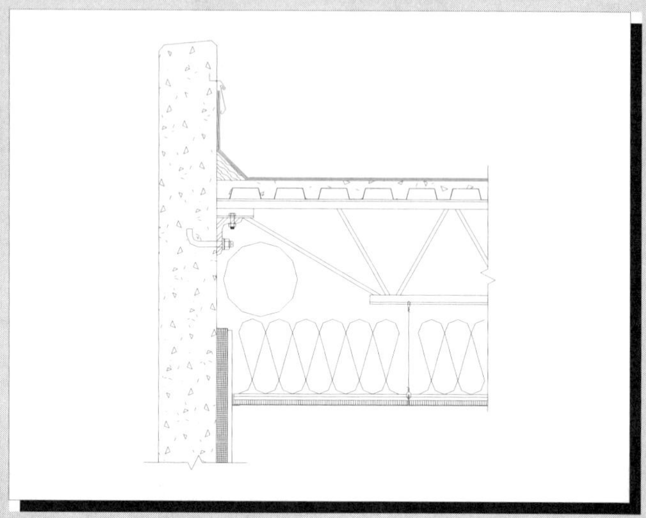

Step 9: Select [Annotate ⇨ Keynote Leader Settings…] from the pull-down menu.

Step 10: Enter the values shown below.

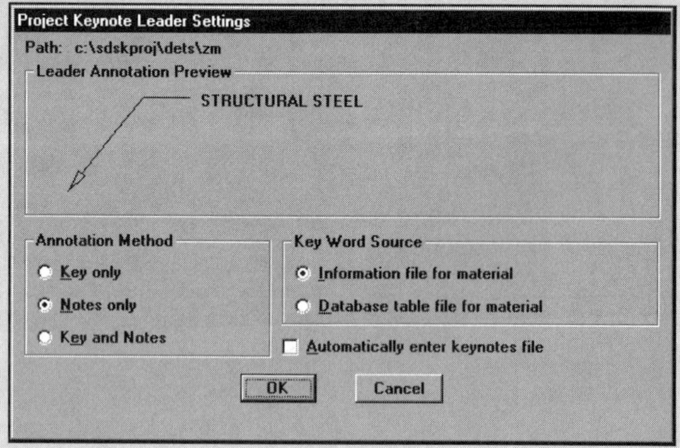

Step 11: Choose the "OK" button to continue.

Step 12: Select [Annotate ⇨ Keynote Leaders] from the pull-down menu and annotate the concrete wall.

Step 13: Annotate the flashing that protrudes from the wall and covers the built-up roofing material.

Step 14: Annotate the rigid insulation on the inside of the concrete wall.

Step 15: Annotate the gypsum wall board adjacent to the insulation.

Note:

You are currently annotating using the CSI Mediumscope descriptions.

Annotate Inert Entities

There is no material assigned to ductwork, ceiling tiles, and ceiling accessories.

- ✔ You can access the keynotes manager when you select an object that lacks a material attachment.
- ✔ The following example shows how to annotate these objects using the keynotes database.

Hands-on:

Step 1: Select [Annotate ⇨ Keynote Leaders] from the pull-down menu and pick a suspended acoustical ceiling tile entity.

Step 2: Enter 095 and press <Enter> in the Key Word edit box located below the Key Word list.

Step 3: Highlight 09510 and the “OK” button to add the note.

Step 4: Select [Tools ⇨ Annotate ⇨ Text Leader] from the pull-down menu.

Step 5: Place a leader that extends from the ceiling support wire.

Step 6: Enter 09100 and press <Enter> when the text prompt appears.

Step 7:	Press <Enter> again and notice that the *Details* module retrieves the description for 90100.
Step 8:	Press <Enter> to exit the text prompt and return to the leader command.
Step 9:	Place a leader that extends from the round supply duct.
Step 10:	Enter ?15880 and press <Enter> twice to enter the keynotes manager.
Step 11:	Highlight 15890 in the Key Word list and choose the "OK" button to add the note.
Step 12:	Press <Enter> again to exit the text prompt.
Step 13:	Press <Enter> to exit the text leader command without drawing another leader.
Step 14:	Select [Annotate ⇨ Keynote Leader Settings...] from the pull-down menu.
Step 15:	Enable the check box which allows you to enter the keynote file automatically and pick the "OK" button.
Step 16:	Select [Annotate ⇨ Keynote Leaders] from the pull-down menu and annotate the 3-ply built-up roofing.

Modify the Keynote Table

You can use the default CSI keynote table to annotate details with consistent notation using industry standard conventions and terminology.

✔ The following example shows how to enter a new keynote.

Hands-on:

Step 1: Pick the "New..." button within the Keynote Manager dialog box.

Step 2: Enter the new keynote information as shown below.

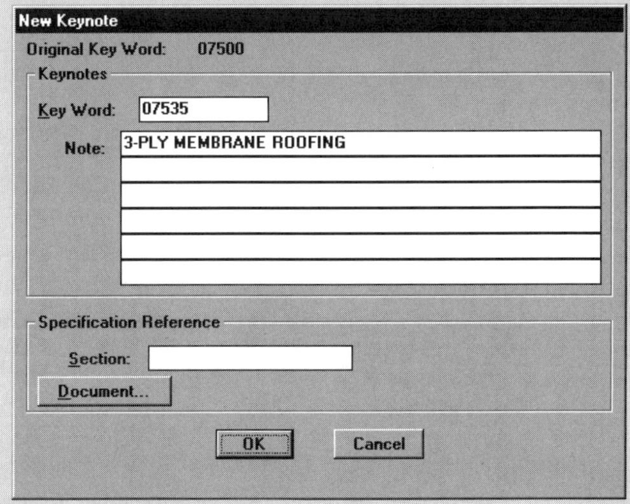

Step 3: Choose "OK" to add the new keynote.

Step 4: Highlight 07535 as the keyword and choose "OK" to annotate the roofing.

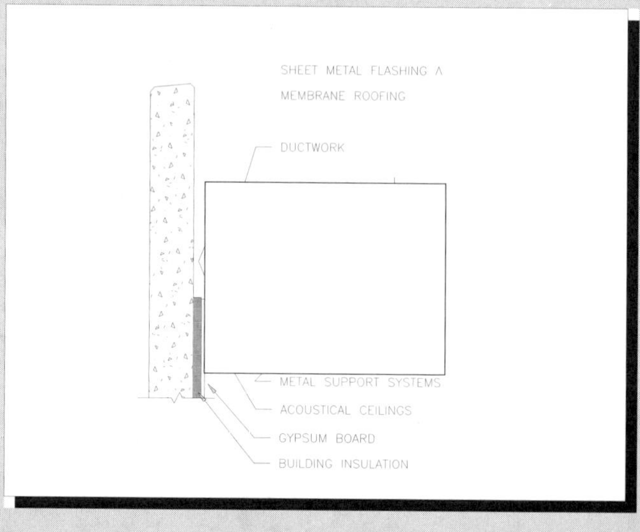

Step 5: Zoom to the extents of the detail.

Step 6: Select [Manage ⇨ Create Detail…] from the pull-down menu.

Step 7: Select a basepoint near the center of the detail.

Step 8: Accept the default of **Yes** at the prompt for automatic selection of objects.

Step 9: Accept the default of **Yes** to save the detail to the library and enter the following information.

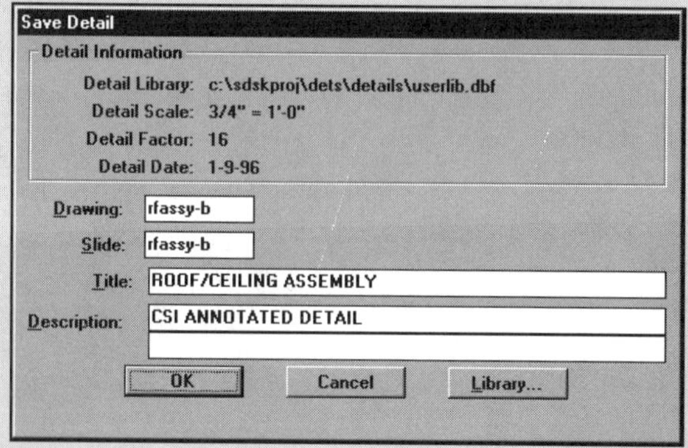

Step 10:	Pick "OK" to save the detail and create a slide.
Step 11:	Enter **No** when prompted to insert the detail.

Utilizing Key Words

The following example shows how to insert traditional annotation using key words.

- ✔ Usually, you delete the existing keynote file from the project and create a new keynote database from scratch.

Hands-on:

Step 1:	Select [Manage ⇨ Insert Detail…] from the pull-down menu.
Step 2:	Select ROOFASSY from the project detail library.
Step 3:	Choose the "OK" button to insert the detail.
Step 4:	Insert the detail into the center of your screen area using the block insertion option.
Step 5:	Enter a rotation angle of **0**.
Step 6:	Enter **No** at the prompt to insert a detail title.
Step 7:	Select [Manage ⇨ Setup Existing Detail] from the pull-down menu.
Step 8:	Insert the exploded detail onto the center of the screen area.
Step 9:	Select [Annotate ⇨ Edit Keynotes File…] from the pull-down menu.
Step 10:	Pick the "New…" button in the Keynote Manager dialog box appears.

Step 11: Enter the information as shown below.

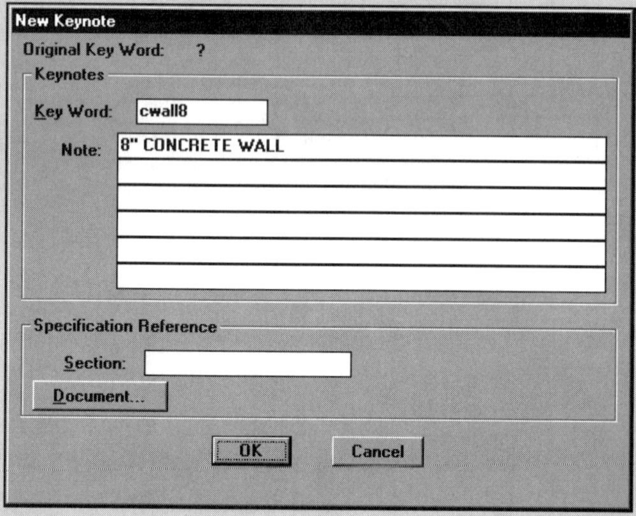

Step 12: Choose the "OK" button to continue.

Step 13: Use the same procedure above and enter the following key words and notes:

rigidin - RIGID INSULATION

battin - BATT INSULATION

buroof - BUILT-UP ROOFING

Step 14: Choose the "OK" button to exit to the command line.

Step 15: Select [Tools ⇨ Annotate ⇨ Text Leader] from the pull-down menu.

Step 16: Draw a leader from the concrete wall.

Step 17: Enter CWALL8 and press <Enter> twice when the text prompt appears.

Step 18: Press <Enter> again to begin another leader.

Step 19: Draw a leader extending from the batt insulation in the ceiling.

Step 20: Enter BATTIN and press <Enter> twice when the text prompt appears

Note:

You must enter key words on lines that are separate from other notes. Keynote searches are case sensitive.

Step 21: Enter 10″ R-30 and press <Enter> twice.

Step 22: Annotate the rigid insulation and built-up roofing using the same procedure.

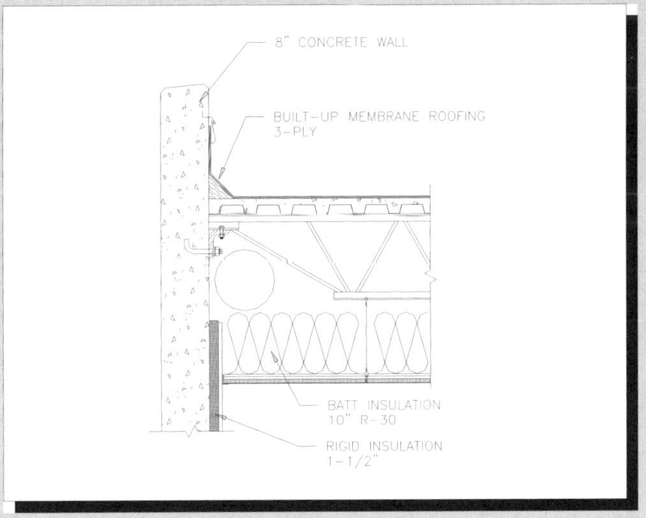

Step 23: Save the detail to the library as RFASSY-C.

ConDoc Keynoting and Title Insertion

The ConDoc annotation method is a narrow scope form of the CSI Masterformat.

- ✔ ConDoc is a system for formatting and integrating construction documentation developed by the American Institute of Architects (AIA).
  - ✗ ConDoc makes construction document creation easier while improving quality.
  - ✗ ConDoc uses the 16 divisions of Masterformat, which is now an AEC industry standard.
- ✔ By using ConDoc methods for annotation and the Masterformat for construction specifications, you create links between construction documents and specifications.
  - ✗ When you annotate a material on a drawing, the number identifying that material includes the Masterformat number.
  - ✗ You can reference this number in the specifications, which provides more detail on how to handle the desired material.
- ✔ This keynote method helps you reduce text on a drawing and eliminates duplication of errors while annotating.

Create Annotation with ConDoc Method

The following shows how to modify details to support the ConDoc method of annotation.

- ✔ Begin by setting up a new detail sheet using a ConDoc title block.
- ✔ The *Details* module applies ConDoc detail titles with margins and generates a keynote chart.

Hands-on:

Step 1: Start a new drawing called *\sdskproj\workshop \dwg\detsht2.*

Step 2: Load the Details module and attach to the project WORKSHOP.

Step 3: Setup a 24x36 ConDoc title block at 1′-0″=1′-0″ scale in model space.

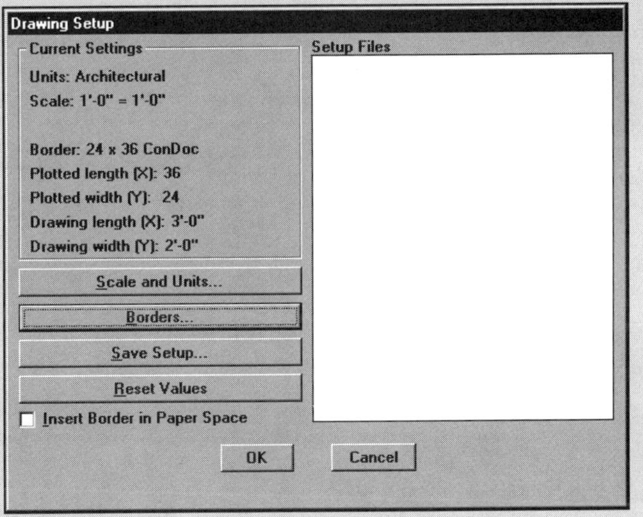

Step 4: Select [Manager ⇨ Title Settings...] and enter the settings as shown below.

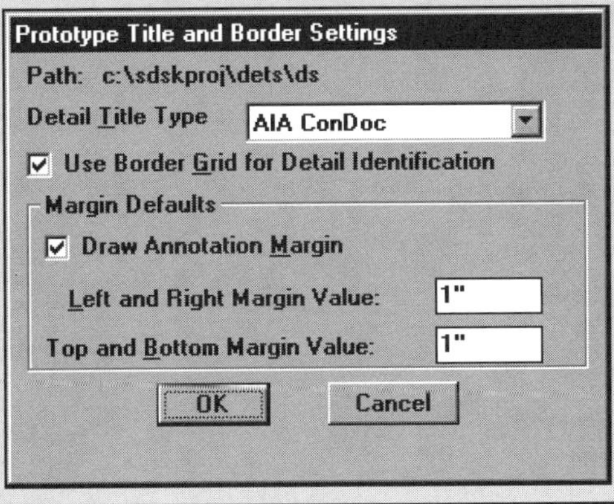

Step 5:	Choose the "OK" button to continue.
Step 6:	Select [Manage ⇨ Insert Detail...] from the pull-down menu.
Step 7:	Select the Project detail library and highlight ROOFASSY as the detail to insert.
Step 8:	Pick the "OK" button to continue.
Step 9:	Choose the "XREF" option for insertion.
Step 10:	Insert the detail into the lower right corner of the drawing sheet.
Step 11:	Leave plenty of room for annotation.
Step 12:	Accept the default of **0** for the rotation.
Step 13:	Accept the default of **Yes** when prompted to insert a detail title.
Step 14:	Enter **A101, A103, A104** at the prompt for the detail reference.

Note:

The detail reference is prompting you for each drawing number where this particular detail is referenced or noted.

Step 17: Locate the title block as shown in the following image.

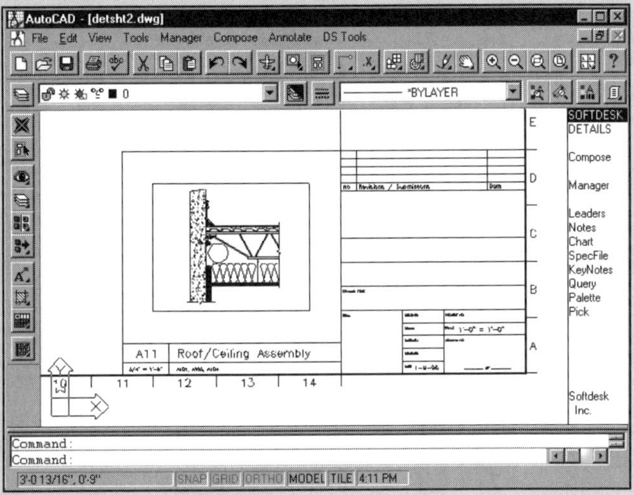

Note:

The margin lines are on the NOPLOT layer. These lines are for reference only and will not plot. The margin is for column grid bubbles and dimensions.

Step 18: Select [Annotate ⇨ Keynote Leader Settings…] from the pull-down menu.

Step 19: Verify the settings as shown below.

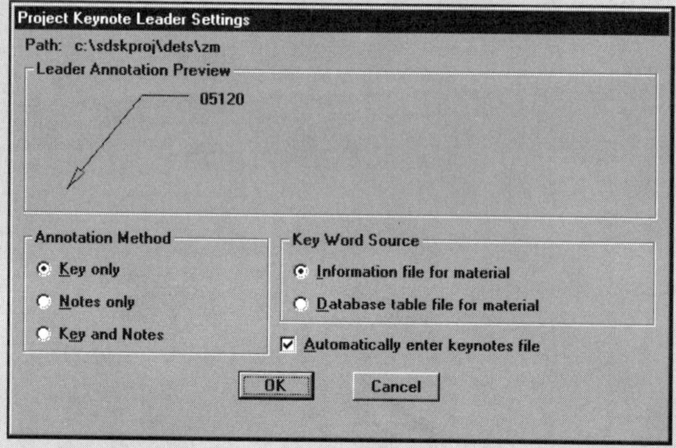

Step 20: Pick the "OK" button to continue.

Step 21: Select [Annotate ⇨ Keynote Leaders] from the pull-down menu.

Step 22: Pick the concrete wall to annotate.

Step 23: Extend the leader as you desire.

Step 24: Pick the "New…" button when the Keynotes Manager dialog box appears.

Step 25: Enter the information as shown below.

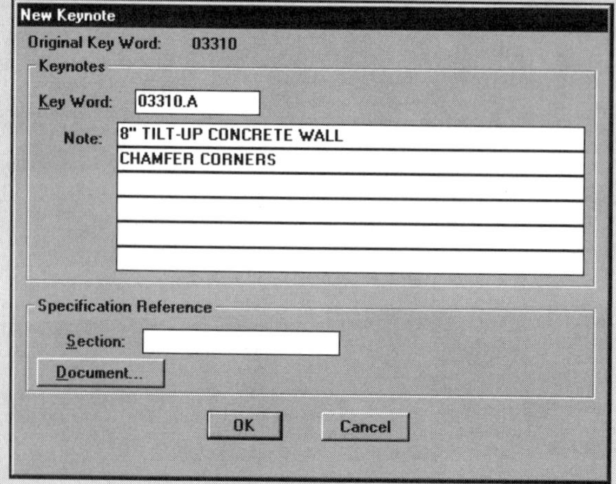

Step 26: Choose the "OK" button to continue.

Step 27: Highlight the keynote entry and choose the "OK" button.

Step 28: Pick the flashing for annotation and extend the leader as you desire.

Step 29: Pick the "New..." button when the Keynotes Manager dialog box appears.

Step 30: Enter the information as shown below.

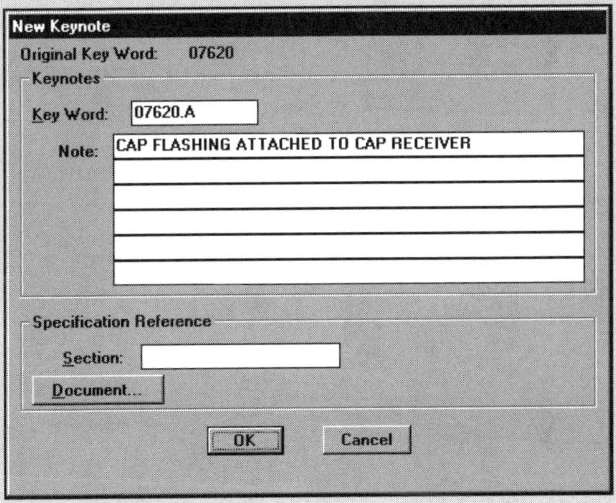

Step 31: Annotate the following items using the same procedures as shown above.

06100.A - CANT STRIP

03310.B - 2 1/2″ CONCRETE SLAB

05310.A - 1 1/2″ 20 GA. RIBBED METAL DECK

05210.A - 14K4 STEEL JOIST @ 30″ O.C.

Insert Grid Line and Bubble

The following example shows you how to insert a grid line and bubble on the detail.

Hands-on:

Step 1: Select [Tools ⇨ Annotation ⇨ Grids and Bubbles...] from the pull-down menu.

Step 2: Highlight Bubbles and Lines and choose the "OK" button.

Step 3: Accept the default bubble type of <Circle>.

Step 4: Enter **A1** as the bubble contents.

Step 5: Type **.X** and pick a point on the outside face of the wall to locate the x location of the bubble.

Step 6: Pick a point within the top margin area to define the YZ location.

Step 7: Extend the line down into the lower margin area and pick a point (approximately 5″ down).

Step 8: Enter "." for none at the prompt for the next bubble contents.

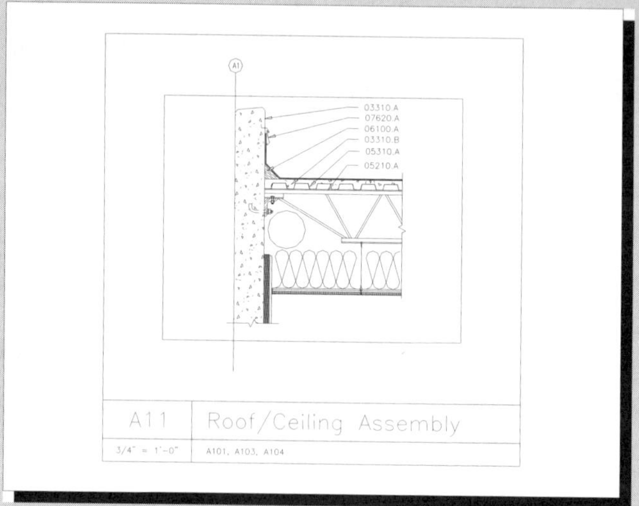

Charting Keynotes

Once you have annotated the details using keynotes, you need to generate a list to identify the association between materials and the keynotes.

Hands-on:

Step 1: Select [Annotate ⇨ Chart Keynotes] from the pull-down menu.

Step 2: Place a window around the detail and its annotation at the select object prompt.

Step 3: Press <Enter> to accept the selection.

Step 4: Place the chart in the "Materials Keying Legend" area of the title block.

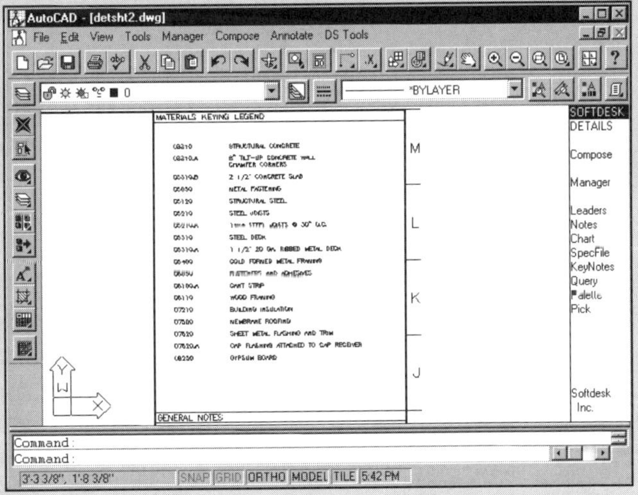

Incorporating Details by Others

You can use details created with regular AutoCAD or imported with DXF from other CAD programs in the Softdesk *Details* module.

- ✔ Use the Softdesk *Details* module to associate the detail information with the materials library, create annotation, and incorporate the detail into the standard libraries.
- ✔ You can also manipulate and regenerate hand-drawn details with Softdesk *CAD Overlay ESP*.
- ✔ The *Details* module also has the ability to incorporate popular manufacturer details for Vertex detail libraries.

Attaching Intelligence to Common Entities

The following exercise shows how to add intelligence to your details.

- ✔ You can import these details or draw them with a program other than the *Details* module.

Hands-on:

Step 1:	Zoom to the extents of the current drawing.
Step 2:	Pan over to display a clear area on the graphics screen.
Step 3:	Use the [Ddinsert] command to insert *\sdskproj\workshop\dwg\deaddet2.dwg*.

Step 4: Use the "Explode" option when you insert the block.

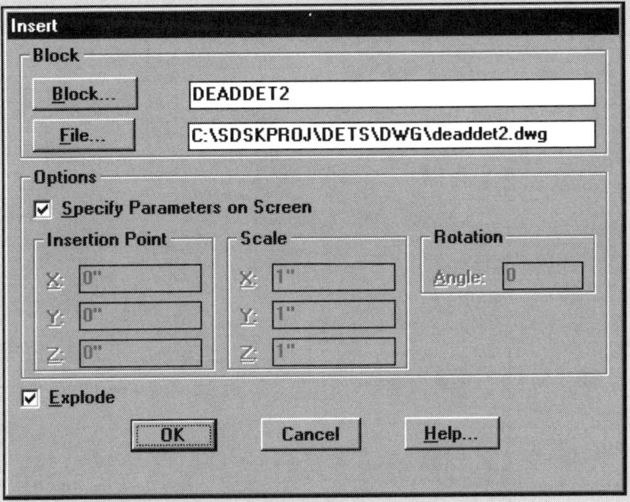

Step 5: Choose the "OK" button to insert the block.

Step 6: Select [DS Tools ⇨ Query Material Object] from the pull-down menu.

Step 7: Pick one of the inserted entities — the command line displays the message "Object is not identified as a material".

Step 8: Press <Enter> to exit the [Query Material Object] command.

Step 9: Select [Tools ⇨ Inquiry ⇨ Distance] from the pull-down menu.

Step 10: Measure the height and width of the floor joists — the width is 1 1/2″ and the height is 9 1/4″.

Step 11: Select [Compose ⇨ Material Compose] from the pull-down menu.

Step 12: Retrieve the 2x10 from the nominal cut lumber material table.

Step 13: Choose the "OK" button twice to exit the Material Retrieval dialog box.

Step 14: Select "Attach" from the side screen menu below the word TABLE.

Step 15: Select all of the entities that compose the 2x10's and press <Enter> at the select objects prompt.

Step 16: Select [DS Tools ⇨ Query Material Object] and pick one of the 2x10 entities — the entities are now associated to the material table.

Step 17: Choose the "OK" button to exit to the command line.

Step 18: Select [Compose ⇨ Material Compose] from the pull-down menu.

Step 19: Retrieve 5/8″ Gypsum Wall Board Retrieval dialog box.

Step 20: Attach the material to the appropriate entities.

Step 21: Repeat the same procedure for the remaining items:

3/4″ Plywood Sheathing (06 - Wood and Plastics)

1x4 Wood Flooring (09 - Finishes)

Step 22: Select [Compose ⇨ Material Compose] from the pull-down menu and retrieve 6″ Batt Insulation.

Step 23: Choose the "OK" button twice to draw the insulation.

Step 24: Draw the insulation as shown below.

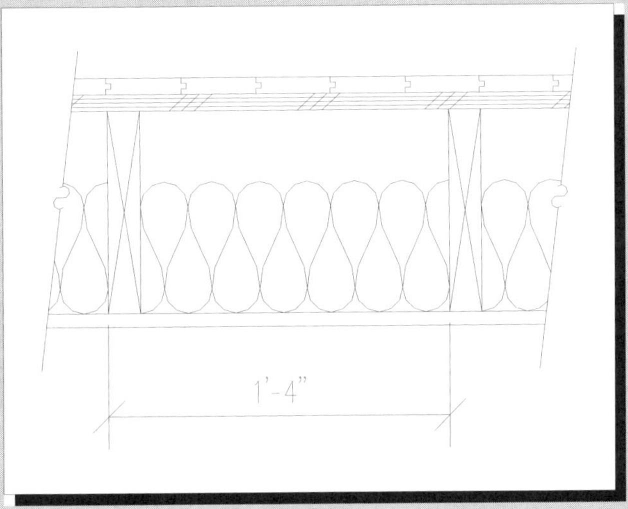

Step 25: Select [Manager ⇨ Setup New Detail...] from the pull-down menu.

Step 26: Set the scale 1 1/2"=1'-0" and choose the "OK" button.

Step 27: Select [Manager ⇨ Create Detail] from the pull-down menu.

Step 28: Pick a point in the center of the detail as the insertion base point.

Step 29: Select all the objects that compose the detail at the select objects prompt.

Step 30: Press <Enter> to accept the selection.

Step 31: Accept the default of **Yes** at the prompt to save the detail to the library.

Step 32: Enter the information as shown below.

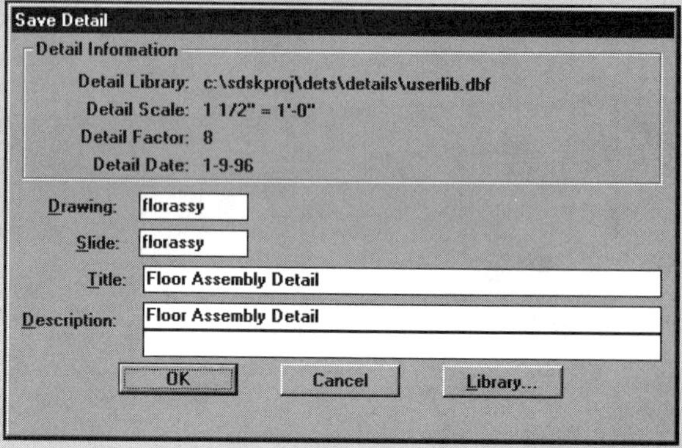

Step 33: Accept the default value of **Yes** at the prompt to insert the detail.

Step 34: Insert the detail as an XREF.

Step 35: Insert the detail within the drawing sheet above the Roof Assembly detail.

Step 36: Allow enough room to add a detail border and annotation.

Step 37: Enter **A102** as the detail reference.

Step 38: Insert a detail title as shown in the following figure:

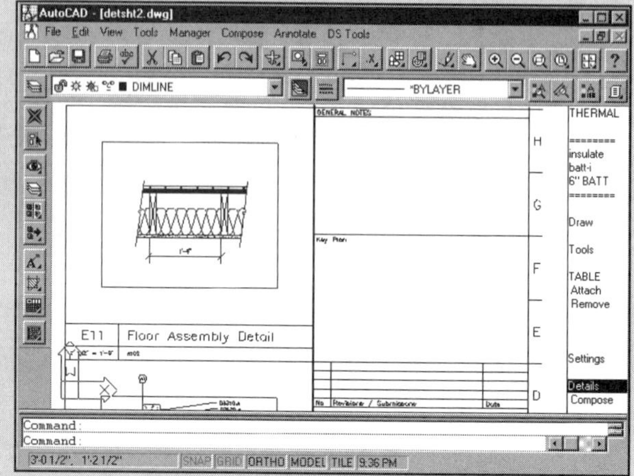

Step 39: Select [Annotate ⇨ Keynote Leader Settings...] from the pull-down menu.

Step 40: Enter the settings as shown below.

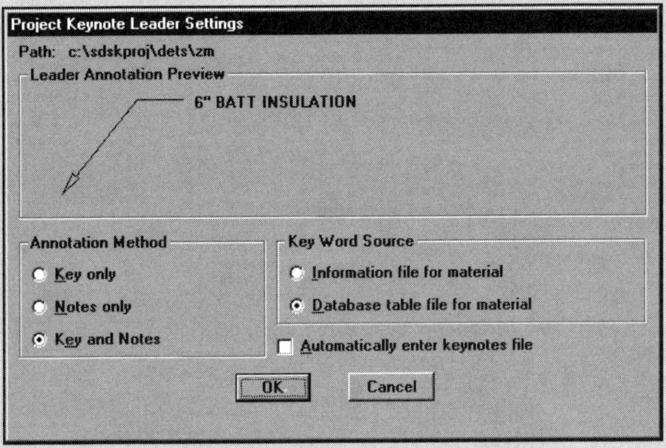

Step 41: Annotate all the materials in the detail.

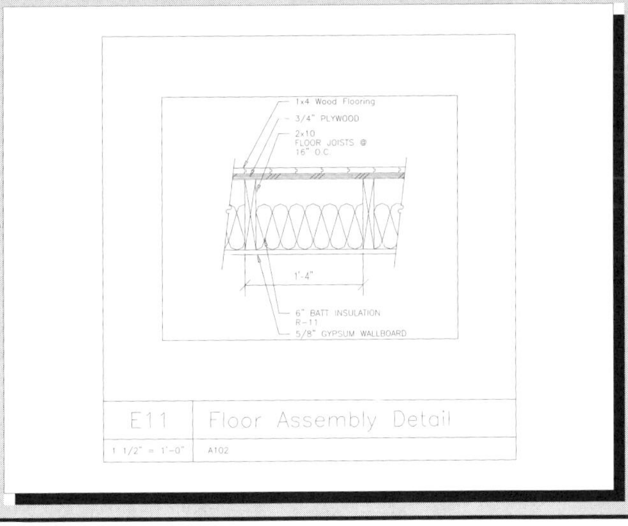

Inserting a Vertex Detail

Vertex details are pre-drawn details that you can import directly into the Softdesk *Details* library or into a Softdesk drawing.

- ✔ These details do not contain the intelligence of a detail created with the *Details* module.
  - ✗ You can easily add this intelligence using the steps in the previous example.
- ✔ The Vertex Detailer Viewer allows you to cycle through the available details one by one.
  - ✗ You can also enter a specific drawing name to search for in the Drawing Search section of the dialog box.

Hands-on:

Step 1:	Select [Manager ⇨ Import Vertex Details...] from the pull-down menu.
Step 2:	Enter the root directory for vertex details as *<drive:>\sdskproj\workshop\vertex*

Note:

You can find the files this routine is looking for in c:\sdskproj\workshop\vertex\dbm\details. *However, you need only direct it to the vertex library location.*

Step 3: Find the c66604v1 drawing.

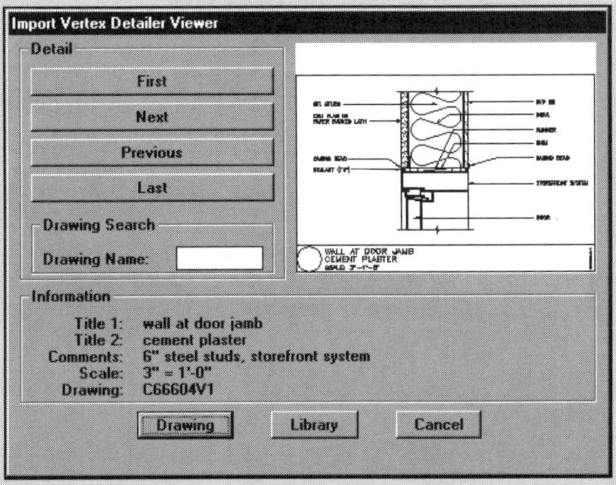

Step 4: Pick the "Library" button to add this detail to the project library.

Step 5: Press <Enter> to save the detail to the current library.

Step 6: Select [Manager ⇨ Insert Detail...] from the pull-down menu to access the library and view the new detail.

Step 7: Scroll to the end of the list and highlight the new detail.

Step 8: Choose the "Cancel" button to exit the library without inserting the detail.

Step 9: Select [Manager ⇨ Import Vertex Details...] from the pull-down menu.

Step 10: Accept the default for the root directory for vertex detail library files.

Step 11: Find the *c66603v1* drawing.

Step 12: Pick the "Drawing" button to insert the detail into the current drawing.

Step 13: Choose the "Block" option for insertion.

Step 14: Insert the detail into a clear space within the drawing and enter a rotation angle of **0**.

Step 15: Select [Manager ⇨ Setup Existing Detail] from the pull-down menu and pick the vertex detail.

Step 16: Insert the detail in a clear area.

Step 17: Erase the detail border.

Step 18: Stretch the leaders in closer to the detail as shown below.

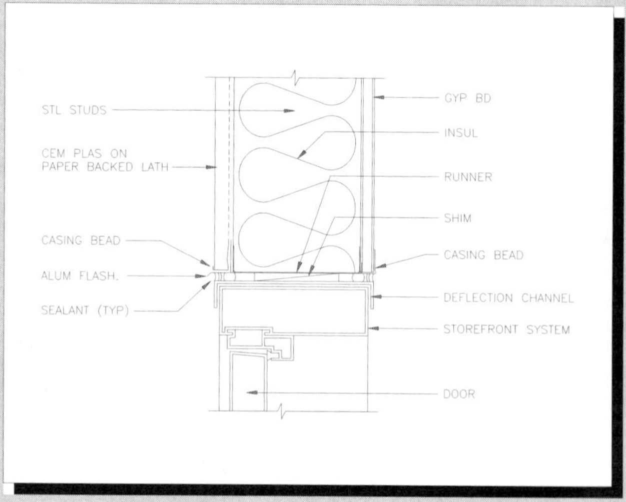

Step 19: Zoom to the extents of the vertex detail.

Step 20: Select [Manager ⇨ Create Detail] from the pull-down menu.

Step 21: Pick near the center of the detail to locate the insertion base point.

Step 22: Accept the default of **Yes** at the prompt to automatically select objects for detail.

Step 23: Press <Enter> to accept the selection.

Step 24: Accept the default of **Yes** at the prompt to add the detail to the library.

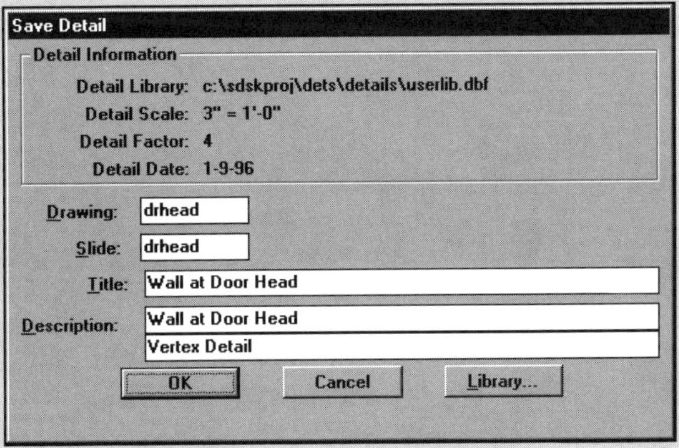

Step 25: Enter **No** at the prompt to insert the detail.

Step 26: Select [Manager ⇨ Title Settings...] from the pull-down menu.

Step 27: Enter the values as shown below.

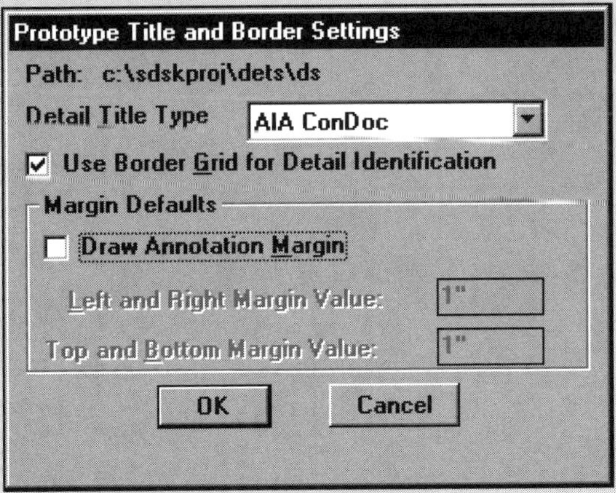

Step 28: Choose the "OK" button to continue.

Step 29: Select [Manager ⇨ Insert Detail...] from the pull-down menu.

Step 30: Highlight DRHEAD and choose the "OK" button to insert the detail.

Step 31: Choose the "Block" option for insertion.

Step 32: Insert the detail above the floor assembly detail with a rotation angle of **0**.

Step 33: Accept the default of **Yes** at the prompt to insert a detail title.

Step 34: Type **A101, A102, A103** at the prompt to enter the detail reference.

Step 35: Insert the detail title as shown below.

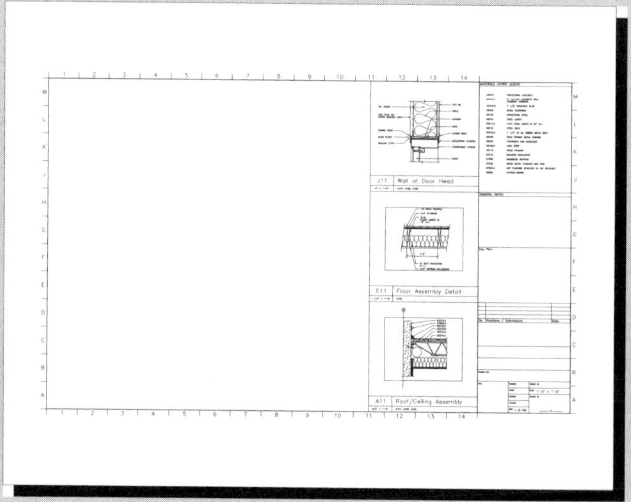

Using Hand-drafted Details

The next section shows how to manipulate hand-drafted details with the *Details* module.

- ✔ Use *CAD Overlay ESP* to underlay a scanned image of the hand-drawn detail.
- ✔ This section shows some *Detail* module utilities for composing detail materials quickly.

Hands-on:

Step 1:	Create a new drawing called *\sdskproj\workshop \dwg\rasdet1*.
Step 2:	Use the [Softdesk Products...] command to initialize *CAD Overlay ESP* and the *Details* module.
Step 3:	Setup a 1'-0"=1'-0" drawing with a 24x36 sheet size — do not include a sheet border.
Step 4:	Verify that *CAD Overlay ESP* is the current application.
Step 5:	Select [Raster ⇨ Image Paste] from the pull-down menu.
Step 6:	Select the *\sdskproj\workshop\details\rfinsul.rlc* file to paste.
Step 7:	Enter **0,0** as the insertion point.
Step 8:	Press <Enter> to accept the default image scale.
Step 9:	Accept the default image rotation angle of **0**.
Step 10:	Enter **8** for the image color.
Step 11:	Select [Raster ⇨ Zoom Image] from the pull-down menu to display the image.
Step 12:	Use the [Softdesk Products...] command to switch to the *Details* module menu
Step 13:	Select [Manager ⇨ Setup New Detail...] from the pull-down menu.
Step 14:	Setup the new detail at 3/4"=1'-0".
Step 15:	Zoom in on the double top plate of the detail.
Step 16:	Select [Compose ⇨ Material Compose] from the pull-down menu and retrieve 2x4 lumber.
Step 17:	Choose the "OK" button to draw the material.
Step 18:	Draw two 2x4's over the existing raster image.

Step 19: Extend a 2x4 in width to represent the studs below the top plate.

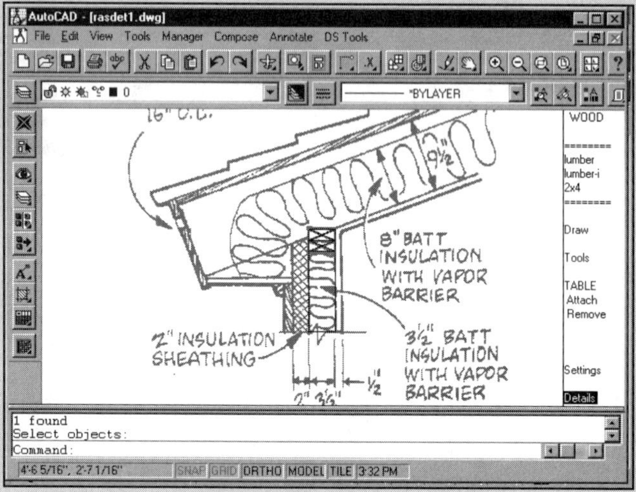

Step 20: Select [Compose ⇨ Material Compose] from the pull-down menu and retrieve 2x10 from the lumber material table.

Step 21: Choose the "OK" button to draw.

Step 22: Choose the default option to draw the material.

Step 23: Choose the width option for the lumber view.

Step 24: Type <Ctrl-W> to access the raster snap options.

Step 25: Pick the "End" button to use an endpoint raster snap.

Step 26: Pick the first point of the rafter.

Step 27: Use the raster snap options to select the second point of the rafter.

Step 28: Pick a point to indicate the side of offset.

Step 29: Press <Enter> when prompted to copy objects.

Step 30: Press <Enter> twice more to exit to the command line.

Step 31: Add the following materials to the detail using the same tools described above.

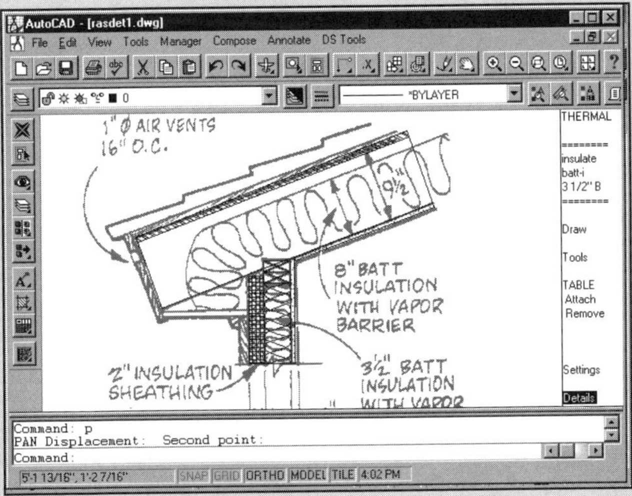

¾″ plywood roof sheathing

½″ gypsum wall board

2″ rigid insulation

3 ½″ batt insulation at wall

Step 32: Type the [Image] command at the command line.

Step 33: Type **OFF** to remove the raster from the screen view.

Step 34: Add materials and annotate as shown below.

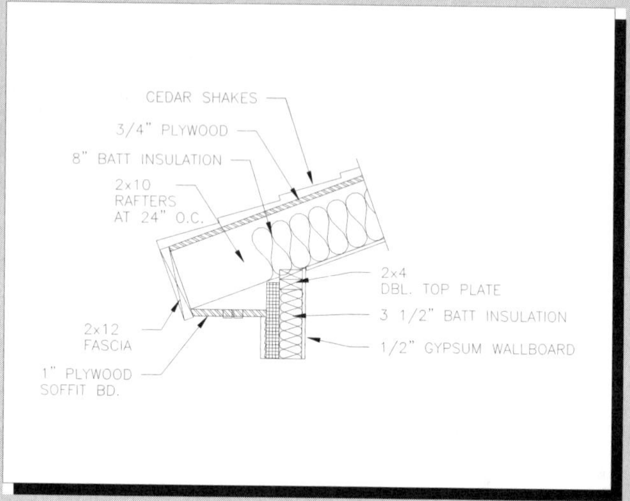

Step 35: Save the detail to the library.

Index

2

3

A

M

N

P

Q

R

S

T

U

V

W

X

More OnWord Press Titles

Pro/ENGINEER and Pro/JR. Books

INSIDE Pro/ENGINEER, 2E
Book $49.95 Includes Disk

Pro/ENGINEER Quick Reference, 2E
Book $24.95

Pro/ENGINEER Exercise Book, 2E
Book $39.95 Includes Disk

Thinking Pro/ENGINEER
Book $49.95

Pro/ENGINEER Tips and Techniques
Book $59.95

INSIDE Pro/JR.
Book $49.95

MicroStation Books

INSIDE MicroStation 5X, 3d ed.
Book $34.95 Includes Disk

INSIDE MicroStation 95, 4E
Book $39.95 Includes Disk

MicroStation Reference Guide 5.X
Book $18.95

MicroStation 95 Quick Reference
Book $24.95

MicroStation 95 Productivity Book
Book $49.95

MicroStation Exercise Book 5.X
Book $34.95 Includes Disk
Optional Instructor's Guide $14.95

MicroStation 95 Exercise Book
Book $35.95 Includes Disk
Optional Instructor's Guide $14.95

MicroStation for AutoCAD Users, 2E
Book $34.95

Adventures in MicroStation 3D
Book $49.95 Includes CD-ROM

Build Cell for 5.X
Software $69.95

101 MDL Commands (5.X and 95)
Optional Executable Disk $101.00
Optional Source Disks (6) $259.95

Windows NT

Windows NT for the Technical Professional
Book $39.95

SunSoft Solaris Series

SunSoft Solaris 2. User's Guide*
Book $29.95 Includes Disk

SunSoft Solaris 2. for Managers and Administrators*
Book $34.95

SunSoft Solaris 2. Quick Reference*
Book $18.95

*Five Steps to SunSoft Solaris 2.**
Book $24.95 Includes Disk

SunSoft Solaris 2. for Windows Users*
Book $24.95

The Hewlett Packard HP-UX Series

HP-UX User's Guide
Book $29.95 Includes Disk

HP-UX Quick Reference
Book $18.95

Five Steps to HP-UX
Book $24.95 Includes Disk

Softdesk

Softdesk Architecture 1 Certified Courseware
Book $34.95 Includes CD-ROM

Softdesk Architecture 2 Certified Courseware
Book $34.95 Includes CD-ROM

ISoftdesk Civil 1 Certified Courseware
Book $34.95 Includes CD-ROM

Softdesk Civil 2 Certified Courseware
Book $34.95 Includes CD-ROM

NSIDE Softdesk Architectural
Book $49.95 Includes Disk

INSIDE Softdesk Civil
Book $49.95 Includes Disk

Other CAD

Manager's Guide to Computer-Aided Engineering
Book $49.95

Fallingwater in 3D Studio: A Case Study and Tutorial
Book $39.95 Includes Disk

Geographic Information Systems (GIS)

INSIDE ARC/INFO
Book $74.95 Includes CD-ROM

ARC/INFO Quick Reference
Book $24.95

INSIDE ArcView
Book $39.95 Includes CD-ROM

ArcView Developer's Guide
Book $49.95

ArcView/Avenue Programmer's Reference
Book $49.95

101 ArcView/Avenue Scripts: The Disk
Disk $101.00

ArcView Exercise Book
Book $49.95 Includes CD-ROM

INSIDE ArcCAD
Book $39.95 Includes Disk

The GIS Book, 3d ed.
Book $34.95

INSIDE MapInfo Professional
Book $49.95

Raster Imagery in Geographic Information Systems
Book $59.95

GIS: A Visual Approach
Book $39.95

Interleaf Books

INSIDE Interleaf (v. 6)
Book $49.95 Includes Disk

Adventurer's Guide to Interleaf Lisp
Book $49.95 Includes Disk

Interleaf Exercise Book
Book $39.95 Includes Disk

Interleaf Quick Reference (v. 6)
Book $24.95

Interleaf Tips and Tricks
Book $49.95 Includes Disk

OnWord Press Distribution

End Users/User Groups/Corporate Sales

OnWord Press books are available worldwide to end users, user groups, and corporate accounts from your local bookseller or computer/software dealer, or from Softstore/CADNEWS Bookstore: call 1-800-CADNEWS (1-800-223-6397) or 505-474-5120; fax 505-474-5020; write to CADNEWS Bookstore, 2530 Camino Entrada, Santa Fe, NM 87505-4835, or e-mail ORDERS@HMP.COM. CADNEWS Bookstore is a division of SoftStore, Inc., a High Mountain Press Company.

Wholesale, Including Overseas Distribution

High Mountain Press distributes OnWord Press books internationally. For terms call 1-800-4-ONWORD (1-800-466-9673) or 505-474-5130; fax to 505-474-5030; e-mail ORDERS@HMP.COM, or write to High Mountain Press, 2530 Camino Entrada, Santa Fe, NM 87505-4835, USA. Outside North America, call 505-474-5130.

On the Internet: http://www.hmp.com

OnWord Press 2530 Camino Entrada, Santa Fe, NM 87505-4835 USA